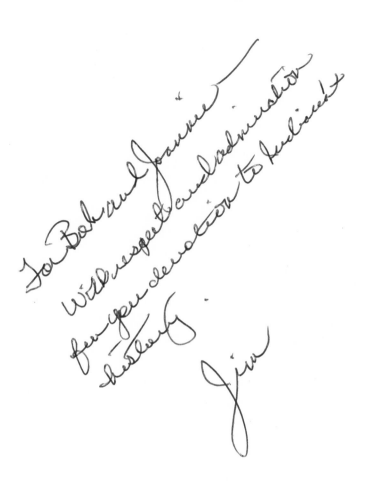

To Bob and Joanne

With respect and admiration
for your devotion to Kuderant

Sincerely

Jim

Thomas Taggart
Public Servant, Political Boss
1856–1929

Thomas Taggart
Public Servant, Political Boss
1856–1929

James Philip Fadely

Indiana Historical Society
Indianapolis 1997

© 1997 Indiana Historical Society. All rights reserved

Printed in the United States of America

The paper in this publication meets the minimum requirements of American National Standard for Information Sciences—Permanence of Paper for Printed Library Materials, ANSI Z39.48-1984. ∞

Library of Congress Cataloging-in-Publication Data

Fadely, James P., 1953–
    Thomas Taggart : public servant, political boss: 1856–1929 / James Philip Fadely.
       p. cm.
    Includes bibliographical references and index.
    ISBN 0–87195–115–0
    1. Taggart, Thomas, 1856–1929.   2. Politicians—Indiana—Biography.
3. Democratic Party (Ind.)—Biography.   4. Legislators—United States—Biography.
5. Businessmen—Indiana—Biography.   6. Indiana—Politics and government.
7. United States. Congress. Senate—Biography.   I. Title.
F526.F33 1997
328.73'092—dc20
[B]
                                    96–29072
                                        CIP

For James Philip Fadely, Jr., a seventh-generation Hoosier

Contents

Acknowledgments

T he writing of history and biography involves many people who assist the author in a variety of ways. This study of Thomas Taggart is no exception, and I wish to thank here those who have given generously of their time and effort to make this book a reality. I must first express gratitude to the Indiana Historical Society for sponsoring this project with a Clio Grant. All Hoosiers are indebted to the Society for the role it plays in preserving Indiana's rich heritage.

The grandchildren of Thomas Taggart have been most gracious in helping with the research required for this work. Their collective insight and information have proven invaluable as this biography progressed. Evelyn Chambers Denny, Dora Sinclair Loutrel, Letitia Sinclair Mumford, Eva Taggart Parsons, and the late David L. Chambers, Jr., have my thanks for their assistance and friendship. Other family members involved in the process were the late Betty Cretors, Diana Chambers Leslie, Nancy Mumford, the late Josephine M. Sinclair, and Elizabeth Mumford Wilson.

I am most grateful to Pam Wasmer, former manuscript librarian in the Indiana Division of the Indiana State Library, for her cheerful and willing assistance for months on end as the researching and writing of this manuscript went forward. The staffs of the Indiana Division of the Indiana State Library, the Lilly Library at Indiana University, the Manuscript Division of the Library of Congress, the William Henry Smith Library of the Indiana Historical Society, and the Melton Public Library in French Lick were also helpful in the preparation of this work.

In French Lick, Paula Mills and Adina Mills assisted in obtaining materials relating to the French Lick Springs Hotel while Auttie Shipman and Claire Kearby graciously granted interviews. Visiting the various Taggart homes helped establish a sense of the family, and I am grateful to Luther James for his tour of Thomas D. Taggart's estate, Mt. Airie, in French Lick; Mrs. Joseph McCarthy for showing me about the Taggart summerhome in Hyannis Port, Massachusetts; and to the staff of Delta Sigma Phi Fraternity for allowing me to roam through the Taggart home in Indianapolis.

My deepest thanks go to Thomas A. Mason, director of publications, Paula J. Corpuz and Shirley S. McCord, editors, and Kathleen M. Breen and George R. Hanlin, editorial assistants, at the Indiana Historical Society for their careful, professional attention to this manuscript. Their encouragement and assistance throughout this project have meant much to me.

My largest debt of gratitude is to my wife, Sally Fehsenfeld Fadely, for her steady and constant support as this book unfolded. In addition to making it possible for me to devote countless hours of research and writing to this work, she also tackled the task of word processing the manuscript. And, finally, I am grateful to my parents, Mr. and Mrs. Harry E. Fadely, for having instilled in me during my early years a love for Indiana and its history.

For all who helped with this book I am grateful. For the errors that remain I alone am responsible.

Introduction

Thomas Taggart, a native son of Ireland, so completely dominated the Democratic party in Indiana at the end of the nineteenth century and during the first quarter of the twentieth century that Hoosier author Meredith Nicholson once wrote: "T. T.— These are the most famous initials in Indiana history. If I were writing a biography of the Honorable Thomas Taggart, I should not spell out the name on the cover and title page, but merely double the twentieth letter of the alphabet and let it go at that."

Taggart's skill and success in both business and politics are legendary in the annals of Hoosier history. Coming from a humble immigrant background, young Taggart worked his way up from clerk at the dining hall at the old Union Depot in Indianapolis to proprietor of two hotels in the capital city. But, most important in a business sense, he was widely known as the person who developed the French Lick Springs Hotel in southern Indiana into a world-class spa for the rich and famous. With his hotels and other far-flung business interests, Taggart became one of Indiana's wealthiest men. His well-heeled lifestyle allowed for mansions in Indianapolis in the winter, Hyannis Port on Cape Cod in the summer, and a deluxe apartment in the French Lick Springs Hotel for various times of the year. He also provided imposing homes for several of his children.

In politics Taggart achieved renown in the Democracy when he won terms as auditor in 1886 and 1890 in heavily Republican Marion County (Indianapolis). He went on to further his fame by carrying Marion County as county chairman for Grover Cleveland over hometown favorite Benjamin Harrison in the presidential contest of 1888, and he did the same for Indiana as state chairman in the presidential election of 1892. Taggart then served three terms as mayor of Indianapolis in 1895, 1897, and 1899. He was elected committeeman from Indiana to the Democratic National Committee in 1900, a post he held for sixteen years. During that time he served as chairman of the national committee in 1904–8 and supervised Judge Alton B. Parker's presidential campaign in 1904 against Theodore Roosevelt. In 1916, upon the death of Sen. Benjamin Franklin Shively, Gov. Samuel M. Ralston appointed Taggart to the United States Senate. He lost the special senatorial election later that autumn to Republican James E. Watson, and he lost again in the Senate race of 1920. Nevertheless, for a third of a century Thomas Taggart was the undisputed boss of the Democratic machine in Indiana. He made governors, congressmen, senators, vice presidents, and even presidents. He was, in essence, the Democratic power in the Hoosier state. His life, so filled with success and achievement, was the epitome of an immigrant's dream of America. This is his story.

CHAPTER ONE

Beginnings

Thomas Taggart entered the world on 17 November 1856 in Amyvale, County Monaghan, Ireland, just a few days after John C. Frémont unsuccessfully led the first Republican battle in an American presidential election. It is said Taggart "was scarce an hour old before he screamed with rage and shook his tiny fist at the name Frémont. Then it was that he joined the party of Jefferson and Jackson."[1] Alas, the future leader of the Hoosier Democracy would become such a political legend that such stories would spring into existence. In actual fact, of course, Thomas Taggart made his worldly entry in a much more inauspicious way.

His father, also Thomas Taggart, was born in Ireland in 1817 and had spent all of his thirty-nine years in the little village of Amyvale. His mother, Martha Kingsbury Taggart, was born in Scotland in 1819, the daughter of Robert Kingsbury, and had moved to Dundine, Ireland, by the time she married Thomas.[2] The newlyweds started their life together in tiny Amyvale in altogether humble circumstances. The elder Thomas Taggart was an only son, believed named for his father Thomas, and he had four sisters, who were described as tall, attractive women and, like the entire family, were Presbyterians.[3]

Thomas and Martha Taggart were already the proud parents of five children before Thomas was born in 1856. His older siblings were Jane (born 1847), Mary (born 1849), Robert (born 1851), Letitia (born 1853), and Sallie (born 1855). All six children were baptized in the Protestant faith at nearby Liss Avaragey. A seventh child, Martha, called Mattie, was born in 1862 after the family immigrated to the United States.[4]

Evelyn Chambers Denny Papers

Martha Kingsbury Taggart, the mother of Thomas Taggart.

Like so many other families in Ireland during this period, the Taggarts saw their best chance for economic survival and success in faraway America. The prospects for a family remaining in northern Ireland at this time were decidedly bleak, so the family's immigration to America began. The elder Taggart's sisters Sallie, Jane, and Ann left Ireland first and located in Springfield, Ohio, prior to 1860. One sister, Mary, remained behind and lived in Armagh in northern Ireland.[5] Then Thomas and Martha pulled

Evelyn Chambers Denny Papers

Thomas Taggart, the father of Thomas Taggart, who brought his family to the United States in 1861.

up their roots in Amyvale in 1861 and made their way to the United States with six children, including five-year-old Thomas. The major Irish immigration to America had already taken place by this time. The conditions on board ship, to be sure, were quite grim, and food was scarce. One story cites young Thomas's determination at an early age declaring that he would stand in line with his tin cup for food from the ship's soup kitchen, gulp it down, and go to the end of the line for another round.[6] Upon landing in New York City the Taggarts made their way west to Xenia, Ohio, where Thomas began a job as baggage master at the Xenia railroad station.[7] His three sisters resided not far away in Springfield, so there was a feeling of family cohesion and emotional support in a land so far away from home. Still, the middle-aged Taggarts must have found the uprooting a tremendous challenge, and the eruption of the American Civil War in the year they arrived also must have contributed to the unsettling nature of the experience.

Despite the fact that Thomas was gainfully employed as baggage master during his first years in Xenia, the family lived in poor circumstances. John R. Malloy, an Ohio Republican leader who knew young Thomas as a child in Xenia, recalled that the Taggarts were poor and kept a pig in the backyard.[8] Young Thomas attended the public schools in Xenia for his primary education and one year at the public high school before he left formal education behind and entered the world of work.[9] He first worked in a railroad restaurant/hotel for a Mr. E. Cory who was succeeded by N. & G. Ohmer of Xenia.[10] Thomas began his work life by cleaning the lunchroom at the Xenia depot. Of his first job he said, "It was the one spot in town where there was activity and noise, where I could touch the hem of romance. Strangers who changed cars there were adventurers."[11]

Characteristics of the adult Taggart began to form and take shape during these early years in Xenia. Taggart himself credited the wife of a railroad division superintendent with starting him on the right track when she told him that having to sweep and scrub floors was no excuse for not keeping his face clean. "From then on, though my clothes were shabby, I contrived to look surprisingly clean." As an older person, when money was no object, Taggart's sartorial appearance was immaculate.[12] His first boss insisted that he scrub clean the corners of the lunchroom floor. Young Tom took all of this to heart and emphasized cleanliness in all of his hotels later in life.[13]

His generosity, which became legendary in subsequent years, was evident also during these early Xenia years. His task every

Evelyn Chambers Denny Papers

Tintype of Thomas Taggart as a young man.

morning was to buy flowers for the depot restaurant. Mrs. John Durand lived in a hotel across the street, and she asked him to get a flower for her each day. The only problem with this arrangement was that Mrs. Durand never paid Tom for her flowers. The small salary that he earned was turned over to his family to help out with household expenses. He paid for Mrs. Durand's flowers with money he earned by doing extra work, sometimes borrowing the money to pay for them. But he was ashamed to suggest that she pay for the flowers, and he knew that at some point she would repay him. "One day she called me to her and handed me $15. At that time it seemed a tremendous sum, and that really was the nucleus of any financial success I have had, and stands out in my life as a memory of a very happy time. That day, with that $15 in my pocket, I would not have exchanged places with any one in the world. And every bloom that grows along the roadside reminds me of Mrs. Durand."[14]

Young Taggart worked at the Xenia depot during the period 1868 to 1875,[15] starting at the bottom as a preadolescent, working hard, and proving his ability to his employer. By age sixteen he had graduated from cleaning floors to working the lunch counter in the depot restaurant.[16] Taggart stated that he was forced to go to work on a half-day basis at age twelve while still attending school. And, in his own words, "my parents gave me every assurance that I was destined never to amount to anything." Fortunately, his teacher tutored him two or three evenings a week so that he could keep up with the rest of his class. This continued for two or three years until he dropped out of high school for full-time work. When he became a United States senator from Indiana many years later, this teacher sent Taggart one of his first and most prized congratulatory letters.[17]

By the summer of 1874 Taggart was ready to declare his intention to become a citizen of the United States, a declaration he made formally on 21 August of that year. Several weeks later, on 13 October 1874, the judge of the probate court in Greene County, Ohio, where Xenia is located, granted Taggart his American citizenship. During the course of the ceremony Taggart had to "renounce and abjure all allegiance and fidelity to every Foreign Prince, Potentate, State or Sovereignty whatever, and particularly to Victoria Queen of Great Britain and Ireland."[18]

Without a doubt Taggart was driven by a strong ambition from his very early years. It would be reasonable to assume this drive was fueled, in part at least, by the relative poverty in which the Taggarts lived. Whatever the cause, he was successful in impressing his employer, N. & G. Ohmer, with his capabilities. The company sent him, at a young eighteen years of age in 1875, to Garrett, Indiana, a key railroad town in De Kalb County in the northeastern corner of the state to manage its depot hotel, the De Kalb House. Taggart's early success was rooted in the immigrant's driving desire to make good and in a remarkably winning personality that was evident in early life. His personality, marked by a genuine interest in others and an ease with people, was perhaps best captured by a line from an article about him that appeared years later: "That hand-to-shoulder style is the natural adjunct of the smile that won't come off, and together they built up Tom Taggart."[19]

"I did everything in the Garrett restaurant. I built the fires and washed the dishes. I carried out the ashes and baked the pies," Taggart recalled toward the end of his life.[20] Clearly he was proving his ability as a jack-of-all-trades in the railroad restaurant/hotel business as he steadily advanced his career. But as important as his two years in Garrett were to furthering his business prospects with the Ohmer company, something infinitely more significant in his life occurred there. He met Eva Dora Bryant.

Eva Bryant's family had been in America since colonial times. She was descended from Stephen Bryant, who landed at the Plymouth Colony in 1632, and Edward Gilman of Ipswich, England, who arrived in Boston in 1638. Eva's great-grandfather David Bryant was a lieutenant in the Continental army during the American Revolution, and his father-in-law Jeremiah Gilman was a lieutenant colonel. This family background qualified Eva for membership in the Daughters of the American Revolution, which she joined on 30 August 1895. Her grandfather Gilman Bryant, a native of Peacham, Vermont, was the first white settler in the Mount Vernon, Ohio, area and had a thriving trade with the local Indians.[21] Gilman Bryant's son and Eva's father, Charles Grandison Bryant of Mount Vernon, married Elizabeth Dean Smith of Mansfield, Ohio, on 1 February 1849. This union produced four children: Douglas (born and died 1849), Charles Dudley (born 1850), Eva Dora (born 5 August 1853), and Mary Elizabeth (born 1858). Tragically, in August 1860 Elizabeth Bryant died at twenty-eight years of age, leaving behind three surviving

Evelyn Chambers Denny Papers

Eva Dora Bryant at age nine.

children. Charles was raised by his grandfather Samuel Smith, a deacon in the Congregational Church. Mary lived as a child with an aunt, then went to Rock Island, Illinois, to live with her father and his second wife Louise Harrison, whom he married in 1866. Mary later married Edwin G. Frazier and lived in Rock Island.[22]

   Upon her mother's death Eva, who was only seven years old, went to live with her uncle, Edwin Douglass Bryant, and his wife

Lucy Viola Inscho Bryant.[23] Her aunt and uncle had been married only three years when they took in their little niece.[24] Eva soon formed a strong bond with her aunt and uncle, thus refusing her father's request that she come live with him and his new wife. Even so, her father maintained a paternal relationship with Eva, giving her, for instance, a piano when she was eight years old. He also looked after her education. He sent her to a Catholic school near Rock Island, but she was so unhappy there that he transferred her to Mount Carroll Seminary in Mount Carroll, Illinois. "My father was very good to me and chose me of his 3 children to live with him after his 2nd marriage," Eva related to her daughter Lucy many years later. When she refused because of her attachment to her aunt and uncle, he took Mary Elizabeth to live with him. Her father had four additional children by her stepmother. There seems to have been no bitterness on Eva's part toward her father, but rather one senses a sentimental attachment to a father who had, in essence, been replaced.[25]

Little is known about this period of Eva's life so it is difficult to determine what amount of time she spent at Mount Carroll. It is known only that she moved to Garrett in her twenty-second year in 1876. Mount Carroll Seminary subsequently changed its name to Frances Shimer, and during the 1920s the school offered four years of academy work and two years of college. Since that time the college has relocated to Waukegan, Illinois.

Edwin Douglass Bryant, commonly referred to as Doug, was in the dry goods trade and moved his business from town to town in both Ohio and Indiana over the years. He started out in Mount Vernon and then moved to Mount Liberty (Ohio), Sparta (Ohio), and back to Mount Vernon. He left Mount Vernon again in April 1876 to take up business in Garrett, Indiana, where the family stayed until May 1878. Leaving Garrett, Bryant moved back to Sparta, Sunbury (Ohio), and finally to Indianapolis in 1885 to be near the Taggarts.[26] Only fragments of his life can be gleaned from the historical record, but it is known that he was a strong supporter of the temperance movement, joining the national Sons of Temperance on 15 April 1856. He also was an admirer of the

Buckeye Copperhead, Clement L. Vallandigham, penning
"Vallandigham a Grand Man" beside an article in his scrapbook
about the Confederate sympathizer's funeral from the *Cincinnati
Daily Enquirer* of 21 June 1871.[27]

According to Eva Bryant Taggart, she and Tom were destined
to meet and raise a family. As she recalled, her uncle Doug had
moved to Garrett ahead of her and her aunt. At that time a gypsy
woman told Eva's fortune, predicting that Eva would have great
changes in her life, marry a man whom she had not yet met with
the initials T. T., and have six children! Eva could only guess that
the gypsy referred to a current admirer of hers, a Tom Thompson.
During this time her uncle started writing about a Thomas
Taggart who worked in the Garrett hotel. It seemed that Tom
bought his groceries from Doug's establishment. Shortly after
Eva's arrival in Garrett with her aunt, Doug introduced the young
couple to one another. Eva remembered Tom at that first meeting as young, kindly, and dapper. He seemed a man of the world
with no self-consciousness. Tom was so polite to everyone, and Eva,
frankly, considered him a fraud at first. She recalled believing that
"no human being could be kind and mean it."[28]

A courtship blossomed between the nineteen-year-old Tom
and the twenty-two-year-old Eva. The next year, 1877, N. & G.
Ohmer Company transferred the up-and-coming Tom to
Indianapolis to work in its restaurant in the original Union Depot.
When he went to the capital city to assume his new position, Eva
Bryant remained behind with her family in Garrett. However, the
relationship continued and the gypsy's prophecy was coming
true: Tom and Eva were to marry on 17 June 1878.

On Monday, 17 June, St. Paul's Episcopal Church in Mount
Vernon, Ohio, was redolent of sweet perfumes from baskets and
vases of rare exotic flowers and plants. One hundred fifty guests
were seated in the pews to witness the union. Shortly after noon
the organist struck up Myerbeer's famous "Wedding March,"
and the couple moved slowly behind the ushers Will S. Sperry and
Charles W. Pyle. The bridal couple was resplendent in their attire.
Eva wore a handsome silk dress in a rich shade of "dregs of wine"

that was cut en Princesse and had point lace trimmings. Her French chip hat was trimmed with marguerites and pompon feathers. Tom was fitted out in a black frock coat, à l'Anglaise, with lavender pants, white gloves, and a white satin necktie. Tom and Eva knelt at the altar rail, and the rector, the Reverend William Thompson, read the Episcopal marriage service. The ritual completed, the couple left the church and boarded a waiting carriage. There was a reception afterwards at the home of Miss Lizzie Elliott, where Eva had been staying as a guest. At 2 P.M. the couple left for Xenia, Cincinnati, and other southern cities. After their honeymoon trip they would start their life together in Indianapolis.[29]

When the newlyweds returned to Indianapolis in the summer of 1878, Tom, twenty-one years old, resumed his duties as a clerk for N. & G. Ohmer at the Union Depot restaurant. Eva, at age twenty-four, set about making a home. By autumn life changed dramatically for the couple. On 4 October Eva gave birth to their first child in Lorain, Ohio. They named their daughter Florence Eva.

Family and children were always the most important things in life to the Taggarts. Florence Eva would be the first of six children born to Tom and Eva over the next decade, bearing out the gypsy woman's prediction. The next five children, all born in Indianapolis, were Lucy Martha, 7 March 1880; Nora, 29 October 1881; Irene Mary, 27 December 1883; Thomas Douglas, 16 July 1886; and Emily Letitia, 19 November 1888.[30] Thus, the couple's family grew quite quickly in the first years of their married life.

As the Taggarts established their family and Tom his career, they lived in several places in downtown Indianapolis. They were living at 153 North Tennessee Street in 1880 when Lucy was born. In the mid-1890s Tennessee Street was renamed Capitol Avenue. The next year, when daughter Nora was born, their residence was listed at 355 North Illinois Street. In 1882, after five years in Indianapolis with the N. & G. Ohmer Company, Taggart was promoted from clerk to superintendent of the Union Depot Dining Hall and had living accommodations in the train station.

The city directories for the years 1882 through 1887 give the Taggart residence as the Union Depot, and both Irene and Thomas were born while the family resided there. It was not until 1888, the year of their youngest child Emily's birth, that they were listed in the city directory as living at 410 North Tennessee Street, today the corner of Capitol Avenue and St. Clair Street.[31]

Tom Taggart had already come a long way in life from the relative poverty of rural Ireland to the bright promise of career and family in Indianapolis. His hard work and driving ambition, coupled with a loving wife and family, all pointed toward a better tomorrow. And, without doubt, one must keep in mind that behind his success lay a winning personality that would soon lead to his rise in the world of politics as well as business.

CHAPTER TWO

Business, Politics, and the
Power of Personality

I enjoyed making friends just as a person might enjoy catching fish," Taggart once commented in discussing his life.[1] And how very true that comment was. There is no one who came into contact with Taggart, friend or enemy, who would ever deny his winning personality and genuine friendliness. In fact, these were traits on which everyone who knew him commented. Taggart was generous to a fault and was truly "a gentleman from Indiana." Indeed, his personality was a powerful asset as he set about combining careers in both politics and business.

To be sure, the old Union Depot Dining Hall put Taggart at the center of things for the leaders of the Democratic party's working organization. In the heyday of the American railroad this was the building through which anyone of importance passed, as well as thousands of everyday citizens. The political organization people gathered, loafed, ate, talked, and shared political intelligence at Taggart's lunch counter.[2] His personality and ambition were like magnets to this field of political activity. It was inevitable, given this combination of forces, that Taggart's business and political stars would rise.

As early as 1884 the twenty-seven-year-old dining hall manager already had attracted enough attention for his party work, as a precinct committeeman and later boss in the old Seventeenth Ward, to be offered the Democratic nomination for Center Township trustee. The Seventeenth Ward, in which the Union Depot was located, was bounded by Washington Street on the north, Merrill Street on the south, Delaware Street on the east, and

Illinois Street on the west. In a move that foreshadowed a lifelong reluctance to run for elective office, he respectfully declined.[3] However, despite this decision Taggart was very much at the center of the local Democratic scene. On a personal note, his affiliation with the Democratic party in Indianapolis came as a great surprise to his father Thomas and his brother Robert, both of whom were Republicans. They reportedly never understood his decision to become a Democrat.[4] One suspects, however, that the decision was not altogether difficult for Tom to make. With his sincere concern for all people, specifically including those less fortunate in material terms, and with the Democratic party's open embrace of the immigrant, the affiliation with the Hoosier Democracy seemed a nice and comfortable fit. And philosophically the evangelical and puritanical bedrock upon which Indiana Republicanism was built did not suit Taggart's temperament.

By 1886 Taggart was more susceptible to a draft to run for public office. Marion County Democrats were delighted when he allowed them to nominate him for the office of auditor. It may be assumed that part of his reluctance to seek elective office had to do with the staunch Republican history of Marion County. The county had never voted for a Democratic candidate for president. But 1886 was an off-year election and a Democrat's chances might be considerably better. Also part of his reluctance to run for office was that he never saw politics as a permanently viable livelihood. The uncertainties of political life were too great for that. And, of course, by the summer of 1886 he had a family of five children to support with the arrival of his son Thomas Douglas on 16 July. Nevertheless, run he did.

His Democratic supporters were sure they saw a winner in personable Taggart, and they did all they could to ensure his victory. One big-hearted Irish woman employee was moved to give him money for his campaign, saying, "Tommy, my boy, you have no money to make your race. You have always spent all your money to get things for the other boys. You are going to be elected sure. Use this to help make it sure."[5] What confidence people seemed to have in him already in his young life. And, as it turned out, that confidence was well placed. The Republican hold on Marion County was broken, and Taggart, just shy of his thirtieth birthday, won the auditor's race with a plurality of approximately 1,700 votes. In a quirk of the election law at the time, Gov. Isaac P. Gray commissioned him as auditor on 13 November 1886 for a four-year term starting almost a year later on 2 November 1887. He went on to win reelection in 1890 by an even larger plurality of approximately 2,580 votes. Again, Gov. Alvin P. Hovey commissioned him on 10 November 1890 for four years beginning 2 November 1891. Thus, Taggart's second term as auditor would not end until November 1895.[6]

Taggart's campaign in 1890 for reelection as auditor highlighted the personal qualities that made him such a success in both business and politics. His Republican opponent that year, whom he defeated, was a friend and a neighbor. On the day after the election Taggart reimbursed his opponent for his campaign expenses so that his account could be replenished to provide for the security of his wife and children.[7]

Taggart's generosity was legendary. His deputy auditor "Dore" Johnson often saw Tom paying off a note he had endorsed for a vagabond or someone down on his luck. Johnson reprimanded Taggart for this practice and reminded him that he had a family to support. Taggart saw the merit of Johnson's argument and said he would stop. Furthermore, he told Johnson he would buy him a new suit if his name were ever again found on a note. Some time later the deputy auditor spied Taggart in his office writing a check to a creditor. When Johnson reminded him of his promise, Taggart replied, "Quit your kicking. I've already ordered the suit."[8]

Unlike many public offices the Marion County auditor's position paid quite handsomely. This, too, surely helped Taggart overcome his reluctance to seek the office. Sources vary about how much the auditor's office was worth when Taggart occupied it, but the numbers range from a low of $20,000 to a high of $50,000 annually for the period 1887–95. The evidence leans more toward the former number being the actual value of the office during

The Taggarts' original house on North Tennessee Street (later Capitol Avenue). This house was later moved to make room for the new Taggart house on the site. Pictured are (left to right) Nora, Emily, Florence, and Tom.

Taggart's terms and the latter number being the estimated value of the $20,000 in later years' money. In any case, even accepting the lower number, a $20,000 annual income from an elective county office in those years was rewarding and lucrative indeed. The source of this considerable income seems to have been the various fees payable to the county auditor's office in the late nineteenth century.[9] Clearly, Taggart profited quite nicely from his eight years as Marion County auditor and could increasingly afford not only a nice lifestyle for his family but also his widely known generosity as well.

Although it is difficult to determine with complete certainty, the evidence suggests that in 1887, the year in which he began his first term as county auditor, Taggart bought the Depot Hotel and restaurant from the N. & G. Ohmer Company and became the sole proprietor.[10] He had worked for the Ohmer company for ten years in Indianapolis. Thus began his career as an owner in the hotel business, a career that would not end until he had two more hotels under his control, one of which was a leading international spa and resort of its time.

With Taggart's parallel rise in both business and politics as hotel proprietor and county auditor, his family's lifestyle made a similar move upward. No longer would they live in quarters provided by the company at the Union Depot downtown. In 1888 the Taggarts and their five young children moved to the northwest corner of Tennessee (today Capitol Avenue) and St. Clair Streets. Their sixth child came along shortly thereafter. This house was referred to as the Samuel Osbourne house after its original owner. Osbourne was private secretary to Governors Joseph A. Wright and Ashbel P. Willard. The Osbournes later divorced, and Fanny, his wife, sold the house to the father of Jacob Piatt Dunn, the Indianapolis historian and civic activist. Fanny went on to become the wife of Robert Louis Stevenson, whom she met in France. The elder Dunn added a second story and changed the structure from a cottage to a house. So, by the time the Taggarts moved into the house in 1888 the house was large enough to accommodate them. Several years later Taggart moved the house to the southwest corner of St. Clair Street and Senate Avenue to make way for his family mansion. Without doubt, the Taggart family was on the way up socially.[11]

Once Taggart proved his ability as a successful vote getter in the auditor's race of 1886, victory-starved Marion County Democrats saw him as their political savior. To achieve Taggart's electoral success in Republican-dominated Marion County was some feat indeed. Thus, when rough times beset the county's Democratic organization in 1888, Taggart was the natural choice to take over the helm. Simeon Coy, the county Democratic boss and chairman, had been accused, along with an associate, of altering voting tally sheets in a local race in 1886. By the time the case worked its way through the judicial process in 1888 Coy and his associate were convicted. The problem, then, was to find a person who not only could lead the organization but also could unite the two factions that had developed within the party. One faction consisted of the Coy crowd and the other of less-active Democrats who resented the control of such an unscrupulous politician as Coy. The choice of the county party to be the new chairman clearly was Taggart.

He served in that role in the relatively brief period of 1888–90. During that time, however, he scored his most impressive political triumph to date. In the presidential election of 1888, with Indianapolis attorney Benjamin Harrison leading the Republican ticket and incumbent President Grover Cleveland the Democratic, Taggart carried Marion County for Cleveland over the hometown favorite. Needless to say, Taggart was now established as a bright star among Hoosier Democrats.[12]

The story of "Corky Pat" while Taggart was county chairman reveals again the generosity that Taggart showed his associates and the respect that they had for him in return. "Corky Pat" was a Democratic political leader in the Kingan pork house district, but his one weakness was liquor. One day "Corky Pat" came into the rooms of the county Democratic committee and was obviously drunk. He asked Taggart for three dollars so that he could buy shoes. The chairman sent a man with him to buy the shoes on the condition that he stop drinking, at least until the campaign was over. "Corky Pat" agreed. Within a week he appeared again and was clearly drunk. When Taggart asked about his promise "Corky Pat" sat down in the middle of the floor, removed his shoes, and handed them over to Taggart.[13]

Continuing his political ascent within the Democratic party, Taggart was elected chairman of the Central Committee of the Seventh Congressional District in 1890, a post he would retain for twelve years. At that time, based on the census of 1890, the Seventh District consisted of Marion and Johnson Counties, with Indianapolis and Franklin the two government centers in the district. Taggart's election as Seventh District chairman, while he served as auditor, further consolidated his control of the Democratic party in the populous Indianapolis area.[14]

Two years after being named district chairman, Taggart was elected chairman of the Indiana Democratic party in January 1892 while still in his midthirties. His rise within the party organization was nothing short of meteoric due to his extraordinary ability to get on with people of all kinds and to his widely recognized organizational skills.

The task for Taggart and the State Central Committee in 1892 was to defeat the incumbent president, Benjamin Harrison of Indianapolis, and elect former president and Democratic hero Grover Cleveland. What Taggart had done for Cleveland against Harrison in 1888 in Marion County he now tried to do across the entire state of Indiana. By this time political eyes all across the country were on Taggart. His remarkable ability for political organization was now known at the national level, and Indiana, of course, was a crucial swing state in the late nineteenth century with its fifteen electoral votes.[15]

Among those watching Taggart carefully and hopefully were William F. Harrity and W. C. Whitney, who were the Democratic managers for Cleveland's presidential campaign in 1892. The former was also chairman of the Democratic National Committee (DNC) and operated out of its offices at 139 Fifth Avenue in New York City. Simon Sheerin, national committeeman from Indiana who also served as secretary of the DNC, was a direct link between Taggart and Harrity in particular. The DNC chairman and Whitney sent for Taggart early in the campaign to seek his advice and help, and they certainly received both. Indiana's former Democratic governor, Isaac P. Gray, had been a candidate for the presidential nomination, and Taggart steered him out in favor of Cleveland. Gray later became United States minister to Mexico in 1893. After Cleveland's nomination in Chicago, Taggart gave a detailed poll of Indiana by school district to campaign managers in New York. According to the *Indianapolis News*, "The Eastern men had been used to sharp politics, but they had never seen anything like it." Indeed, Taggart was living up to his reputation.[16]

But the real test, of course, would be if Taggart could carry the whole state of Indiana for Cleveland over favorite son Harrison.

He applied all of his considerable political energy to that end. And, one must keep in mind, he conducted this statewide campaign while simultaneously serving as auditor, owner of the Depot Hotel, and father of six young children. He vigorously set about

the task of perfecting the state party organization for Cleveland. Representative of his approach, Taggart asked his friend Samuel M. Ralston, a Democratic lawyer from Lebanon, to help the county chairmen in Ralston's district perfect their organizations. For example, Taggart sent Ralston to speak in little Fortville because there were members of the People's party there whom he wanted to win over. The key was attention to detail. Summing up his feelings as well as his style in September Taggart wrote, "Indiana, I am satisfied at this time, is reliably democratic, if every man will do his duty from now until election day."[17] As he traveled about the state that year he was introduced as the man who had "redeemed Marion County from republican misrule." Hoosier Democrats clearly pinned their hopes for victory on Taggart's leadership.[18]

"Indiana is all right and will have safe Dem. maj.," Taggart wired Ralston on 9 November.[19] How safe it was is debatable, but the youthful state chairman did indeed produce a Cleveland plurality in Indiana of 7,125 votes. Benjamin Harrison had been defeated for reelection not only nationally but also in his home state. And Democrat Claude Matthews, son-in-law of James Whitcomb, Indiana's first Democratic governor, was elected the state's chief executive.[20] Taggart had done his work so well that Harrison was defeated in his home state, county, and precinct.[21] The confidence that the Hoosier Democracy had placed in Taggart was well deserved: he delivered results. Truly, "He was the toast at every Democratic gathering and at every banqueting board."[22]

William Harrity, W. C. Whitney, and Grover Cleveland sat down with Taggart in New York after the election and asked him what he would like in return for delivering Indiana into the Democratic column. His reply: "Nothing you can give me."[23] Taggart was a loyal adviser and supporter of Cleveland. Even though Taggart feared that Cleveland's appointment of Hoosier Republican Walter Q. Gresham as his secretary of state would not go over well with regular Democrats, he expressed his support of the decision in February following the election. Taggart also knew that Gresham, an independent Republican, had voted publicly for Cleveland and had been helpful in Indiana. As time went by Taggart, along with many Hoosier Democrats, came to support Gresham for the Democratic presidential nomination in 1896.[24]

Taggart, to be sure, was at the top of his political game. He had gained local, state, and national recognition for his political skills by the close of 1892. Inevitably, a movement to draft him to run for mayor of Indianapolis began to gather momentum among Marion County politicos. In 1893 he was chosen to head the city Democratic committee. His terms as both county auditor and state chairman, having been reelected to both offices in 1890 and 1894 respectively, would end in 1895, the year of the next municipal elections. In the end he succumbed to the politicos' requests and ran successfully for mayor that year. With those expanded responsibilities Taggart declined reelection to a third term as Democratic state chairman in December 1895, leaving that position after conducting one statewide presidential contest.[25]

Taggart's business career was booming simultaneously with his success in Hoosier politics. He was a natural for the hotel business. The best evidence suggests that he sold the Depot Hotel in 1894, having owned it for seven years. By that time he had become the proprietor of the Grand Hotel in 1892–93, which he owned until about 1904, and had acquired a partnership interest in the Denison Hotel. While the complexities of business transactions and the passage of time have muddied the historical record, evidence suggests that Taggart had management responsibility for the Denison beginning in 1904. Daniel P. Erwin, a wealthy Taggart associate from Indianapolis, purchased the Denison Hotel about 1901.[26] Most sources refer to the fact that Taggart was associated first with the Grand and later with the Denison.[27]

The Grand Hotel, built in 1873 at the southeast corner of Illinois and Maryland Streets, had become the hub of activity for the Democratic party in Indianapolis. The party's connection with the hotel was so strong by 1886 that about three hundred delegates to the Marion County Democratic convention bought an interest in the hotel. Democratic meetings, strategy sessions, events, gatherings, and parties all happened at the Grand. Thus, it seemed altogether fitting that the city's most prominent Democrat should acquire this building. The transaction highlighted Taggart's ability to convert his political connections into business success. His political and civic involvement helped him make connections and opened up opportunities for him in business. Through politics Taggart knew everybody.[28]

Taggart, by all accounts, was a shrewd businessman with sound judgment. He always had an eye toward the future and improving his family's financial and social position. His investments began as soon as he was able to spare the cash. "My first investment was in Dakota," Taggart remembered later. "I had saved from my salary $1,800, when a prominent man I knew came to me and said, 'Tom, would you like to make some money?' 'Yes,' I replied, 'but I don't want to take any chances.' 'Well,' said my friend, 'I will guarantee you making ten percent on this.' He then advised me to buy some lots in Dakota. Dakota seemed a long way off for a first serious investment, but I had plenty of confidence in human nature, and especially in this man. I invested my $1,800, and within ninety days I sold out for $6,000. Some of my friends urged waiting for $6,500, but I thought $6,000 was good enough, and I was glad I did, for a few weeks after I could not have realized $4,000."[29]

In his landmark history of Indianapolis published in 1910, Jacob Piatt Dunn, a fellow Democrat and contemporary of Taggart's, referred to Taggart and a group of Indianapolis men securing control of a bonanza copper mine in Mexico and all of them making fortunes. That point was repeated in various articles published in 1929, 1966, and 1970.[30] True enough, Taggart was part of a business syndicate that owned copper mines in the state of Sonora in northern Mexico. The group of investors who formed the Indiana-Sonora Copper and Mining Company (there are also references to the Cananea Consolidated Copper Company), included Taggart, then mayor; Samuel E. Morss,

United States consul general to Paris (1893–97) and proprietor of the *Indianapolis Sentinel,* the city's Democratic newspaper; Dr. Henry Jameson, an Indianapolis physician; Crawford Fairbanks, head of the Terre Haute Brewing Company; Peter H. Pernot, former editorial writer for the *Sentinel;* W. H. Schmidt; E. C. Cothrill; and John McCarthy, former superintendent of public works in Chicago. The officers were Morss, president; Fairbanks, vice president; Jameson, treasurer; and Taggart, secretary. In addition to these four men McCarthy completed the board of directors. Offices were located in Indianapolis. The mine properties were acquired through the efforts of Pernot who acted as prospector and agent for the company and made the deal. Taggart, Morss, Jameson, McCarthy, and Schmidt visited the properties in April 1900 and purchased them shortly thereafter from Lycurgus Lindsay and Bracey Curtis. The company incorporated with capital stock of $2,500,000 and in the spring of 1901 rejected an offer of $1,500,000 for its Sonora properties. The company was privately held and, while there are no details available about profits taken from the mine properties, there is little doubt that the investors did quite well. The monies discussed above were indeed substantial sums at the beginning of the twentieth century. Eventually the mine properties were sold to the Phelps-Dodge Corporation.[31]

The article from 1929 cited earlier was part of a collection of tributes to Taggart upon his death. Noting Taggart's customary generosity, the article explained how he had arranged a berth on a train long ago for a woman and baby who had been put on board by a poor mining prospector who could afford only a seat for them. The train was traveling across New Mexico at the time. Several years later Taggart received a letter from the miner thanking him for that courtesy and saying he had grown up with a Tom Taggart in Ohio. "Later on he struck it rich in mining," he wrote. "And the first money he took out of his mine went to buy a handsome stickpin, which he sent to me for old acquaintance sake."[32]

By the mid-1890s the Taggart household was a veritable beehive of activity. The children now ranged from the earliest primary

Indiana State Library

Thomas Taggart residence on the northwest corner of N. Tennessee (later Capitol Avenue) and St. Clair Streets, built in 1893–94. It was considered one of the finest houses in the city at the time.

grade to the oldest secondary grade. Florence, the oldest, was described as gentle and sweet with sterling Christian qualities and attended St. Mary's Church Academy, an Episcopal school in Illinois. Lucy was artistic, played the violin, and attended the Girls' Classical School. Nora, Irene, young Tom, and Emily attended public school. Life was full and complete for Tom and Eva Taggart. To accommodate his large family and reflect his social, political, and business standing in the community, Taggart moved the house in which they had lived a block west along St. Clair Street and had Scott Moore build a beautiful new residence in its place in 1893–94. So the family remained on the northwest corner of Tennessee and St. Clair Streets, only now in much more elaborate surroundings. Outside, the new house had a large, well-kept lawn. Inside there was an oriental-style reception hall with a terra-cotta fireplace, and the house was described as cheerful and artistic throughout and was considered one of the prettiest and finest in Indianapolis. This is very much in keeping with Taggart's well-developed sense of aesthetics that was evident in all of his hotels as well as his homes.

Eva Taggart unquestionably and necessarily ran the domestic side of the family's life. While her husband was virtually consumed by business and politics, Eva focused on being a devoted wife and mother. She also did a great deal of charity work quietly, one of her favorite projects being the free kindergarten. The majority of parties and dances at the Taggart house were given for her children.[33] However, Eva was also attentive to her own social obligations and sometimes entertained on a grand scale. In February 1896, for example, she gave a card party at her home for seventy-five ladies at eighteen tables. She served a supper and, as was usual at any Taggart gathering, had bunches of flowers—pink roses and American Beauty roses, tall stalks of Bermuda lilies, and jonquils—placed throughout the library, parlor, and hall.[34]

Of all the Taggarts' various memberships and affiliations at this time, the one for which Eva was most responsible was St. Paul's Episcopal Church. Eva was a devout Episcopalian, and the family became a pillar of St. Paul's, located not far from the Taggart residence on the southeast corner of Illinois and New York Streets. All six of the children were confirmed at St. Paul's, beginning in 1893 with Florence and Lucy.[35]

Tom, for his part, held several memberships that were exclusively his and reflected personal interests. His earliest affiliation in Indiana was with the Masons. He became a Master Mason in 1877 at the recently chartered Garrett City Lodge Number 537. He transferred his membership to the Mystic Tie Lodge Number 398 in Indianapolis on 6 September 1882. Taggart also was a member of both York and Scottish Rites, an active Knight Templar, and a Mystic Shriner. He also had joined the most noted Democratic clubs in the state, the Cleveland Club and the Hendricks-Gray Club. As a lover of horses, Taggart was active with the Indianapolis Driving Club and was a patron of harness racing in the state. The University Club of Indianapolis, established in 1894 by the college-educated upper crust of Indianapolis men, welcomed him as a member on 16 September 1899. Taggart, poorly educated in comparison to this group, must have taken particular delight in this affiliation.[36]

Edwin Douglass Bryant and his wife Lucy Viola, Eva's aunt and uncle who served as her foster parents, essentially were grandparents to the Taggart children. The senior Thomas Taggart died in Ohio in 1895 and had been far removed from the family. But Uncle Doug and his wife had settled in Indianapolis in 1885 when Bryant established his grocery business at 151 and 153 West Washington Street. His letterhead read, "E. D. Bryant—Dealer in Staple and Fancy Groceries, Produce, and all kinds of Fresh and Salt Meats." He sold the business two years later in 1887 and went to work in the Marion County auditor's office with Taggart. He served there throughout Taggart's tenure as auditor and then did the same as an employee of the city comptroller's office while Taggart was mayor. The Bryants lived out the remainder of their lives in Indianapolis near Tom and Eva's family.[37]

A personality marked by congeniality, kindness, and generosity can be a powerful force for achievement and success, a point demonstrated so well in Taggart's life. By the mid-1890s he had served as county auditor, an elective post that served him well financially, and chairman of the city, county, congressional district, and state Democratic committees in the world of Hoosier politics. In business Taggart had risen in the Ohmer organization, purchased the Depot and Grand Hotels and an interest in the Denison Hotel, and had some lucrative investments. Consequently the Taggarts were viewed as quite successful and socially prominent, and rightly so. In late 1895 the *Indianapolis News* published a list of people and corporations in Indianapolis with assessed property valuations of $10,000 or more. The lineup included such well-known Indianapolis names as Henry Schnull $329,250, Matilda L. Schnull $104,240, H. P. Wasson $135,380, Maj. Gen. Lew Wallace $120,350, Eli Lilly $56,505, Thomas Taggart $14,525, Eva D. Taggart $13,800, and Clemens Vonnegut $16,800. The

Taggarts' worth as measured by property valuation was now roughly half of the Eli Lilly family. Clearly the immigrant with the ever-present smile had made good.[38]

CHAPTER THREE

Mayor of Indianapolis:
Triumph and Tragedy, 1895–1901

Part I: Political Triumph

Tom Taggart and his family realized great political triumph in this period with his election three times as mayor of Indianapolis in 1895, 1897, and 1899. As Taggart's second term as county auditor wound down in 1895, the pressure mounted on him to run for mayor. By late summer the Democrats were overwhelmingly of the opinion that Taggart was the man who could capture city hall for the party. When the Democratic city convention met on 29 August the consensus was that Taggart would be nominated. After John W. Kern, chairman of the convention, gaveled the meeting to order, W. S. Budd of the Second Ward arose and placed Taggart's name in nomination for mayor. Two other names, Edwin St. George Rogers and Fielding T. Lee, were also placed before the convention for its consideration. When the votes were counted the tally read Taggart 552, Rogers 81, and Lee 9. Taggart was then nominated by acclamation, and at that point he came to the hall to address the gathering. "Were I to consult my own feelings in this matter I would not accept this nomination," he said, "but I feel it to be my duty to respect the call of my party and I accept this nomination, coming as it does, unsolicited by me." This pattern of being drafted for political office despite his reluctance was evident throughout Taggart's career. One suspects the reluctance was genuine, usually if not always, because Taggart always considered his hotel business, not politics, as a more reliable source of livelihood. He went on to note in his speech that the

duties of the mayor's office were largely of a business character and
should be conducted on sound business principles. Thus, Taggart
launched his first campaign for mayor of Indianapolis hoping for
success once again on election day, 8 October.[1]

Preston C. Trusler, Taggart's Republican opponent in 1895,
never stood a chance. Trusler had served as comptroller for the
outgoing mayor, Caleb S. Denny, and was thus closely connected
with his administration. The public perception was that Mayor
Denny's board of public works had undertaken too many expensive street and sewer projects and that enforcement of
the Nicholson Law, which regulated bars, had been a bit too
strict. Along with his association with the Denny regime, Trusler
was not a good political personality. The straw that broke the
camel's back for many city Republicans was that they believed
Trusler had voted for Grover Cleveland over Benjamin Harrison
in 1892.[2] Consequently, the election results were Taggart
(Democrat) 17,491, Trusler (Republican) 13,769, Philip McNab
(Prohibitionist) 247, and S. M. Shepard (Populist) 244. Taggart
had a winning margin of 3,722, the largest plurality ever given to
a mayor up to that time. Taggart's time-honored political touch
had held yet again.[3]

The municipal campaign had been hard fought and nasty as
usual in Hoosier politics. The Republicans charged in their newspaper, the *Indianapolis Journal*, that Taggart was simply a saloon
keeper and had been arrested the year before for being open on
Sunday. The *Indianapolis Sentinel*, the Democratic paper of the day,
set the record straight by pointing out that Taggart was in fact the
proprietor of the Grand Hotel and that a barkeeper had indeed
been in the barroom without authority on a Sunday and that
Taggart had promptly fired him for his action. The tenor of the
campaign reflected the intense partisan wrangling common to
Indiana's political culture.[4]

None of this squabbling and name-calling, however, put a
damper on the voters' enthusiasm for the contest. Election night
found fifteen thousand people milling around on one block of
Washington Street, between Meridian and Illinois Streets, outside

the *Indianapolis News* building to see election results flashed across a screen by a stereopticon. It took fifteen policemen to clear the streetcar tracks on Washington Street. When Trusler's picture appeared on the big screen there was faint cheering, but Taggart's image brought vigorous applause. The crowd did not learn the actual results of the municipal election until after 8 P.M. when the official figures came in. The *News*, a Republican-controlled paper, described the noise arising from the throng as "hideous" and "diabolical." Various loud sounds came from horns, washboilers tied together by rope, and drums, all signs that Hoosiers practiced their politics with noisy and rowdy enthusiasm.[5]

The *News* called Taggart's Democratic victory a "municipal revolution," and in certain respects it was. All six Democratic candidates for city councilmen at large were elected, and eight of the fifteen city councilmen elected from the city's fifteen wards were Democrats. Along with Taggart as mayor, Charles H. Stuckmeyer was elected city clerk and Charles E. Cox police judge. It seemed clear after the election that the Democratic ticket had been swept into office by a large black vote and by other usually dependable Republicans who had scratched. Once his election was assured Taggart reiterated his plans as mayor, "As I said before election, I am in favor of a clean business administration, and I shall try to give such an administration to the city. . . . Those who are expecting a wide-open policy, with a reign of gambling and drunken blackguardism will be disappointed. I expect that most of that talk was brought forward for campaign purposes, and we shall not hear so much of it now." He pledged to enforce all laws on the books with reason and common sense.[6]

Just before noon on Thursday, 10 October 1895, Taggart took the oath of office as mayor of Indianapolis. He was thirty-eight years old; his next birthday was a little over a month away on 17 November. True to his personality and style Taggart wanted an inauguration open to the public. Both big doors to the mayor's office in the basement of the Marion County Courthouse were thrown open for the first time in a long while, and over two thousand people filled that area of the building to witness his

installation. Taggart was a bit early for the ceremony and joked to
those there, "Well, you see I am rather in a hurry. I resigned my
office up-stairs at 10 o'clock, and I've lost nearly two hours already.
I want the salary down here to begin as soon as possible." When
elected mayor he was still state Democratic chairman and had
twenty days remaining on his second term as county auditor.
The county commissioners would soon meet to appoint a successor
to the latter post. The crowd demanded a speech from the new
mayor, and big "Bill" Flynn hoisted him up to the top of the
table. Taggart promised "to give to the people of this city an
honest, economical and business-like administration." Then,
amid the applause, Sam Dinnin, owner of the Fan saloon who had
climbed up to the transom over the mayor's office door so he could
peer in, shouted, "Three cheers for Tommy Taggart, by God." Thus
Taggart and his fellow Democrats ushered in the "municipal
revolution" that the *News* feared.[7]

Taggart soon appointed people to various positions in city
government. As his private secretary he named Herbert Spencer,
who had worked for him at the state committee, auditor's office,
and the hotel. The twenty-four-year-old graduate of Notre Dame
was paid one thousand dollars annually.[8] Taggart appointed
James B. Curtis, city Democratic chairman, as city attorney after
John W. Kern, a Taggart political associate and later United States
senator, reportedly withdrew by letter from contention for the position. Curtis then appointed Joseph E. Bell, later to become mayor
himself, as deputy city attorney.[9] Most surprising, in many ways, was
Taggart's appointment of Thomas F. Colbert as superintendent
of police. The appointment was especially interesting because
Colbert had been employed by the Indianapolis Brewing Company
and Taggart had been attacked during the campaign on the
liquor law enforcement issue. Predictably, however, Colbert vowed
to enforce vigorously all liquor and gambling laws.[10] Some people, particularly the political opposition, felt that Taggart's election was a signal that gamblers could return to the city with their
games of roulette, faro, keno, poker, craps, and other forms of
chance. The mayor himself felt obliged to declare, "No gam-

bling will be permitted in this city while I am mayor and the sooner the gamblers realize this the better it will be for them. They might as well understand now that I mean what I say."[11] The public debate about both liquor and gambling law enforcement in Indianapolis reflected the political theory that pietistic evangelicals, overwhelmingly Protestant, tended to support the Republican party while those people from a liturgical background, Roman Catholics and some Protestants, voted Democratic. The latter were much more reluctant to enforce government-ordained morality, especially since it often conflicted with their cultural tradition. Roman Catholics in the city always supported Taggart because they had confidence in his justice and impartiality on these and other issues of the day.[12]

The opposition press, however, aggressively attacked the new mayor on the liquor issue. During one of its own investigations the *News* found in February 1896 that twenty-two of the twenty-five saloons that it surveyed were doing business on Sunday in violation of the law. The newspaper discovered that saloon side rooms along the alleys did business illegally while the main saloon remained closed in obedience to the law.[13] In June the *Daily Journal* pointed out that the barroom in the Grand Hotel, owned by the mayor, was going strong at midnight during the Democratic state convention, clearly an unlawful hour to sell liquor in the city. The crowd of two hundred patrons in the bar was loud, and one front door was wide open while the curtains were drawn.[14] Even with the partisan tone of this article it is highly unlikely that the mayor did not know the practices of his own hotel. But, again, the enforcement of liquor laws was of relatively minor importance to the local Democratic organization. It must also be kept in mind that the electorate had reacted the year before, in part against Mayor Denny's strict regulation of the city's bars.

The Indianapolis over which Taggart presided was experiencing explosive growth and development. The city's population jumped from 105,436 in 1890 to 169,164 at the turn of the century, an increase of over 60 percent in a single decade. Residential and commercial development burst out of Alexander Ralston's original mile square boundaries for the capital, but the city, with some exceptions, still lay largely within Center Township. The discovery of natural gas in north central Indiana fueled the growth of industrial enterprises, and residential expansion soon followed. The well-to-do lived on the city's north side along the leafy upper reaches of Meridian, Pennsylvania, Delaware, and Alabama Streets, while working-class and various ethnic communities located to the south, east, and west. Horse-drawn carriages or streetcars were the major modes of transportation within the city, and railroads converged on Indianapolis with its central location and connected the city to the region and the nation. This connection to the national rail network did much to spur the city's growth and development. The invention of the automobile by Elwood Haynes in 1894 in Kokomo had yet to impact the Indianapolis of Taggart's tenure. As a symbol of the expanding Hoosier capital city, the 284-foot Soldiers and Sailors Monument slowly rose from 1889 until its completion in 1902. This monument in the very center of the city saluted both Hoosier veterans of the Civil War and a new and vibrant Indianapolis.[15]

Unquestionably Taggart's greatest achievement as mayor of Indianapolis for six years was the implementation of his vision for a public park system. A good part of the beautiful municipal parks of Indianapolis today stand as a lasting legacy to him. His leadership in the national urban parks movement put Taggart at the fore of a major progressive issue of the day. The needs to conserve natural resources and to provide urban green space for a newly industrialized society were evolving as some of the cutting-edge issues for the Progressive movement at the turn of the century. Indeed, Taggart was seen as a fresh young leader of the progressive faction of the Hoosier Democracy.

The public parks movement in the United States dated back to the development of Central Park in New York City in the late 1850s by Frederick Law Olmsted, the father of American landscape architecture. European cities, of course, had long appreciated the aesthetic, reflective, and recreational qualities of parks, but the concept was relatively new to America.

The seeds of the park idea had been planted in the American experience with the village green, or common, in colonial New England. The New England common, however, began with the practical purpose of grazing animals in a central location on commonly held land. As industrialization gathered speed at the time of the Civil War, some forward-looking people understood that green places needed to be preserved in urban America before the landscape was nothing but buildings and concrete.

The completion of Central Park revealed Olmsted as a visionary in this arena and in a profession that still lacked a name. He went on to great success with well-known designs for parks in Boston, Brooklyn, Buffalo, Detroit, and Montreal, the grounds of the United States Capitol, and George W. Vanderbilt's famous Biltmore estate near Asheville, North Carolina. Perhaps the Olmsted-designed park plan nearest to Indianapolis was that for Logan Place in Louisville in 1892. Olmsted's philosophy of urban landscape design, that the natural beauty found in parks had a civilizing influence on people and provided a psychological retreat from the pressures of daily life in the city, struck a chord in the Indianapolis of the late 1890s and elsewhere as the City Beautiful movement took hold. However, by the time Taggart's park plan came to fruition Olmsted was retired and in poor health, dying in 1903. Nevertheless, there was a direct Olmsted connection to the development of a park plan for Indianapolis. The board of park commissioners hired John C. Olmsted, stepson of Frederick Law Olmsted, to report on the city's park and parkway needs. His findings influenced Taggart on this issue.[16]

The Taggart administration laid plans to make Indianapolis the "park city" of the continent.[17] The concept of an urban green space in the Hoosier capital had existed since the founding of the city. Ralston, who laid out the city plan for the new capital in 1821, urged that land for parks be purchased, but that suggestion was slow to gain acceptance. In 1868, when the heirs of pioneer settler Calvin Fletcher tried to donate thirty acres to the city to be improved as a park, the city refused the gift, claiming that the whole city was like a park with its broad streets and large residential lots.

As the pace of industrialization increased, however, people began to feel differently about the idea. By the time Taggart became mayor many people were receptive to his park initiative. And, indeed, Marion County's topography offered good potential for a park system with its heavily wooded areas and four waterways: White River, Fall Creek, Pogue's Run, and Pleasant Run.[18]

The Indiana General Assembly passed a law in 1895 authorizing a board of park commissioners expressly for the city of Indianapolis. The Indiana Supreme Court later ruled the law unconstitutional, and the legislature subsequently reenacted the law with minor changes. Not until the period 1909–15 did park boards come to other large cities across Indiana.[19] The previous Republican administration had begun the process of planning a park system that provided primarily for a boulevard and a chain of parks, mainly along Fall Creek. J. Clyde Powers, an engineer and superintendent of the park system, had devised the plan.[20] With the change in administrations, political tension soon pervaded the parks process. At the beginning of 1896 Taggart's cabinet of city department heads passed a resolution asking for the resignation of the Republican-appointed park commissioners because they never attended cabinet meetings. Taggart commented at the time that he "guessed" there was a park board. He also made clear that he hoped the park board would not contract for any improvements that would put the city in debt, especially for the chain of parks along Fall Creek.[21] In May 1896 Taggart appointed Albert Lieber, a Democrat and head of an Indianapolis syndicate of breweries, to the park board, making it a three to two Republican board. Lieber, whose father was a consul in Germany, had studied parks in German, Austrian, English, and American cities.[22] By July Taggart came up with his own plan for park development in the city. He proposed buying patches of land, a square each, for parks and distributing them evenly throughout Indianapolis for maximum access by the maximum number of people. The park system would start with four or five squares, and the Fall Creek plan would be put on hold until the city was better able to build it. Importantly, Taggart signaled his discomfort with parks along Fall

Creek because they would not be accessible to all citizens. "The Fall Creek plan would be all right for the rich, those who can afford their carriages and conveyances, but, in my opinion, it would not do for the poor," the mayor observed.[23] Even the Republican *News* joined in supporting Taggart's call for several small parks across the city, but the paper still favored the large Fall Creek park plan as well.[24] Finally, a key event in the unfolding of a park plan occurred in 1896 when the city paid off $500,000 of Belt Railway bonds. This transaction freed the sums needed to finance an expanded park system and brought the vision one step closer to reality.[25]

In 1897 Taggart brought his plans for a new park system in Indianapolis to fruition. That year the city parks department was reestablished by an act of the legislature, and a new board of park commissioners was formed,[26] following the state supreme court's invalidation of the previous law. On 4 March the city council passed an ordinance authorizing the issuance of park bonds in the amount of $350,000—$300,000 for parkland acquisition and $50,000 for improvements.[27] Four months later on 9 July the council approved the purchase of 953 acres in single strips on both sides of White River northwest of the city for $230,000. At the same time the council also bought Brookside Park for $25,000, Highland Square for $23,500, and Indianola Square for $8,000. In all, the council appropriated $286,500 of the $300,000 available to acquire parklands.[28] Clearly Taggart had shifted the park focus from Fall Creek, favored by the Republicans, to White River. The reason seems to have been that property owners along Fall Creek had inflated their prices in anticipation of the acquisition while land along White River could be purchased at reasonable rates. Nevertheless, the newly acquired parkland became known as "Taggart's Folly" among many, especially the political opposition.[29] Soon, however, people began to see the value and importance of the purchase, and improvements to the park started early. The 1900 park board report reveals that a nine-hole golf course was built at Riverside for $1,513.[30] In 1916 another forty acres north of Thirtieth Street were added to the park, making the total purchase price $243,500. Riverside Park then contained 976 acres, averaged three-fourths of a mile in width, and extended two and a half miles from the Sixteenth Street bridge on the south to the southern boundary of Washington Township (now Thirty-eighth Street) on the north.[31] Thus, Tom Taggart created a legacy for the people of Indianapolis and demonstrated initiative and leadership on an issue dear to the hearts of many Progressives.

During Taggart's mayoral years, certainly in the latter half of those years, the winds of Progressivism were beginning to blow through the American political culture. This movement, urban and upper middle class in composition and committed to ameliorating social problems and opening up the political system, was fueled by the Populist movement that preceded it.

The Populist or People's party came into being in July 1892 at a convention in Omaha, Nebraska, that nominated James B. Weaver of Iowa as its presidential candidate for that November election. The Populists consisted primarily of western and southern farmers united by agrarian discontent, but their hope was to attract the eastern industrial working class and, thus, form a broad coalition to advance their cause. Among many things, Populists demanded the free coinage of silver at a ratio of sixteen to one, a graduated income tax, government ownership of railroads, telegraphs, and telephones, restriction of immigration, an eight-hour workday, and the direct election of senators. Alas, the hoped-for coalition did not materialize, although Weaver did receive over a million votes and carried Colorado, Kansas, Idaho, and Nevada for a total of twenty-two electoral votes. Populist issues would have to wait for another day.

That day came sooner rather than later with the arrival of Progressivism in the late 1890s. Taggart's years as Indianapolis mayor coincided with the beginning of the movement and his last attempt at public office, the United States Senate race in 1920, with its demise in the aftermath of World War I. Progressivism, in essence, was a response to the industrialization and urbanization of America. Resulting problems, such as the emergence of powerful economic interests unresponsive to the popular will, the exploitation of workers, including women and children, social ills related to the spread of slums, crime, and poverty, and the corruption in urban government had to be addressed. Such muckraking journalists as Lincoln Steffens, Ida Tarbell, and Ray Stannard Baker exposed these and other problems in American life and assisted academicians and religious leaders in challenging social Darwinism and classical economics, the underpinnings of the laissez-faire state.

The Progressives were notably successful in achieving their agenda, working through both major political parties. In fact the two presidents most identified with progressive reform, Theodore Roosevelt and Woodrow Wilson, came from different parties. The Progressives obtained the breakup of concentrated corporate power through antitrust legislation, federal regulation of large business in the public interest, child labor laws, the eight-hour day for labor, accident insurance for workers, prohibition, the commission and city-manager forms of municipal government, direct election of United States senators, woman's suffrage, the direct primary, and the initiative, referendum, and recall.[32]

Finding himself in the midst of this national political revolt, Taggart carved out his own niche on the political stage. Taggart, first and foremost, was a man who believed in the power and process of the Democratic organization. That political organization, composed of party workers from the precinct level up to the state central committee and the party boss, is sometimes referred to as a "political machine." The machine expected the officials it elected to be responsive to its wishes and to those of its constituents, largely the lower and middle classes. A great deal of party discipline was inherent in this type of political structure. To a fault, Taggart was completely loyal to the Democratic party organization at all levels. Under this traditional system of politics the kingmakers were few, and he wanted to be the chief kingmaker. However, at the same time Taggart sympathized with many Progressive policy goals. He had great empathy for the underprivileged in society, probably a result of his own background, and felt honor bound to deliver good government, both as an elected official and as a boss. In fact, the trait that most characterized his years as an elected public servant was the application of sound business principles to government. In a review of the book *Traveling on the Democratic Donkey* in the *New York Times* in 1925, Taggart and his machine were cited for delivering good government to Indiana. The reviewer added that when Democrats Thomas R. Marshall and Samuel M. Ralston occupied the governor's office, "Taggart served notice on his machine that any crook or grafter who tried to pick a quarrel with the Governor would have him to reckon with."[33]

While Taggart promoted such Progressive issues as efficient and good government, municipal ownership of the water supply, conservation of natural resources in the public interest, and taxes on the wealthy, he likewise opposed Progressive measures that would dilute the power of the Democratic political organization. He saw the organization as effective in delivering government services to the people and, just as importantly, he enjoyed exercising that power. Like the Progressive movement itself, Taggart embodied certain contradictions when it came to placing him on the political spectrum. He could often be seen as a Progressive in the kind of government that he produced for the public, but he was utterly opposed to the open-access mechanics of government that were so much a part of the Progressive agenda. Always he was an organization man.

While Taggart could agree with reformers on various policy issues, indeed even take the lead on an issue such as urban parks, he strongly disagreed with them when it came to the inner workings of the political process. On no issue was this more apparent than that of civil service for government employees. Taggart was an unabashed believer in rewarding one's political supporters with government jobs after success at the polls. Very simply, he favored the spoils system with its political patronage because it was the glue that held the party organization together. As a matter of practical politics, more people will work harder for a candidate if there is an anticipated reward with victory. Taggart had seen this up close as city, county, congressional district, and state Democratic chairman as well as in his own campaigns for auditor and mayor. Therefore, when he was elected to the latter position there was a question as to how he would handle civil service for municipal employees.

Shortly after his election he announced that there would be a civil service board and asked his cabinet to form new rules and regulations for it. He refused to be bound by the previous administration's civil service procedures. Immediately the Republican *Indianapolis Journal* declared that Taggart was "forced" to say there would be a board since he was actually opposed to the creation of such a board.[34] A month after taking office the mayor told William Dudley Foulke of Richmond, president of the Indiana Civil Service Reform Association, that his [Taggart's] recent firing of policemen and firemen was in the interest of better service, but others had been fired because he wanted to replace Republicans with Democrats. He reiterated to Foulke that he would not be governed by procedures from the Denny administration.[35] Several days after Taggart's meeting with Foulke the Indiana Civil Service Reform Association and its president issued a highly critical report concluding that Taggart's policy "signifies a return from the merit system to the spoils system, a retrograde movement from the reform which is everywhere making headway throughout the cities of the country to the unclean and corrupt methods of Tammany Hall." Its investigation found that the mayor ignored civil service laws and appointed people to city jobs before naming a board to formulate rules. The report noted that supposedly his cabinet, which consisted of the heads of the departments of finance, law, public works, public safety, and public health and charities, would put together the rules for civil service.[36] The *Civil Service Chronicle*, published in Indianapolis, also took aim at Taggart. In its January 1896 issue the periodical reported, "There has been no change in the situation in this city. The mayor, Tommy Taggart, pursues his way, evidently ignorant that the tendency of the times is not backward to Tammany methods but forward to such methods as shall reform the Taggarts out of politics."[37]

Thomas Taggart as mayor of Indianapolis in 1900.

There is much to suggest that historian Ari Hoogenboom's theory that the civil service reform movement fit an "outs" versus "ins" pattern contains much truth. He argues that the reformers, finding the post–Civil War political world much different than they expected, blamed the professional politicians for their political powerlessness. Thus, the reformers struck at the spoils system, the very source of the machine politician's strength. No doubt many reformers acted from a genuine conviction that civil service policies would result in better government, but the underlying notion may well have been that better government came about when they and their kind held power.[38]

The mayor's cabinet adopted civil service rules on the evening of 29 November 1895. There would in fact be no civil service board established; each department would be left to judge its own employees.[39] Thus the municipal civil service reform effort came to a grinding halt in the city.

The people of Indianapolis obviously approved of Taggart and his administration since they returned him to office in 1897 and again in 1899. In 1897 Taggart actually increased his margin of victory, defeating Republican William M. Harding by 3,914 votes. The race in 1899 was much closer and has been described as the fiercest municipal election battle ever fought in Marion County to that time. One big issue that year was the Republican charge that Taggart had squandered vast public funds with the purchase in 1897 of the Riverside and Brookside "bogs." Nevertheless, the mayor prevailed over Charles A. Bookwalter by the thin margin of 347 votes. The final tally was Taggart 20,388 and Bookwalter 20,041, and the city council now had an eleven to ten Republican majority.[40] Taggart had served three two-year terms as mayor by the autumn of 1901, and it was time to move along to other things. He intended to turn the full force of his attention to a business opportunity and vision that intrigued him in the little town of French Lick in southern Indiana.

The achievements of Taggart's six years as mayor of Indianapolis were many and varied. Certainly at the top of the list would be his implementation of a park plan for the city. Not only did he acquire Riverside, Brookside, and Indianola Square parks, but he also started the development of Garfield Park, the city's oldest. Taggart increased the size of the city from 19.38 square miles on 1 January 1896 to 28.15 square miles on 1 January 1902. He achieved this by annexing the suburbs of Haughville, Mount Jackson, Brightwood, and West Indianapolis, plus much of the interlying area. The administration also made great strides in public works. The mileage of constructed sewers increased from 48.41 to 128, asphalt streets 26.88 to 43.09, brick streets 15.76 to

25.75, wooden block (creosoted wood) streets 1.60 to 15.77, and cement walks 34.91 to 154.99. The total cost of public works for the period 1896–1901 inclusive was $4,015,090.42. In 1899 he initiated the policy of building permanent bridges over the city's waterways. In 1899 the city constructed the Melan arch bridges over Fall Creek at Meridian Street ($55,000) and Illinois Street ($50,000). These permanent bridges were made of concrete with ten-inch I beams running lengthwise through the arches and faced with Bedford limestone.

Taggart added to his list of achievements by settling the city's street railway franchise problem that was brought to a head when the state legislature passed a law authorizing Indianapolis to grant a new franchise that would run for thirty-four years. The act stipulated that fares should not exceed five cents, that the company must pave around its tracks, and that the city could acquire the company's property at any time at cost. With Taggart's leadership the city entered into a contract with the street railway company that contained not only the legislature's provisions but also provided that the company would spend one million dollars on improvements and that it would pay the city $30,000 annually for twenty-seven years and then $50,000 per year for the remaining seven years of the contract. Upon reaching this settlement the mayor declared, "Indianapolis has now the best street railway franchise of any city in the United States." Many hailed this agreement as significant because for the first time the city shared in the street railway system's income. One prominent lawyer and former high official summed up the feelings of many about Taggart's tenure at the helm of Indianapolis, "As mayor of Indianapolis he has made a record unprecedented in the history of the city."[41]

There is no doubt that Taggart worked hard to deliver the "business-like administration" that he first promised in 1895. No issue better illustrates that point than his effort to keep the city clean, literally clean. He met with the Board of Public Works and all street sweeping contractors the morning of 8 November 1895 and laid down strict rules for clean streets: downtown streets were to be swept daily and outlying streets three times per week.[42] Ever vigilant, he got up at 5:30 A.M. each day and drove around town in his buggy, looking for alleys that needed to be cleaned. He later commented, "It may sound boastful, but I am certain the city had never seen such clean streets."[43] Similar efforts and the commitment to give the taxpayers their money's worth were hallmarks of Taggart's political career.

When Taggart was first elected mayor in 1895 speculation mounted throughout the press and political circles that he would soon move to higher office. In fact, even before his election the *News* reported an "understanding" among Democratic leaders when Taggart consented to run in the mayoral race that Taggart could have anything he wanted if he "redeemed" the city. It was further reported that the general impression was that Taggart could get the Democratic nomination for governor in 1896 should he wish it.[44] When the Democratic State Central Committee and two hundred to three hundred invited Democrats converged on the Grand Hotel in early December 1895, two movements or booms took shape. One movement was for Gov. Claude Matthews for president and the other for newly elected Mayor Taggart for governor the next year. The mayor's response discouraged such talk, "Oh, now, do not start that. I have troubles enough already. I have got one office, and there is trouble enough in it for one man."[45] The opposition *Indianapolis Journal*, however, reported that a close friend of Taggart's said Taggart was a candidate for governor "for all he is worth." The reported strategy was that Taggart not appear to be a candidate too early and thus become a target.[46] One possible roadblock to his nomination for governor, should he have wanted it, was that the law barred judicial officers from running for other offices during the term to which they were elected. This may have applied to Taggart's situation since the mayor had a judicial role in that he could revoke licenses. And, as the law read, resigning would not resolve the matter.[47] As it turned out there was no reason to test the meaning and scope of the law.

Despite Taggart's public lack of interest in running for governor, pressure and speculation continued to mount in April and

May for him to do so. In early April he felt obliged to state that he would not be a candidate even if the convention were to nominate him: "I shall decline the nomination. I am fixed in my determination in this matter, and no amount of argument can change my purpose. I was elected mayor of Indianapolis for two years, and it would be unfair to the people who elected me to resign that office to be a candidate for another. I owe something to the people who made me mayor of this city, and I do not intend that my name shall be used in connection with any other office this year."[48] However, it should be pointed out that not all Democrats were clamoring for Taggart's nomination. No one can be involved as long and as intensely as Taggart in politics and not have political enemies, both within and without one's own party. One prominent Democrat told a reporter that John Kern would make a better gubernatorial nominee than Taggart. "I tell you, the democratic party does not want Taggart," he declared. He accused the mayor of standing back in bad times for the party "but every time he thought the prospects were good he came forward with his smiles and soft words." This man felt that Kern was intelligent and well read and if elected "he would not have to depend on some other man's brain to carry on the affairs of the state."[49]

Nevertheless, Taggart continued to be the choice of most leading Democrats, which prompted him to state in mid-May, "I am not and will not be a candidate, neither could I accept the nomination for governor if tendered me." He thanked his friends for the high honor of being mentioned for governor.[50] Taggart must have sensed that Democratic prospects were not at all good in Indiana or across the country in 1896 with the party split between sound-money Gold Democrats, the faction of which he was a member, and the free silver people. The fight for the free silver cause was led by debtors, farmers, and westerners, where the silver mining interests were located. These people wanted to expand the money supply through the "free," or unlimited, coinage of silver at the pre-1873 ratio of one ounce of gold to sixteen ounces of silver. The free silver people welcomed an easy money policy that put more currency in the hands of the people, but conservatives, largely easterners and banking interests, feared the devaluation of the dollar. The political infighting over this issue was fierce, all of which Taggart was keenly aware. So Hoosier Democrats ended up nominating Benjamin Franklin Shively for governor. He went down to defeat in November at the hands of Republican James A. Mount.

The money question caused no end of trouble for Taggart in 1896. In early June he was elected chairman of a statewide sound-money committee that had connections in every one of the ninety-two county seats to influence county delegates to the state convention. John P. Frenzel, a Taggart political ally and prominent Indianapolis banker, was elected treasurer of the committee and Pierre Gray secretary. There was considerable speculation that the upcoming Democratic National Convention in Chicago would split over the money issue and that a second Democratic ticket, a sound-money ticket, would emerge so that Democrats would not be forced to vote Republican.[51]

Taggart, ever the loyal party organization man, declared in midsummer that the state and national conventions, both dominated by free silver forces, had decided the Democratic party's money policy for the campaign. He indicated that he knew of no effort by the free silverites to depose his successor as state chairman, Sterling R. Holt, a sound-money man.[52] Within a few weeks, however, Chairman Holt did in fact resign his position, citing "free silver abuse" as one of the reasons he was leaving. This was early September, and the autumn campaign loomed. The Hoosier Democracy had been shaken to its very foundations by the money question. Party leaders, as usual, begged Taggart to lead the fractured party by again assuming the state chairmanship. He flatly refused, saying, "I'm out of solder. It takes solder, and plenty of it, to join this thing together."[53] With Taggart's refusal the state central committee chose Parks M. Martin of Spencer, the free silver chairman of the second district, as state chairman.[54]

Taggart in fact had barely escaped being deposed by the free silverites as chairman in his own Seventh District. In mid-August, at the Seventh District congressional nominating convention in Franklin, Charles M. Cooper, a free silver advocate, had been nominated for Congress. After his nomination there was a move to remove Taggart from effective campaign control by naming a "congressional chairman" with a committee of one person from each township in Marion and Johnson Counties, the two counties that made up the Seventh District. Taggart defeated the challenge on a close vote after addressing the convention and vowing to resign the district chairmanship if the motion passed.[55]

To be sure, the year was not an easy one politically for the Democrats in Indiana or across the nation, but Taggart tried to bridge the factional gaps with calls to party loyalty. In the case of Gov. Claude Matthews's favorite son bid for the presidential nomination in 1896, Taggart also called on his fellow Democrats' Hoosier loyalty. Of the delegates to the national convention from the Seventh District he said, "There is no longer any doubt in the matter. It makes no difference if the delegates chosen from this district are free silver men, gold men or any other kind of money men, they will support Governor Matthews from start to finish."[56] The presidential nomination went to William Jennings Bryan after his "cross of gold and crown of thorns" speech, which fired the passions of the free silver and Populist forces. But, alas, votes count more than passions as the final arbiter of elections, and the national ticket suffered a solid defeat at the hands of William McKinley.

In all of the debate about the money question one of Taggart's characteristics shone through: a lack of pretension. When reporter Louis Ludlow, later a member of Congress from the Indianapolis area, asked him for an interview on the silver question in 1896 Taggart replied, "Now, what in Sam Hill do you suppose I know about the silver question?" Ludlow found his response candid and refreshing. "His reply was unanswerable. He didn't know much about it, but at that he knew a hundred times more than most of those all-wise persons who pretended to know all about it."[57]

The election of 1900 brought more speculation about Taggart's political career, but this time the speculation included national

Indiana State Library

Silver punch bowl presented to Thomas Taggart by the city of Indianapolis when he was mayor.

office. There were rumors that a deal had been struck to place the mayor on the national ticket as its vice presidential candidate. His alleged response to this talk about the vice presidency was, "I'm ineligible. I was born in Ireland. I'll never be President or Vice President."[58] Whether the quote is indeed his or not, the point was true enough. The Twelfth Amendment (1804) to the Constitution bars the foreign born from serving as vice president of the United States. Despite his ineligibility for the top two offices of the land, Taggart did move to a level of national influence within the Democratic party in 1900 when he was named committeeman from Indiana. Now, with his appointment to the Democratic National Committee, a post he would hold until 1916, Taggart could play out his political role on a much larger scale.

Part II: Personal Tragedy

The six children of Tom and Eva Taggart were their special joy. Unquestionably Taggart always considered his family his most prized possession, even after accumulating so many of this world's goods. As their first child, Florence Eva understandably occupied a special place in the hearts and affections of the Taggarts. By late 1898 Florence was twenty years old and had already spent three years at St. Mary's Church Academy, an Episcopal school in the small town of Knoxville, Illinois. That autumn she and three classmates at the academy, Florence Yocum of St. Louis and Marjorie Woodland and Miss Leffingwell of Chicago, decided to spend the winter and spring at Clearwater on Florida's Gulf Coast. Col. Harry Yocum, Florence's father, owned a cottage in Clearwater, and he organized a yachting trip for the girls to reach their destination. Misses Taggart, Yocum, and Woodland would go by yacht and Miss Leffingwell would join them in Clearwater once they arrived. Colonel Yocum had engaged a yacht named the *Paul Jones* after Paul Jones and Company of Louisville, distillers and dealers in bourbon and rye whiskeys. The yacht, with Capt. J. S. A. Sturtevant at the helm, set out on 6 December from Louisville and was scheduled to reach Clearwater on 15 January 1899. In anticipation of the upcoming trip Florence Taggart had entertained Florence Yocum and Marjorie Woodland at the new Taggart residence on Capitol Avenue where they met many members of Indianapolis society.

The yachting party made its way down the Ohio River from Louisville and then down the Mississippi River to New Orleans. Four mishaps, including a fire and an engine breakdown, befell the yacht as it made its way downriver, perhaps serving as omens of what was to come.[59] Nevertheless, Colonel Yocum and the party left New Orleans on New Year's Eve and remained at the lighthouse ninety miles below the city at the entrance to the Gulf of Mexico until 3 January 1899. On that day the *Paul Jones* set sail for Pensacola in exceedingly foggy weather. According to the

Diana Chambers Leslie

Florence Eva Taggart (1878–1899), the eldest of the six Taggart children.

Western Union manager at New Orleans, Yocum had hired the best pilot on the coast, "a man that would take no chances with a craft of this character."[60] Tragically, no one on board the yacht would be seen alive again.

Finding out what happened to his daughter Florence and the others on the *Paul Jones* became the all-consuming passion of Mayor Taggart and his family in those first days of 1899. The thought of losing their eldest child in the prime of her youth was utterly devastating to the Taggarts. The sense of family held firm as they pulled together to provide support for one another during this personal crisis. Second child Lucy, now eighteen years old and fresh from her first semester at Smith College as a member of the class of 1902, left the Massachusetts school and remained in Indianapolis with her family as the tragedy unfolded.[61]

Taggart spent the next four and a half months desperately trying to solve the mystery of his daughter's disappearance. In the beginning, true to character, he took charge of the search for Florence. The mayor left Indianapolis for the Gulf Coast in mid-January and spent the next two weeks directing all the search efforts. Taggart requested and received a list of all ships clearing New Orleans on the third through the sixth of January. When he contacted these ships to ask if they had seen anyone from the *Paul Jones,* the universal response was "nothing sighted."[62] During the search telegrams shot back and forth between the coast and Indianapolis. Taggart made his way gradually from Mobile, Alabama, to Biloxi, Mississippi, and finally to New Orleans and its surrounding area. Sen. Charles W. Fairbanks and Cong. Jesse Overstreet worked with the secretary of the treasury and arranged for two revenue cutters to search the coastal waters for the missing yachting party. All involved held out hope that the *Paul Jones* was stranded on one of the many small islands that dot this part of the Gulf of Mexico.[63]

The desperate father was encouraged on 18 January when members of a fishing party told him that they had seen the yacht at the Chandeleur Island lighthouse on 5 January and all had been well. Chandeleur Island was approximately one hundred miles from where the party started on 3 January. Taggart wired his wife from Mobile, Alabama, "This in my opinion confirms the fact that they are safe on one of the small islands."[64] Taggart's hopes were deflated later in the day when fishermen, dragging nets off Bird Island, found a couple of trunks. In one trunk were stockings marked "F. E. Taggart." On 19 January Taggart identified the garments as his daughter's and searched Chandeleur Island in vain.[65] By 21 January all hope disappeared. "There is no longer any doubt in my mind about the result," he telegrammed from Biloxi, Mississippi. "I go to New Orleans this afternoon."[66] Lucy replied by wiring him the same day in New Orleans, "Mama and the children are all well. Keep up bravely Father Dear."[67] Eva Taggart collapsed soon after learning from her husband that there was now little doubt about Florence's death. Attended by two physicians and two nurses, she was completely prostrated at the Taggart home. Reports at the time indicated that Mrs. Taggart had opposed Florence's going on the ill-fated trip but had given way in the face of her husband's approval.[68] After a week of further inquiry in New Orleans Taggart gave up all hope for Florence's survival and returned to Indianapolis at the end of January. The emotional pain and anguish must have been overwhelming for the family, especially since there was no final resolution to Florence's fate. Despite the information provided by the fishing party Taggart believed that an accident had happened the night of 4 January about ten to fifteen miles from shore while the yacht was at anchor. Whatever had happened, the pilot, who had thirty years of experience in these waters, could not prevent it.[69] The only thing Taggart now knew for sure was that his daughter was dead.

As the realization spread that Florence was dead, an outpouring of sympathy enveloped the Taggart family. The case was a high profile one because of Taggart's prominence in Indiana and, to some extent, across the nation. Business associates from the Indiana Hotel Keepers' Association, of which Taggart was president, sent their condolences.[70] Political associates, even opponents such as Senator Fairbanks, did what they could to help in the face of such numbing personal tragedy. Schoolmates of Misses Taggart, Yocum, and Woodland at St. Mary's Church Academy held a memorial service in their chapel during the first week of February for the three young women. The service was conducted by the Reverend Doctor Leffingwell who was the rector of St. Mary's Episcopal Church. The music was provided by a choir of sixteen young women attired in black dresses and white veils. The floral tributes included a pillow of white rosebuds with violets in the centerpiece with a cross and crown on an "S.E." monogram that represented the Sigma Epsilon sorority. Doctor Leffingwell eulogized the three girls as gentle, happy, and kind with a love of their fellow students and teachers. The Eucharist was celebrated at the conclusion of the beautiful service.[71] Many felt the sorrow of the Taggarts and sought to express their feelings in appropriate ways.

Despite the acknowledgments of Florence's demise, Taggart continued to be haunted by a nagging desire to locate his daughter's body and bring this sad chapter in their lives to a conclusion. Also, there is evidence to suggest that Eva had not yet accepted the fact of her daughter's death, holding out a mother's desperate hope that her first-born child had somehow survived. So in May the mayor planned to take his wife and their daughter Lucy to New Orleans so that Eva could see that the Louisiana coast was not tropical enough to offer food and shelter to castaways. Taggart wanted Eva to understand once and for all that Florence was gone, if not from the accident itself then from starvation along the inhospitable coast.[72]

As the family was preparing to make its way south to New Orleans to bring some closure to the matter, word arrived that a body had been found and that it might be Florence. Upon arriving in the Crescent City, the Taggarts checked into the St. Charles Hotel. Two days later they took a packet boat downriver into the Delta to Buras and Venice to identify the body. They must have thought it was hoping against hope to believe that of the eight victims of the *Paul Jones* tragedy the body recovered would be their daughter's.[73] But this time their hope was justified. Amazingly, the body, found on a sand strip called Grand Gosier Island and almost hidden by a log, was indeed Florence's.[74] Commenting on the unusual preservation of the body Taggart said, "The teeth and mouth were as perfect and natural as mine are today. . . . The condition of the remains simply astounded me!" This was due to the fact that the movement of the waves had covered the body with white sand, thus creating a natural grave.[75] Taggart told the *Indianapolis News* at the time, "The discovery is a relief, provided for the family only by Providence. The Almighty alone could have preserved this body, of all those lost in the manner in which it was saved: Washed by the gulf waves to the only spot where it could be safe, and found by a fisherman who might be one of half a dozen to visit the sand strip in a year, we can thank the Almighty for its deliverance."[76] The Taggarts could now face this tragedy head-on and deal with the emotions connected to the loss of a loved one.

How had this terrible accident happened? Amid all of the inevitable speculation one theory seemed most plausible. For whatever reason the gasoline tanks on the yacht probably exploded. The *Paul Jones* was a fifty-seven-foot yacht, and the gasoline tanks took up about four feet in the bow. Searchers later found one-half of the hull, and it measured fifty-three feet in length. The theory was that the explosion split the hull in half and completely blew away the four feet of space the tanks occupied.[77] George Woodland of Chicago, father of Marjorie Woodland and vice president of the Prairie State Bank, reported in June that a majority of opinions in the New Orleans area supported the explosion theory. Sadly, he had just returned from a fruitless search of nearby islands for his daughter's body. Despite the weight of opinion behind the explosion theory Woodland held out the possibility that they might have hit a reef and split the keel.[78]

Once a positive identification of the body had been made by the Taggarts, the mayor sent for a metal casket and two undertakers from Indianapolis.[79] The Taggarts returned to Indianapolis with Florence's body on 17 May. The body was taken by H. W. Tutewiler to the family's home and placed in the south parlor. The closed coffin was covered with magnolia blossoms, Florence's favorite. The parlor, too, was filled with flowers. The funeral the next morning, attended by relatives and close friends, was a simple Episcopal service said in the parlor by the Reverend Gustav A. Carstensen,

Diana Chambers Leslie

Florence Taggart died in a tragic yachting accident in the Gulf of Mexico.

rector of St. Paul's, the Taggart family's parish church. Father Carstensen read the 130th Psalm, the lesson, the litany, and the prayers. Out of respect for Mayor Taggart and his family, all city offices were closed throughout the morning hours. The body was placed temporarily in a vault at Crown Hill Cemetery where concluding rites were held.[80] Later Florence's remains were placed in the Taggart family plot at Crown Hill. After four and a half agonizing months, the Taggarts' heartbreaking ordeal was finally over.

Thus, as Taggart prepared for his difficult mayoral reelection battle in the autumn of 1899, he had suffered what was likely the most painful period of his life. The death of a child before a parent is fundamentally unsettling and out of the normal scheme of things. It took great personal strength to face a fierce political campaign after this kind of tragedy. In fact, Taggart did try to beg off from making this race, citing family considerations and the state of his own health. However, the wish that he seek a third term was so overwhelming among Indianapolis Democrats that Taggart finally consented to run.[81] In addition to the loss of Florence, that year Taggart's only brother Robert died at age forty-eight. For many years Robert had been in charge of the Ohmer railroad restaurant in Terre Haute, but about fifteen years before his death he purchased the railroad depot restaurant in Decatur, Illinois, which made him fairly well-to-do. While distance separated them, Robert, his wife, and five children were in touch with the Tom Taggarts at least annually at the Taggart family reunion.[82] The family's healing from Florence's loss was sufficiently well along that Lucy decided in the autumn to move to New York City to study art rather than return to Smith. Her artistic talent had long been recognized and had been cultivated at May Wright Sewall's Girls' Classical School, which Lucy had attended. Now the first daughter, Lucy exhilarated in her father's narrow reelection triumph that October. From her new residence at 204 West 78th Street on the Upper West Side she wired: "Hurrah Papa is reelected."[83]

CHAPTER FOUR

The French Lick Springs Hotel

By the time Taggart's third term as mayor of Indianapolis came to a close in October 1901 he was completely committed to a business venture at French Lick in Orange County in southern Indiana. This venture into the resort hotel business would over time bring him international fame and a substantial fortune.

According to legend, George Rogers Clark is credited with naming French Lick. There once was a French fort and trading post at the approximate site of the hotel, and the salt licks of the area were well known. Thus, the designation French Lick, whatever its actual source, fits the spot. The Lost River valley of Orange County also had another very noticeable characteristic: sulphuric mineral springs that bubbled to the earth's surface throughout the valley. Thus many people refer to the area simply as the "Springs Valley." One of the favorite stories in the valley claims that a German immigrant rode into the area on horseback around 1800 and although he found the hills and valley lush and verdant, he was accosted by a violent odor that smelled like gunpowder mixed with spoiled eggs. "Drive on, John," said the German to his son, "Hell's not half a mile from this place."[1]

French Lick had over a half century of history as a resort before Taggart's arrival. Without a doubt Dr. William A. Bowles was the single most important person in the early history of the French Lick Springs Hotel property. Bowles was described as six feet two inches tall, two hundred pounds, handsome, "self-confident, pleasant, and magnetic." While all of that was surely true, he also was a constant center of controversy. Bowles had been married three times and divorced twice by the time he died, and he had been expelled from the Baptist Church twice, once for suing his brethren for nonpayment of medical bills and again over a point of doctrine.[2] Bowles, who was a physician, Baptist minister, and politician, stirred up a storm of controversy during his service in the Mexican War of 1846–48. At the beginning of the war Bowles was named captain of a company of the Second Indiana Regiment. He then was promoted to colonel and led the regiment in combat. During the course of the conflict he became friends with Jefferson Davis who commanded a Mississippi regiment in Mexico. This friendship would prove another source of controversy for Bowles during the Civil War. Davis later stated that except for Bowles and a few other Hoosiers, the Second Regiment had "fled ingloriously" from the Mexican battlefield at the Battle of Buena Vista. The soldiers claimed bitterly that Bowles had ordered their flight. Whatever the case, Bowles's friendship with Jefferson Davis, then president of the Confederacy, turned into outright sympathy for the Confederate cause during the Civil War. Bowles became head of the Knights of the Golden Circle, formed in Shoals, Indiana, to lend support to the Southern effort. The authorities arrested him and charged him with treason, and he was sentenced to be hanged. Pres. Abraham Lincoln commuted this sentence to life imprisonment at the request of Gov. Oliver P. Morton. Bowles was pardoned after the Civil War.[3]

Bowles and his brother Thomas purchased fifteen hundred acres, including the site of the present French Lick and West Baden hotel properties, from the state in 1832.[4] The state had drilled unsuccessfully for salt on the lands prior to the sale.[5] Several years later, most likely in 1845, Bowles built the first hotel building on the French Lick site, although there is no agreement on the exact year it was built. Most sources, in fact, place the date as early as 1840. But in 1844 Bowles was living in Paoli, the Orange County seat, running a drug business and often away on political business, leaving little time for a hotel at the springs. The following year, however, the 10 July edition of Paoli's newspaper, the *True American*, detailed a Fourth of July celebration: "The festivities of the day were closed by a splendid dance, at Doctor Bowles' new

building, at the French Lick."[6] At about the same time Bowles
leased the West Baden Springs portion of his property to Dr.
John A. Lane, who built the first hotel there. At the end of his five-
year lease, circa 1850, Lane purchased the West Baden tract from
Bowles.[7] Bowles's hotel was called the French Lick House.
According to an 1855 advertisement for French Lick, patrons were
advised that there were daily stagecoaches from New Albany to the
springs via the New Albany and Vincennes Turnpike. Also, there
were hacks from Orleans for those who came on the railroad or
the west stage. The same advertisement for French Lick indicated that the "watering season" began on 15 June.[8] Indeed,
Bowles played up the therapeutic value of the mineral waters for
such ailments as "dyspepsia, chronic dysentery, diarrhea, loss of
appetite, jaundice, affections of the liver, spleen and kidneys,
diseases of the skin and ulcers."[9]

The French Lick House was certainly a simple beginning for a
hotel property that later would become a world-famous spa under
Thomas Taggart. A. J. Rhodes recorded this description of the first
hotel building, "I can not tell of what order of architecture it was,
but, as I remember its peculiar style, I conclude it was his own conception of a building of that kind, and that it was original. I think
it was perhaps 80 to 100 feet long, rather narrow and three stories
high. The house was a frame with a strange appearance. The rafters
on the north side reached three-fourths of the way across the
top and was rather flat. The south side rafters were nearly

The French Lick House built by Dr. William A. Bowles, ca. 1845.

Indiana State Library

perpendicular. A two-story structure extended south perhaps
some forty feet."[10] A history of French Lick and West Baden
written in 1904 was more blunt, calling the first hotel the "ugliest
and most unsightly building" ever constructed in the area.[11]
However unattractive it may have been, the French Lick House
gave rise to the community of French Lick as settlers were drawn
to the area by the waters. Bowles, in fact, helped charter the
town of French Lick in 1857.[12]

After having leased the hotel to Dr. Samuel Ryan for several
years, Bowles died in 1873. Bowles's private life mirrored the tur-
moil and controversy of his public life. He had married his third
wife in the year of his death and left no living children. Two
grandchildren from his first marriage pressed a claim of fifteen
thousand dollars against his estate, and the hotel was sold at a sher-
iff's sale in 1880 to satisfy the judgment. At the time of the sale four-
teen thousand guests visited the hotel annually. Two men from
Paoli, Hiram E. Wells and James M. Andrews, purchased the
property and after several years of improvements and advertising,
the hotel was a successful operation. In 1887 Wells and Andrews
sold the hotel to a syndicate from Louisville, with Wells retaining
a one-fourth interest until 1891. The Louisville businessmen
made extensive improvements to the property, such as adding a
general power plant, and made it a year-round place rather than
a summer resort. That year on 1 April the Louisville, New Albany,
and Chicago Railroad, better known as the Monon, completed its
line to the springs. Two years later, in 1889, the hotel and the
Monon signed a contract for a railroad right-of-way on the property and a depot. By the next year round-trip tickets to French Lick
could be purchased from any railroad running through Indiana,
Illinois, Ohio, and Kentucky. The Louisville investors built the
Clifton building in 1888, which was separate from the main building, the Windsor. The Pavilion, a large white frame building,
was also constructed in 1888 for dances and entertainments.
Unfortunately the Windsor building burned in 1897. The
Louisville syndicate used the insurance money to rebuild the
main building and the front wing of the present hotel and to build

a new dining room and hotel kitchen and to add steam heat to the property. Nevertheless, after the fire the Louisville syndicate was ready to sell.[13]

Enter Thomas Taggart, hotel man and the mayor of Indianapolis. Throughout the decade of the 1890s Taggart frequently visited the French Lick and West Baden hotels. Then, in the winter and spring of 1898–99 Taggart conceived the idea of building his own health resort in the Lost River valley.[14] He soon began to turn his dream into a reality. In April 1900 the mayor and three partners purchased the Andrews Tract in Orange County, an eighty-acre parcel of land adjoining the French Lick Springs property owned by the Louisville syndicate. The three partners were W. M. McDoel, president of the Monon Railroad; Crawford Fairbanks, owner of a brewery in Terre Haute; and Col. Livingston T. Dickason, owner and operator of extensive quarry and mineral interests in Indiana and Illinois. The partners quickly contacted an architect and made plans for hotel buildings, a mineral water bottling plant, a bathhouse, a park, and a golf course. A year later, on 19 April 1901, Taggart, Fairbanks, and Dickason entered into an agreement with the Monon whereby the railroad would subscribe to $250,000 of the first mortgage bonds while the partners would subscribe to $100,000.[15] In a surprise change of plans the next month, however, Taggart offered $150 per share for the French Lick Springs Company at a company board meeting in Louisville on 27 May. Why the change in course? Taggart later stated that the partners realized it would be wiser to purchase and improve an existing hotel rather than build a new third resort in the Springs valley. Shrewd as he was, one must wonder if the purchase of the adjacent Andrews Tract was not part of a strategy to get favorable terms from the Louisville people. In any case, the deal was consummated. On 17 June a new agreement was drawn up with the Monon in which the railroad would now subscribe to half of the $600,000 in 5 percent gold bonds to be issued for the property. Two days later Articles of Association for the French Lick Springs Hotel Company were set out, specifying capital stock of $600,000 with six thousand

shares at $100 each. The corporation was to have a fifty-year life
and would have a branch office in Chicago. The seven incorpo-
rators also composed the board of the company. The French Lick
Springs Hotel Company filed its Articles of Association with
Union B. Hunt, secretary of state, on 25 June. The next day
there was a board meeting of the French Lick Springs Company
in Louisville at which seven new directors were elected as the previous Louisville board resigned in succession. The new board
then elected Taggart president, Daniel Erwin vice president, and
Henry Hickman secretary and treasurer of the French Lick
Springs Hotel Company.[16]

The deed was done. Taggart and the others had purchased a
resort property of approximately 350 acres with a collection of
buildings and attractions. But this was just the beginning of
Taggart's dream. He was driven to realize his vision for French Lick.
As the *Hotel Monthly*, an industry trade publication, put it, "Thomas
Taggart put his soul into the property."[17]

When Taggart and his partners formed the French Lick Springs
Hotel Company mineral springs resorts were enjoying their heyday in American life. Almost ten million dollars of mineral water
was sold annually in the United States, and Indiana alone had
nearly thirty mineral springs resorts in 1900.[18] One of these
resorts was at nearby West Baden Springs. Ownership of that
property had passed from Doctor Lane about 1884 to a group of
five men (John T. Stout, Amos Stout, George W. Campbell, Elvet
B. Rhodes, and Dr. James Braden). Then, just three years later, the
West Baden Springs Hotel was purchased by Lee W. Sinclair of
Salem, Indiana. It was Sinclair who developed the site into a
competitive hotel property during the years that Taggart visited
as a guest. Tragically, a fire destroyed Sinclair's wooden hotel in
the early hours of 14 June 1901, just as Taggart was arranging the
purchase of the rival Springs valley resort. With fierce determination the Sinclair family rebuilt the hotel into one of the modern wonders of the world.[19] The new West Baden Springs Hotel,
completed in 1902, featured the largest unsupported dome in the
world, a distinction it held until the construction of the Houston

Astrodome in 1965. The fear of fire was understandable at this time, and the new hotel trumpeted its fireproof construction. "Persons intending to visit West Baden or French Lick will do well to keep in mind that the new West Baden Springs Hotel is thoroughly modern, up-to-date and strictly fire-proof. Nor should the fact be overlooked that it is the only fire-proof hotel in this valley," a hotel publication advised.[20] The French Lick-West Baden rivalry would continue and intensify as it was played out on a national, and sometimes an international, stage.

In the first year of the Taggart partnership's ownership of the French Lick Springs Hotel, 1901–2, over $200,000 was spent on improvements to the property. The most important change came in the front wing facing east, the part of the hotel complex rebuilt with insurance money after the 1897 fire. This section was enlarged and faced with the trademark yellow, or buff, French Lick brick. This brick was an expensive and elegant design element of the period. New furnishings were added as well as a new power-house.[21]

Despite the concerted effort of the partnership to move forward quickly with improvements to the property, friction among the partners soon developed. Taggart, as manager of the hotel and largely dependent on his salary as such, wanted to plow profits back into further expansion. His partners, wealthy men living off their investments, wanted to take out hotel profits in dividends. So Taggart launched an effort about 1905 to buy out his partners so that he might set the course for the hotel and implement his vision for it. The arrangement provided that each partner become, essentially, a sales agent who had thirty days to bring in bids for his shares. In the end there were two other bids, but Taggart's was one hundred thousand dollars higher. The final numbers meant that the other partners received five times their original investment in the deal. Taggart secured the necessary financing within ten days, and his partners sold out. He paid off this debt in three years using hotel profits.[22]

The first expansion of the hotel under Taggart's sole ownership came in 1905–6 when he built a six-story annex to the south end

Indiana State Library

The Pluto spring house on the hotel's grounds, one of the property's three principal mineral springs.

of the front wing. A sixth floor was also added to the entire front wing, and additions were made to the bathhouse and the powerhouse. The spring houses at the property's three principal mineral springs, Pluto, Proserpine, and Bowles, were rebuilt at this time.[23]

The main wing of the French Lick Springs Hotel under construction in 1910–11.

The second phase of the expansion involved the construction of the hotel's main wing in 1910–11. It, too, was a six-story addition faced in yellow brick and was fireproof. This wing cost over $400,000 to put up, so Taggart was certainly sending the message that this hotel was to be topflight. An additional $130,000 was spent on a new bath building, a new marquee over the main entrance, and to modernize the lobby, kitchen, and dining room, leaving no doubt that the French Lick Springs Hotel ranked as a first-class establishment.[24]

The third expansion came in 1914–15 with the building of the deluxe wing, or A wing, at an angle back of the main wing. This wing cost nearly $300,000 and featured the most luxurious rooms in the hotel. At the top and back of the deluxe wing, on the fifth and sixth floors, were new family apartments for the Taggarts. Tom and Eva had the sixth-floor suite and their son the suite below, both connected by a circular iron stairway. Prior to their move the Taggarts lived in a two-story frame house on a hillside behind the hotel. This building later housed employees before it was demolished. The deluxe wing now stood where the old Clifton building had been. The addition of this wing took Taggart's hotel to an even higher level of elegance for the society people who flocked there. In 1914 he also built a modern dairy barn for the herd of Jersey and Holstein cattle that served the hotel's needs.[25]

Indiana State Library

Thomas Taggart at a family gathering at the Taggarts' cottage at French Lick Springs. The Taggarts lived here until they moved into a penthouse apartment in the new deluxe wing.

The final phase of expansion under Taggart ownership took place in 1924–25 when the north wing, or convention wing, went up. At a cost of more than $500,000, the new six-story wing had one floor for the convention hall, one floor of parlors, and four floors of rooms. Now the hotel could compete effectively for convention business, increasingly the lifeblood of the hospitality industry.[26]

The last two phases of expansion, the deluxe wing and the convention wing, were overseen by son Tom who graduated from college in 1909. After attending the Benjamin Harrison public grade school in Indianapolis, young Tom boarded first at Howe Military School in northern Indiana and then at Betts Academy in Stamford, Connecticut, for his secondary studies. He continued his education in Connecticut by enrolling at Yale, where he graduated with a Ph.B. from the university's Sheffield Scientific School. After commencement he went to work at the French Lick Springs Hotel, starting in the storeroom so he could learn the business

Mr. and Mrs. Thomas Taggart horseback riding at the French Lick Springs Hotel. Their hillside cottage is in the background.

from the ground up. By 1912, with his father absorbed in his many and varied political and business activities, young Tom had taken over the day-to-day management of the hotel.[27]

The town of French Lick, as well as the hotel, benefited substantially from the Taggart years in the valley. When Taggart arrived in 1901 the town had five hundred residents, cheap buildings, muddy streets, and no water or electric systems. In June 1902 the town's board of trustees granted Taggart the right to build, operate, and maintain an electric light plant and system for French Lick. At the same meeting the trustees also gave him the right to build, operate, and maintain an electric railway system in the town. The board of trustees in neighboring West Baden did the same, and on 9 November 1903 the French Lick and West Baden Railway inaugurated service on its 9,999-foot track between the valley's two resort hotels. The car ran at thirty-minute intervals until its last run on 10 July 1919.[28] In July 1905 the French Lick town board granted Taggart the right to build, operate, and maintain a water plant and system for its residents.[29] Unquestionably the Taggart investment in town and hotel enhanced the quality of life in the little Orange County community. By the time of Taggart's death in 1929 the town of French Lick boasted brick streets, three thousand residents, and water, electric, and sewage systems.[30]

Even so, life in French Lick was far from ideal. During World War I the West Baden Springs Hotel was used as an army general hospital. In April 1919 the commanding officer reported to the Board of State Charities on the sanitary conditions of West Baden and French Lick, citing unsanitary conditions that were pervasive throughout the Springs valley with the exception of the French Lick Hotel and the Homestead Hotel. And the prevalence of vice and prostitution was mentioned as major social ills of the area.[31] The sanitary conditions at the French Lick Springs Hotel were always a major concern of the cleanliness-conscious Taggart, especially after an incident in 1903 shortly after he had purchased the hotel. There had been high water from spring rains, and sources reported that hotel sewage had backed up, which allowed microbes and bacteria into the water table. Soon thereafter typhoid fever, or something similar, broke out and affected especially the Chicago colony at the hotel. One Chicagoan died, and four were quite ill. Hoosier author Booth Tarkington was also sent home to Indianapolis with typhoid.[32] Aside from the human tragedy of the situation, this kind of negative publicity could kill the resort's business. So a sewage system for the town and hotel was put in place, and the streets were bricked. Hotel promotional literature now pointedly stated that drainage and sewage systems had been installed by "America's most expert sanitary engineers," the hotel's drinking water was piped from a natural freshwater spring, the streets were paved with brick, and that there was no malaria.

While Taggart, with his usual congenial and compassionate manner, worked hard to improve the quality of life in the valley, he could turn shrewd and determined when his plans encountered opposition from the local folks. One such situation developed when he wanted to dam a creek near the hotel to create a pond for his livestock, and the farmers downstream objected and threatened to sue. Taggart invited the farmers to a big dinner and dance at the hotel, free of charge, as a neighborly gesture. Virtually everyone went and signed the guest register as they arrived. Several days later the farmers noticed work on the dam had begun. When they protested Taggart told them that they had signed a release form allowing him to proceed. The farmers responded that they certainly had not. Then he told them that they had signed the release when they entered the hotel for his dinner and dance.[33]

Spring and autumn were the big social seasons at French Lick Springs. The social set converged on the valley in the spring on their way home from Palm Beach and other resorts in Florida. The biggest time of the year in French Lick was the first Saturday in May with the running of the Kentucky Derby in nearby Louisville. Both Taggart and his son had a love of horses, so Derby time was all the more festive. The French Lick Springs stables often competed in the Derby and other races as well. The guest register at French Lick read like a who's who of American society. Names linked to great fortunes such as Vanderbilt, Whitney, and Rockefeller appear, as well as many from the political and entertainment worlds. The resort really began to attract national notice after Taggart, as chairman of the Democratic National Committee, headed Judge Alton B. Parker's presidential campaign against Theodore Roosevelt in 1904. The expansions and improvements to the hotel made it competitive with the best resorts in the world, and the French Lick Springs had virtually anything one could want. The mineral water from the springs attracted many for its therapeutic value at a time when spas were popular in the United States and Europe. The bath department at French Lick, an elaborate organization, offered every kind of spa treatment available. There were control tables for Aix, Vichy, Scotch, Fan, Rain, Circular, Steam, and Perineal douches; Turkish and Russian rooms; rooms for colon irrigation and massages; Nauheim tubs; sulphur baths; dry and wet packs; enemata; and rubdowns with

salt, alcohol, cocoa butter, and oil, to name some of the spa's offerings. The entire bath department was under the supervision of a
medical staff.[34]

Golf, a relatively new sport in America when Taggart bought the
hotel, held a prominent place at French Lick. The old French Lick
Springs Company had started to build a golf course when Taggart
acquired the property. He went ahead and developed what is today
the Valley Course into an eighty-acre, nine-hole course, expanding the course by 1910 to eighteen holes.[35] In 1920 the Taggarts
built a championship course on ground they purchased just two
miles southwest of the town of French Lick. The new Hill Course
was 6,777 yards long and played to a par of seventy. The clubhouse
had thirty sleeping rooms, lockers for two hundred men and
thirty-five women, a broad veranda that wrapped around the
building, a large living room with an open fireplace, and a beautiful dining room finished in Chinese lacquer. The Hill Course,
designed by Donald Ross, hosted the Professional Golf Association
(PGA) Championship in 1924 that was won by the colorful Walter
Hagen.[36]

Recreation, in virtually all its forms, was the name of the game
at French Lick. There was horse riding and driving on fifty
miles of trails, tennis on grass courts, bowling, billiards, swimming,
a gym, walking on the electrically lighted "track" just north of
the hotel, bordering the Valley Course with its benches and
labeled trees, fine dining with the superb cuisine of Chef Louis
Perrin who had been at the hotel since about 1895, and dancing
in the lobby to the hotel orchestra.[37] And, of course, there was reading and rest and relaxation in peaceful silence and beautiful surroundings. Taggart's aesthetic eye focused on his property at
French Lick. Flowers and plants and their arrangement were
important to him, so he sought to make the visual landscape as
pleasing as possible. Taggart hired several horticulturists before
he found Charlie Springer, a native of French Lick, who got
everything to grow. He once said of Springer's work, "His gardens
are as good for your soul as are the sulphur baths for your random
aches and pains."[38] Springer returned the compliment, "Mr.

Indiana State Library

The Formal Garden at the French Lick Springs Hotel developed by horticulturist Charlie Springer.

Taggart wishes flowers by the armload to give to the people. . . . Mr. Taggart likes flowers, and I've got to make this formal garden very pretty for him; and I do my best. They are fine people, the Taggarts—the only thing as trouble between us is they treat me better than I do them."[39] Very little on his hotel property, which eventually consisted of three thousand acres, escaped Taggart's aesthetic instinct. Even his hilltop dairy barn was landscaped with potted shrubs.[40] While the entire property was landscaped extensively, two gardens, the Formal Garden and the Japanese Garden, were the most beautiful. The Formal Garden spilled in terraces down a gentle hillside to the new deluxe wing. From his apartment at the top of the wing Taggart could enjoy Springer's careful work. The Japanese Garden was near the walking "track" and the Valley Course. This garden was a meticulous and faithful effort to re-create a Japanese garden. Each stone had a name and its proper place. The garden featured a miniature lake with water lilies and goldfish, a hillside waterfall, a torii gate and rustic bamboo fence, a little island, foot bridges, stepping-stone pathways, Japanese benches, stone lanterns, wildflowers, and Japanese evergreens.[41] There was indeed a serenity that could be found amidst all the hustle and bustle of resort activity.

The hotel also had additional fashionable amenities of the day. A new Monon railroad station was built in 1907, and fifty yards to the left of the hotel's main entrance was a parking track just for private railroad cars. There was a branch office of Logan and Bryan, Brokers with direct wires to all of the principal exchanges. There was even a French Lick Special Station of the United States Weather Bureau, recording mean temperatures of 53.9° in spring, 76.6° in summer, 55.9° in autumn, and 33.3° in winter.[42]

One could reasonably argue, however, that the amenity that lured most visitors was gambling. French Lick and West Baden were names synonymous with gambling throughout the nation, and the people came. There were two seasons on the gambling calendar in the valley: April, May, and part of June in the spring and September, October, and the first half of November in the autumn. The casinos in the area catered to the high-rolling, big-spending crowd. Ed Ballard's casino, connected by a twenty-foot by three hundred-foot double-decked walk to the West Baden Springs Hotel, supposedly had only one rival in grandeur—the Monte Carlo Casino in Monaco. Full evening dress was required of its patrons, and the dealers were decked out in tuxedos. Big-name bands entertained as wealthy guests let the good times roll. The stakes were high for games such as roulette, baccarat, chemin de fer, bird cage, and the slot machines. The play at Ed Ballard's in West Baden was estimated at two million dollars annually in 1903, with 5 percent, or $100,000, going to the house. These kinds of profits earned Ballard the title "the prince of the Indiana Monte Carlo."[43] The second upper-crust casino was Brown's, immediately across the street from the French Lick Springs Hotel. Brown's was quite grand in its decor and sense of decorum and over the years became a renowned gambling spot. Brown's Casino was so named because Al Brown owned it until about 1908 when Ed Ballard took over.[44] Finally, The Gorge was an elegant supper club and casino located in the rolling hills of the countryside outside French Lick. The tables at The Gorge sported china, crystal, silver, and napery, and the lawns were beautifully landscaped with gardens and statuary. The menu featured steak and chicken dinners—solid Hoosier fare. The Gorge was built in 1919 by George Haur and purchased by Joe Ballard,

Ed's brother, in 1925. If you were of fairly average means there were many gambling options also available. Those establishments were mainly in West Baden and included the Club Chateau, Sutton House, Oxford Hotel, Ritter House, Colonial Club, Indiana Club, Kentucky Club, and the Homestead. The Homestead had been built by Ed Ballard about 1912 with a casino in the basement. It sat right across the street from the entrance to the West Baden Springs Hotel.[45]

Charles Edward Ballard stood at the center of the major gaming operations in the Springs valley during the first third of the century. Ed Ballard was a poor local boy who found a vertical route to financial success. Before he died he owned interests in gambling establishments around the country as well as in the valley. With his growing wealth he also formed the American Circus Corporation, a holding company for several circuses, and owned the West Baden Springs Hotel during the period of 1923–31. To confirm his new socioeconomic status and provide a home for his family Ballard built "Beechwood," an imposing brick mansion on the French Lick side of West Baden. Ballard spared no cost when it came to building and decorating his home, importing black walnut paneling from Circassia on the Black Sea, marble fireplaces from France and Greece, and fountains and statuary from Italy. He filled the house with antiques, paintings from all over the world, a custom concert grand piano of hand painted bird's-eye maple, and many other beautiful objects. "Beechwood" was Ballard's monument to legitimacy. By the time of his death in November 1936 his wealth was estimated anywhere from twenty to one hundred million dollars. He met his demise in Hot Springs, Arkansas, at the hands of a disgruntled business associate, Robert Alexander of Detroit. Ballard, sixty-three years old, met Alexander in a Hot Springs hotel room where five shots were fired. People speculated that the two men argued over a $250,000 breach of contract lawsuit that Alexander had filed against Ballard, that Alexander had shot Ballard, and that he then turned the gun on himself.[46]

Gambling in French Lick and West Baden during these years was in flagrant violation of state law. For his part Taggart always maintained vehemently that he had no connection with the illegal gambling that was going on all around him. However, the question persists as to his exact relationship with Ballard and the area's famous gaming operations. Charles Edward Ballard, Jr., wrote in 1984 that Taggart asked his father to set up a casino in a white frame cottage on the hotel grounds in the autumn of 1901, shortly after Taggart purchased the property.[47] James Ballard, Ed Ballard's nephew, confirmed that Taggart was his uncle's silent partner in local gaming operations, but nothing was ever put on paper. James Ballard pointed out that young Tom Taggart even sent Elmer Thacker to manage Brown's Casino at one point after Ed Ballard's death.[48] Pamphlets about the early history of the French Lick Hotel make open references to a combination bowling alley/dice room in the middle of the Japanese garden on the hotel grounds.[49] The *Indianapolis News* speculated in early 1903 that Taggart received $50,000 annually for the gambling privilege at his hotel's casino. In 1905 the *Chicago Tribune* ran a story contending that Taggart doubled his take that year from $26,000 annually to $52,000 for the Monte Carlo privilege on his property. When Al Brown, then the holder of the French Lick Springs Hotel casino lease, refused to pay, Taggart cut off utilities to the building. Brown's revenge was to let a contract to the Terre Haute architect who built the French Lick hotel for a $200,000 casino building to rival Taggart's operation.[50] Brown's Casino, purportedly later a joint Taggart-Ballard operation, even shared the same heating system at one point with Taggart's French Lick Springs Hotel.[51] While it is true that Taggart's name cannot be connected on paper to the gambling operation in any absolute sense, it stretches the imagination to believe he was not connected in some way. And, of course, great numbers of guests at his hotel were lured by the Monte Carlo offerings of the valley and openly patronized the casinos.

Charlie Bennett, resident manager of the French Lick Springs Hotel under young Tom after his father's death, once noted that control of the area's gambling was strictly local, and organized crime was kept out. "The gambling was locally controlled, and I

The casino on the grounds of Taggart's French Lick Springs Hotel.

never saw or heard anything that would lead me to believe there was any criminal organization involved," he stated. He did reminisce about carrying bags of money to Taggart's office from slot machines set up openly in the hotel lobby and on the mezzanine.[52] Even though Ballard and the Taggarts maintained local control of the valley's gambling, organized crime made at least one serious attempt early on to muscle in for part of the action. In 1906 hoodlums from Chicago descended on the Springs valley and demanded "protection" money from the owners of the French Lick and West Baden Hotels. Taggart simply chose to ignore their demands. Consequently the thugs dynamited the veranda at the French Lick Monte Carlo and blasted the gaming room at the West Baden Springs Hotel.[53] All evidence points to the fact that Taggart successfully resisted organized crime's overtures to get a share of the gambling operation. To be sure, Al Capone was known to frequent the valley, but the story goes that Taggart even denied Capone permission to hold his wedding reception at his hotel.[54] Ballard and the Taggarts made a good combination in controlling the area's gambling because the Ballards were

Indiana State Library

Republicans and the Taggarts were Democrats. Since gambling was a violation of Indiana state law, there had to be some kind of "arrangement" with the governor to keep such flagrant and widely known gambling going. There is evidence to suggest that money flowed from the gaming tables of French Lick and West Baden to the governor's office in Indianapolis. One longtime trusted Taggart employee recalled taking bags of money by car from French Lick directly to the office of the governor in the state-house. "[Thomas D.] Taggart and Ballard would get ahold of some fella going to run for governor and they'd find out if he would let them gamble. And he would. They would spend enough money to get him elected. Then they'd give him $500 a month," the employee recalled.[55] The most alluring amenity of French Lick, the gambling, came to a grinding halt on Derby weekend in 1949 when Gov. Henry Schricker, a Democrat, sent in the state police to shut down the illegal gaming operation. By that time, however, son Tom had sold the hotel for the family, in late 1946, and he had passed away in January 1949. Only then did almost fifty years of illegal gambling stop in the Springs valley.

Dr. Joseph G. Rogers, who visited French Lick in 1869 to make the first extensive analysis of the waters and who named the spring Pluto's Well, would have been shocked to learn how large a business Pluto water became over the years.[56] After Taggart had owned the hotel for a while, the Pluto operation became a solid source of profit for him. Exploiting the spring waters for commercial purposes extended all the way back to Bowles, who boiled down the mineral water in iron kettles so guests could take home larger quantities in smaller packages. This product was a precursor to Pluto concentrate.[57] Doctor Howard of the Louisville syndicate bottled the water and had the Henry Drug Company of Louisville handle its marketing. After selling the property to the Taggart group, Howard bought another property half a mile away for an inn, drilled a well, and lowered the Pluto spring. Taggart obtained an injunction that prevented Howard from further pumping, and a court later decided against Howard for wasting natural resources.[58] The mineral water business could be quite hazardous, as Howard's effort proved, and as Taggart learned over the years when the springs at French Lick twice temporarily stopped flowing.[59]

Taggart saw very early the potential for the Pluto water business at French Lick. In October 1901 he filed papers with the secretary of state's office in Indianapolis registering trademarks for the words Pluto, Pluto Concentrated, Concentrated Pluto, America's Physic, French Lick Springs, and French Lick. He also registered pictures of Pluto or the devil used in any way to advertise mineral spring water.[60] The hotel began to advertise the water extensively in 1910 and claimed it was helpful for "diseases of the stomach, intestines, liver, gall bladder and ducts, auto-intoxication (toxins in the system), intestinal indigestion, gout, rheumatism, diabetes, obesity, under nutrition, diseases of the blood, diseases of the heart and blood vessels, diseases of the urinary system, diseases of the skin, and diseases of the nervous system." The marketing effort modestly claimed that the water was not advisable for weak heart action or shortness of breath, dropsical conditions, advanced kidney disease, and arteriosclerosis.[61] In 1915 Harry Everett Barnard, Ph.D., chief of the division of chemistry at the Indiana State Board of Health, did mineral analyses of waters from Pluto, Proserpine, and Bowles springs. "Our results," he concluded, "both chemical and bacterial, show the waters to be of excellent sanitary quality." Evidently Pluto water was both therapeutic and safe.[62]

Shortly after Taggart bought the property in 1903 the bottling works were improved, and concentrated Pluto water was made available for sale across the United States. Sales that year reached the $52,000 mark, in 1910 they were over $290,000, $368,000 in 1911, and over $500,000 in 1915. Things were going so well for this end of his business that Taggart built a modern Pluto bottling plant across from the hotel in 1913 for over $80,000. By 1919 business was booming as over 450 railroad carloads of Pluto water were shipped in a year, and sales reached $1,249,401.08. A substantial part of Taggart's income and profit margin could now be traced to the sale of Pluto water.[63] Pluto water was sold over drugstore counters around the world and took first prize at the World's Fair

E. C. Kropp Co. Provided by Miss Betty Cretors

Slogan that promised the laxative benefits of world-famous Pluto water.

in Paris.[64] Taggart's address book listed entries for Pluto salesmen all over the country, including New York City, Boston, Philadelphia, Pittsburgh, Chicago, Dallas, and Los Angeles.[65] The red devil Pluto symbol stuck vividly in the public's collective mind. People who searched their drugstores for various items encountered the Pluto trademark peering down from the shelves. Those living near railroad tracks saw the Monon boxcars hauling Pluto water emblazoned with the famous red devils rolling across the countryside.[66] And for the guests of the hotel there was always the memory of Yarmouth Wigginton, a man dressed in a flaming red devil suit, who served Pluto water while telling wonderful stories.[67]

Sylvester Graham, a nineteenth-century food faddist, had a lot to do with Taggart's success in the hotel and Pluto water businesses. Graham convinced a generation or so of people that alimentary immaculateness was a necessity of good health.[68] Thus, those who could afford it went directly to the many mineral springs that were available. Those who could not afford the trip visited the local drugstore and purchased a bottle of Pluto water. Either way Taggart came out a winner. As the years passed and medical sci-

The Pluto water bottling plant, built in 1913, across from the French Lick Springs Hotel.

ence advanced Taggart modified his claims for the therapeutic qualities of the water. "The waters are not a cure-all," he later said. "Like any other forms of therapy, they have their own particular field."[69] In the early 1940s, well after Taggart's death, a suit was brought against the hotel for false advertising regarding Pluto water. In 1948 the Pluto operation became completely separate from the hotel, and it ceased production altogether in the early 1970s.[70] The business that produced the golden profits for the Taggarts finally outlived its usefulness.

The French Lick Springs Hotel was the crown jewel in Taggart's collection of business enterprises over his long career. It became his principal asset and the fountainhead of the Taggart family's wealth. When Taggart purchased the hotel he gave one share of French Lick Springs Hotel Company stock to his wife and one share to each of his surviving five children, retaining 5,994 shares of the company for himself. A similar family ownership was arranged for the French Lick and West Baden Railway Company. According to an internal revenue report in December 1920 he had later given his son controlling stock in the company and split the

"THE HOME OF PLUTO WATER"

FRENCH LICK SPRINGS HOTEL, FRENCH LICK, IND.

Postcard showing the completed French Lick Springs Hotel under Taggart ownership.

remaining shares with his family. Then in late 1922 the capital stock of the company was increased from $600,000 to $3,000,000, with 30,000 shares at $100 each. As of 30 November 1922 the stockholders were Eva B. Taggart (8,000 shares), Thomas D. Taggart (8,000), Thomas Taggart (6,000), Lucy Taggart (2,000), Nora Taggart Chambers (2,000), Irene Taggart Young (2,000), and Emily Taggart Sinclair (2,000). For young Tom to have controlling stock at this point he would have needed voting control of at least another 7,001 shares, perhaps his mother's or his sisters' shares. Clearly Taggart's strong sense of family and his commitment to his wife and children are reflected in his financial arrangements for the hotel in French Lick.[71]

With a rich history dating back to Bowles, the French Lick property was developed by Taggart into an elegant world-class spa with its baths, recreational opportunities, and gambling. French Lick and Taggart became synonymous in the new century as both moved onto the national and international stages together.

CHAPTER FIVE

Chairman of the
Democratic National Committee

I n 1904 Thomas Taggart decided to take on two of the most powerful men in American life, President Theodore Roosevelt and William Randolph Hearst. Roosevelt, elected vice president with Republican William McKinley in 1900, had become president in 1901 upon the assassination of McKinley. In 1904 the Republican National Convention nominated him for a four-year term as president in his own right. Hearst, a powerful publishing magnate and member of Congress from New York City, desperately wanted the Democratic presidential nomination in 1904 and the right to oppose Roosevelt in the autumn campaign. Taggart opposed both that year, helping defeat one and losing to the other. The impact of his decisions and involvements in 1904 would be far-reaching indeed.

As winter turned into spring in 1904 the two leading candidates for the Democratic nomination for president appeared to be Hearst and Judge Alton B. Parker, both from New York. Hearst hoped to capture William Jennings Bryan's followers, especially in the Midwest, with a reformist presidential campaign. Therefore, to achieve that goal Hearst broke with political boss Charles F. Murphy, leader of New York City's Tammany Hall Democratic organization, who had helped elect him to Congress. Murphy's political machine was much admired by Taggart, who appreciated to his very core the mechanics and the game of politics. In fact, the *Indianapolis Sentinel*, the city's Democratic newspaper that Taggart controlled, referred to Tammany Hall as "the greatest of American political organizations."[1] Over the years Murphy and Taggart became close associates, the former spending time at

French Lick Springs for recreational pursuits and political strategy sessions. Clearly the boss of the Hoosier Democracy would harbor no sympathy for the Hearst candidacy. And that led to trouble between the two. Hearst launched a vigorous effort for the important Indiana delegation to the national convention, pouring what the *Indianapolis Journal* called a "flood of gold" into the Hoosier state to win its support. Taggart, for his part, led the charge for Parker, a Democrat with whom he was much more comfortable. The ensuing struggle for the allegiance of the Indiana delegation was bitter.[2] When the Democratic state convention met on 12 May in Indianapolis more than one thousand delegates supported Parker and less than five hundred were for Hearst. At that time state party conventions instructed their delegates to national conventions as to whom they should support for president. Thus Taggart prevailed, and the state's thirty votes at the summer convention in St. Louis went to Parker. Furthermore, the state convention delegates recommended Taggart for national chairman and campaign manager.[3] This recommendation made perfect sense to Hoosier Democrats who had witnessed up close Taggart's superb organizing and vote-getting skills. He had remained active in state and national politics after purchasing French Lick Springs and leaving the mayor's office in 1901. Also, he had served on the Democratic National Committee since 1900, and he coveted the national chairmanship of the party. The state delegation knew that other party leaders across the country would give their suggestion serious consideration not only because of Taggart's skills but also because of Indiana's importance on the electoral map.

The effort that Hearst and his people put forth in Indiana was matched in other parts of the country as well. Hearst was determined that the Democratic presidential nomination would be his in 1904 and nothing would stand in the way. His bitterness over Taggart's effective opposition in important Indiana was long-standing. Even though Hearst had broken with Tammany Hall and machine politics, he still had a very powerful source of political influence, his newspapers. In 1904 he owned the *New York Journal*, the *New York American,* the *Chicago American,* the *Chicago Herald and Examiner,* the *Boston American,* the *Los Angeles Examiner,* and the *San Francisco Examiner.* These seven papers gave Hearst a powerful voice in national affairs from coast to coast. There was an explicit understanding that his newspaper staffs and reporters were to plug his candidacy across the United States. His campaign manager Max Ihmsen organized Hearst Clubs across the country, and a William Randolph Hearst League was set up nationally. Before it was over Hearst had spent an estimated $600,000 on his campaign. But this whopping sum of money was spent to little avail because only 263 delegates at the St. Louis convention voted for Hearst for president, and Parker became the Democratic nominee. Even to the end of his unsuccessful quest Hearst was spending a good amount of money. His headquarters at the Hotel Jefferson in St. Louis outdid those of his rivals for display with electric lights, streamers, flags, and all the latest Belasco stage devices. Of some consolation to Hearst was his reelection to Congress.[4]

The Democratic National Convention adjourned in St. Louis on Sunday, 10 July, having nominated Parker for president and Henry Gassaway Davis of West Virginia for vice president. Davis, at eighty-one years of age, was a wealthy Democrat, reportedly worth forty million dollars at the time.[5] Parker, too, was wealthy as a result of a successful career in law and on the bench. His family home, Rosemount, was on a beautiful estate at Esopus, New York, along the Hudson River. The two Democratic candidates in 1904 were far removed from William Jennings Bryan and his unsuccessful campaigns of 1896 and 1900, much to Taggart's delight. One of the most substantive differences was Parker's returning the Democratic party to the gold standard. Even though the party platform remained silent on the money issues, Parker wired this message to the convention upon his nomination:

> I regard the gold standard as firmly and irrevocably estab-
> lished, and shall act accordingly if the action of the con-
> vention today shall be ratified by the people. As the
> platform is silent on the subject, my view should be made

known to the convention, and if it proves to be unsatisfactory to the majority, I request you to decline the nomination for me at once, so that another may be nominated
before adjournment.[6]

Parker, for all his wealth and patrician manner, was a self-made
man. Born to a family of modest means, he began teaching at age
sixteen to earn enough money to continue his education. He did
so, was admitted to the bar, and became a justice of the New York
State Supreme Court at thirty-three years of age. Thirteen years
later he won election as chief judge of the Court of Appeals.
Parker had known both great joy and pain in his personal life. He
and his devoted wife Mary lost their only son John when he was
seven years old. Their daughter Bertha then became the center
of their lives and, as a result of her marriage to Charles Mercer Hall,
gave them two grandchildren, Alton Parker Hall and Mary Hall,
four years old and two years old respectively in 1904, on whom the
couple doted. The family property, Rosemount, which was situated
one hundred feet above the Hudson River, was historic, the oldest part of the house being in existence in 1777 when the British
dropped anchor just below it during the American Revolution. For
his daily routine Parker, an expert swimmer, took a dip in the
Hudson first thing each morning and then rode one of his sad-
dle horses about the estate surveying his operation. He was a practical farmer whose special hobby was a herd of blooded cattle.
Parker reserved the time from luncheon to dinner each day for
business matters, political and otherwise. To be sure, Parker and
his lifestyle were the epitome of the quiet wealth so prevalent along
the Hudson.[7]

Taggart, undoubtedly, was the key to Parker gaining the
Democratic presidential nomination in 1904. Just when Parker's
candidacy was languishing Taggart threw him Indiana's support
at the state's convention in May. That move may well have been
pivotal to Parker's chances of success. With good reason Taggart's
friends assumed that the national chairmanship had been
promised in return, or, whatever arrangement may or may not

have been made, that the chairmanship would be forthcoming. However, when they approached William F. Sheehan, a Parker confidant from New York, they received an unsatisfactory response.[8] This came as a great surprise to the Hoosiers who must have viewed Sheehan's response as an act of eastern ingratitude. The eastern leaders were so opposed to Taggart, in fact, that they had offered Indiana the vice presidential spot on the ticket if Taggart would stop his quest for the chairmanship. The day before the vice presidential nomination Taggart had gathered his friends and said he would give up the effort. "John Kern can have the nomination for Vice-President," said Taggart, "if I will get out of his way, and I propose to get out. It is time for the Indiana delegation to meet and indorse Kern for second place." The delegation did meet and unanimously voted not to present Kern's name. One delegate summed up the Hoosiers' feelings, "We have pinned our faith to Taggart and we propose to stick to him."[9]

To continue eastern opposition to Taggart, Sheehan held a meeting in the early hours of 10 July with national committeemen Norman E. Mack of New York, Daniel J. Campau of Michigan, and Col. James M. Guffey of Pennsylvania in order to delay the reorganization meeting of the national committee. In spite of Sheehan's efforts a majority of the national committee members met at the Hotel Jefferson immediately after the convention's adjournment. The Parker people claimed the committee had no right to meet, but the meeting convened anyway and those present named Taggart chair of the gathering. They then adjourned until 4 P.M. that afternoon. When the meeting reconvened thirty-seven members were in attendance. August Belmont, another New York confidant of Parker's, was the only representative of the presidential nominee present. The members made it clear that they did not like the efforts by Parker and Belmont to dictate to the national committee. Furthermore, the committee made known its intention to organize and run the national campaign. Then, in an unprecedented move, the members passed a resolution over Belmont's objection that stated, "It is the sense of this meeting that Thomas Taggart, of Indiana,

should be elected chairman of the National Committee." There
was only one "no" vote. By tradition the presidential nominee
named the national chairman, but this year the other regional
groupings of the Democratic party, especially westerners, were not
willing to subject themselves to dictation by their eastern brethren.
So they coalesced around Taggart and pushed his attempt to
become chairman. For the likable gentleman from Indiana this
national position of leadership would not come easily.[10]

John W. Kern, a longtime Taggart friend and ally in Hoosier
politics, now proved central to Taggart's quest for the chairmanship. Kern, who had been defeated for governor of Indiana
in 1900, was also a close personal friend of Parker's. In fact, the
relationship was such that Kern was persuaded by the New Yorker
to be the Democratic nominee for governor again in 1904 to help
the national ticket in critically important Indiana.[11] To further
the cause of his friend Taggart, Kern served as intermediary
between Taggart and Parker and made a trip to Rosemount on
16 July to broker some kind of agreement. The press reported that
Kern and Parker met, took a walk, and then made a short trip over
to see Sheehan for further discussions. The day wrapped up
with dinner, and Kern spent the night at Parker's estate. The next
morning, 17 July, a Sunday, Kern joined Parker and party in his
launch *Niobe*, which was going downriver so they could attend
Episcopal services at the Church of the Holy Cross in Kingston
where Parker's son-in-law Charles Mercer Hall was rector. Kern,
however, did not attend the services and was taken for a ride
instead. Reports of Kern's meeting in Esopus indicated that
Parker felt kindly toward Taggart and that he himself would
not select the chairman. Kern apparently told the nominee that
the ticket might not do well in the Hoosier state if Taggart were
not named chairman of the national committee. Kern also let
Parker know that he would place Taggart's name before the
meeting in New York that would select the party's new chairman.[12] Earlier in the week Parker wrote former president Grover
Cleveland soliciting his advice and apparently expressing some
reservations about having Taggart at the helm. Cleveland wrote

back, "We need Indiana; and if the Taggart Chairmanship will help us get it, it might be well to remember that after all the Chairman of the Executive Committee of the New York Headquarters is the important man."[13]

Kern left Rosemount on the morning of 18 July and headed south along the Hudson River to New York City where he attended an evening political meeting at Hoffman House on 34th Street, the national party headquarters. At that gathering Democratic leaders from the West insisted that Taggart was the man to be the next chairman. They left no doubt that he was their choice for the party's top post. Word was put out also that Taggart would not head up the presidential campaign in the West from the auxiliary headquarters to be opened in Chicago if he were not named national chairman. Clearly, western leaders were turning up the heat on Parker's people as they jockeyed for power in the campaign and the national party. The man who embodied these aspirations for power and influence was Taggart.[14]

Finally, after all the behind-the-scenes maneuvering, the Democratic National Committee met on 26 July in New York City to organize for the coming campaign. The fight against Taggart, however, was not yet over. The eastern forces tried to persuade Sen. Arthur P. Gorman of Maryland to run for chairman, but he refused their pleas. Then, in a desperate last-ditch effort to prevent Taggart's election, the easterners moved to adjourn the 1 P.M. meeting. They were rebuffed by Taggart's supporters who then moved for his election after Kern placed his name before the group. At long last, in a superficial show of party unity, Taggart was elected chairman by a unanimous vote.[15]

"If the Eastern Democrats will do what they say they can do, and carry their States, I'll get the West and Judge Parker will be our next President," Taggart declared on the day of his selection. His words of optimism carried a less than veiled challenge to those in the party who had opposed him so vigorously. Taggart had certainly fought his way to the top of the national party; he had earned the honor. At age forty-seven and only a four-year veteran of the national committee, this immigrant boy from Amyvale had come a long way indeed. He now would be presiding over the Democratic party and guiding the campaign for its nominee for president of the United States. As Taggart took over the reins of party leadership he exhibited caution and courtesy toward Parker, fully aware that his election had come about in a most unprecedented way. He announced that he would not name the party's executive committee or finance committee until he had a chance to sit down and talk with Parker.[16]

Three days after his election, on 29 July, Taggart made his political pilgrimage to Esopus to consult with Parker. While he must have felt somewhat uneasy about the meeting since Parker's aides and eastern supporters had opposed him so strenuously, he also had Kern's assurances that the nominee looked upon him in a favorable way. Whatever his feelings, Taggart's finely honed political instincts must have told him that there were many challenges ahead. When he arrived at the railroad station in Esopus, Parker's coach met him and took him to Rosemount. Party chairman and presidential nominee retired to Parker's library for an hour-long conference that revolved around the makeup of the party's executive committee. Belmont wanted three or four New Yorkers on the seven-man committee, but Taggart reportedly told Parker at their meeting that New York should have no more than two seats. After they conferred Taggart said that Parker had expressed no opinion on the matter and the candidate would take it up with Belmont and Sheehan.[17]

Taggart returned to Indianapolis to wrap up some personal business and to get his affairs in order before locating to New York City for the next three months to run the national campaign. Indianapolis Democrats turned out by the thousands to welcome him home with a parade of five thousand marchers and a rally at Tomlinson Hall. The atmosphere was electric with enthusiasm. Once back in the Hoosier capital Taggart was dumbfounded to receive letters from Belmont and Sheehan thanking him for their appointments to the executive committee. In fact, Parker, acting alone, had appointed the entire executive committee, with Sheehan as chairman. Clearly the sting of Taggart's election had not subsided, and the struggle for power and influence within the party continued. Kern, friend to both men, was angered by Parker's action. In the end, as a conciliatory gesture, Taggart struck only one name from Parker's list of appointments, that of Michigan's Campau who had worked so hard to defeat Taggart. As these scenes were played out on the national stage, Theodore Roosevelt and the Republicans must have been encouraged. The bitter divisions within the Democratic party gave the Republicans every reason to hope for victory in November. And, of course, everyone was aware that the Democrats had been in power during the Panic of 1893 and had dropped the last two elections in 1896 and 1900 with William Jennings Bryan at the top of the ticket.[18]

Despite the Indiana-New York feud that pitted west against east the campaign moved forward. Before Taggart took up residence at Hoffman House in New York, he announced important appointments from Indianapolis in the first week of August. The vice chairman would be De Lancey Nicoll (New York), a corporation lawyer, and the treasurer would be philanthropist George Foster Peabody (New York). Members of the executive committee were William F. Sheehan (New York); August Belmont (New York), financier; John R. McLean (Ohio), publisher of the *Cincinnati Enquirer* and multimillionaire; Sen. Thomas S. Martin (Virginia); Col. James M. Guffey (Pennsylvania), petroleum magnate; former Sen. James Smith, Jr. (New Jersey), who had vast corporate holdings; and Timothy E. Ryan (Wisconsin).[19] The organizational structure would eventually flesh out with Urey Woodson (Kentucky) serving as secretary, Myron D. King (Indiana) as auditor, Judge Daniel McConville (Ohio) as head of the speakers' bureau, George F. Parker and Thomas B. Fielders as heads of the literary and press bureaus, and F. C. Penfield in charge of the department of documents.[20] The executive committee acted as the party's court of last resort and financed the presidential campaign since Taggart had merged the executive and finance committees. Certain individuals were assigned responsibility for key states: executive committee members Sheehan and Belmont had

New York; Ryan, also of the executive committee, was given Wisconsin; vice presidential nominee Henry Davis had West Virginia; and Senator Gorman had Maryland. Taggart, of course, was to win Indiana for the ticket. The new chairman certainly believed in delegating power from the national party to the state organizations, earning him the label "home ruler" in this regard. He felt that the state parties should do most of their own planning and managing. This policy reflected Taggart's Jeffersonian approach to politics and government in general. Having essentially dictated the party platform at the convention and the composition of the executive committee afterwards, the eastern Democrats were fortunate to have Taggart to woo the West.[21]

The national media now recognized the power of Taggart's personality and its effectiveness in the political process. The *Review of Reviews* attributed his success in Indiana squarely to his personality, good nature, and patience. He was acknowledged, in everyday lingo, as a "good fellow" and as a man with a "smile that will not wear off." It was pointed out that he was never addressed as "Mr. Taggart" in Indiana but always as just "Tom."[22] Even *Harper's Weekly*, which referred to most of its subjects as "Mr." or "Mrs.," labeled Taggart in its columns as simply "Tom."[23]

Taggart's friendliness, kindness, and lack of pretension extended to his own employees and they, in turn, gave him their devotion and loyalty. One such example of devotion came in 1904 upon his election as chairman of the national committee. Charlie Washington, a Taggart employee who had been a slave before the Civil War, was very attached to Taggart and wanted to accompany him to New York for the campaign. Taggart told him that he must stay behind and help take care of Mrs. Taggart and the children. Thinking that was the end of the matter, Taggart settled his other affairs in Indianapolis and French Lick and left for New York. When he arrived in New York he was met at the train by none other than Washington. Sure that his employer needed someone trustworthy to look after him in New York City, Washington had some acquaintances on the train crew help him pull off this surprise. Devotion and loyalty to Taggart were genuine.[24]

The Democratic presidential campaign of 1904 got under way on 10 August when Parker gave his address of acceptance at Rosemount. According to the practice of the day the candidate was formally notified of his nomination for the presidency at his home where he then gave a speech accepting the honor. The notification speech afforded a newly anointed nominee an opportunity to set forth the major themes of the coming campaign. Parker, for his part, focused his remarks on high tariff rates under Republican rule, a traditional Democratic issue, and on criticism of American imperialism in the Philippines. In addition to addressing these two questions Parker surprised observers by vowing to serve only one term if he were elected president. The issues of the tariff and imperialism were issues on which there was much intraparty agreement and could, therefore, help bridge the chasm between the Democratic parties of the conservative, business-oriented East and the more populist, agricultural West. Hope ran high that Roosevelt, untested as a presidential candidate himself and unpopular with many in his own party, could be turned out of office by this fellow New Yorker.[25]

Organization was the key to political success in America before the age of mass media. And the Democrats knew early on that there was much work to be done. In mid-August, shortly after the notification at Rosemount, New York's Democrats devised a comprehensive organizational plan based largely upon dividing the state by school districts. Cord Meyer, chairman of the New York State Central Committee, had his headquarters at Hoffman House in New York, such was the importance attached to carrying the nation's most populous state. To help implement its plan the state committee asked Parker to write all of the county chairmen urging them to get behind the organizing effort.[26] The new party chairman, known far and wide as a master of political organization in the Hoosier state, devoted himself to perfecting party organizations in states considered "doubtful" for the Democratic ticket. Taggart would apply the "Indiana system," renowned in political circles for its success, to these state party machines in need of repair. The Hoosier system of doing things was very simple. One person from the Democratic organization was assigned to each precinct in the countryside and to each block in every city and town of the state. Each designated party person had a list of every Democratic voter in his precinct or block and was responsible for seeing that all of his Democrats voted on election day. Properly implemented, this system of political organization could increase Democratic turnout at the polls and make even doubtful states possible for the Parker-Davis ticket to win.[27]

Parker made the decision, possibly a fateful one, that he would spend the campaign at home in Rosemount rather than go on a stumping tour of the country. This was not an unusual decision for a presidential candidate at this time for it was still considered more dignified to conduct a campaign for such high office through subordinates and the print media rather than in person. William McKinley had successfully waged just such a "front porch campaign" against Bryan in 1896. Thus Parker stayed home, conferred with aides, issued statements to the press, and received delegations of supporters. In hindsight, however, Parker could have used every minute of exposure to fight Roosevelt's power of incumbency and to heal the deep divisions in his own party. Nevertheless, he remained in Esopus, riding twenty miles on horseback over his estate each day and following the dignified routine of a gentleman candidate.[28]

Taggart, on the other hand, left family and home, rolled up his sleeves, and went to work in the rough-and-tumble world of national politics. He was responsible for devising and implementing a comprehensive plan that would elect the Democratic ticket. Once that plan was established he would then concentrate on strengthening organizations in states difficult for a Democrat to win. And, of course, the national committee would be a source of support and encouragement for all state party organizations as they developed and implemented their strategies for victory in November. The goal was to capture the necessary 239 electoral votes in the 476-member electoral college. To reach the magic number of 239, Taggart's strategy reportedly was to win New

York, the most important prize with its 39 electoral votes, Connecticut, Delaware, New Jersey, Maryland, and West Virginia, plus the 151 electoral votes of the solidly Democratic South. Having won these states, the ticket would then need only twelve more electoral votes to put it over the top. There were three options, as Taggart saw it, that could bring success: win Indiana and its 15 votes; carry the 13 electoral votes of Wisconsin; or capture the combined 14 votes of Idaho, Montana, Nevada, and Colorado. Making an honest assessment of what he considered possible, Taggart believed the four silver states in the West would be difficult to carry, but there was an even chance in both Indiana and Wisconsin.[29] Others in the press, however, saw a more difficult challenge ahead for Taggart and the Democrats. For example, one newspaper, the *New York World,* counted only the South and Delaware, Maryland, and West Virginia as solid for Parker and Davis, with a total of 169 electoral votes. The ticket, therefore, needed to find another 70 votes in order to win. The paper also saw three possible options for the Democrats to achieve victory. Taggart needed to win one of these combinations of states: 1) New York, Illinois, and Colorado; 2) New York, Indiana, New Jersey, and Colorado; or 3) New York, Wisconsin, New Jersey, Nevada, and Colorado.[30] Whatever combination prevailed, the paper pointed out that New York was essential to Democratic chances and that the other fight would be in the Middle West. To be sure, Taggart and the Democrats had their work cut out for them in the weeks ahead.

To help unify the Democratic party and promote the Parker cause Taggart asked William Jennings Bryan, still widely popular from his presidential campaigns of 1896 and 1900, to speak in Indiana. Bryan agreed to do so and delivered a total of fifty-two speeches in eight days as he crossed the Hoosier state. In the interest of party unity he also spoke in West Virginia, Ohio, Illinois, Missouri, and Nebraska. Bryan's support was important if the party, now controlled by the eastern gold Democrats, was to have any hope of capturing the free silver people of the West and elsewhere in the nation.[31]

Now that Taggart was chairman of the Democratic National Committee and playing a key role in the party's presidential campaign, public interest in him and his family naturally followed. The hotel man and former mayor of Indianapolis began to attract notice and scrutiny from the national media. In the middle of September Tom and Eva Taggart gave an interview to the *New York Herald* that was unusually revealing about their private lives. Eva, described by the reporter as tall with clear brown eyes and a well-poised head, indicated that they lived in a cottage at French Lick Springs and had their main residence in Indianapolis. The home in the Hoosier capital was described as roomy and with extensive grounds. Eva was careful to point out, however, that the house was not too fancy. "Our home is not a pretentious one at all, but very homelike and simple. Simplicity has been the keynote of all our plans and I have always been so grateful that my children have not been given to affectation, not even the small schoolgirl affectations that girls usually have; for instance, writing their names differently." The couple spent a good deal of the interview discussing four of their five surviving children. When Eva spoke about Florence and the "Yokum disaster" of five years earlier, she was very composed and stoically showed no sign of grief. The article recounted that Lucy had studied art in New York at the Art League and the Chase Art School, conducted by native Hoosier artist William Merritt Chase; Nora had graduated from Vassar the year before with an interest in music; and Emily was determined to go to Vassar, too, just like her older sister. Eva seemed to worry a bit over young Tom because "my son's life has been made very easy for him, in comparison with his father's early struggles." She saw her role clearly as that of wife and mother and, uncharacteristically, revealed to the reporter the impact that her own mother's early death had on her. "My six children were born in the first ten years of my married life, and thus I found my life's work cut out for me. The unfolding of their lives is quite enough interest for the usual woman. Before I was old enough to realize my loss my mother died, and all my life I have yearned so much for that mother love that I have tried to fill every niche of my children's lives." As for her wifely role, she stated a belief typical of women of her day—that each man should be allowed the freedom to plan his life's work without being hampered by his spouse. This philosophy surely was comforting when married to a man like Taggart who was absorbed by business and politics and who was away from home much of the time. The chairman's wife was described as optimistic, believing the world was a beautiful place and that life was a great pleasure. She expressed as her only regret that people were usually so near the grave before learning how to live. When asked if she had attended the Democratic convention in St. Louis, she replied that she had not. "I was interested, naturally," she said. "I could not calmly endure the excitement, and I dislike a display of emotions as much as I dislike anything else extravagant." Poised, stoical, unpretentious, and a devoted wife and mother summed up Eva Taggart.

Despite all of his business and political interests, there was no doubt that his family was the center of Tom Taggart's life. He spoke to the *Herald* reporter about his relationship with his wife. "The happiest occurrence in my life from every standpoint was the day when I married my wife. So close to me has she been in all my career that when I came to New York alone, because she concluded I would be too busy to have her about in the early days of the campaign, I was lost without her. She is my inspiration. Yes, my happy family and their love and interest have helped me over many difficult places." The candor of this politically hardened man was strikingly genuine. Taggart revealed more of himself when asked what he enjoyed in life. "What do I enjoy in life? Why, my child, I enjoy every phase of life. When in politics I enjoy that more than anything. My diversions are whatever may happen to my hand, but particularly I enjoy duck shooting. A morning ride with some or all of my family gives me a great deal of pleasure. We have never been able to travel very much, I have been so busy. We like to enjoy things together, but that is in the future. I look forward to seeing my own and other countries with the keenest pleasure." His widespread reputation for friendliness and kindness got a further boost when he recalled the circumstances of his entry

into the political process. "My political career began in a very peculiar way. An acquaintance was running for Councilman, and as he
had a little money I discovered that the 'boys' were allowing him
to spend it, and then laughing at his aspirations. The whole thing
seemed to me so brutal and unfair that I jumped in and worked
for him and we managed to elect him. After that I became so
intensely interested in the political game that I have been in it ever
since." Taggart's attitude and approach were witnessed and experienced by countless people who came into contact with him
over the years. The interview with the New York paper gave an
unusual glimpse into the Taggarts' private lives and thoughts.
Surely its most humorous moment came when Eva stated that she
read to her husband after a tiring day and that he was especially
fond of history. "If he is very weary," she said, "I can read him to
sleep quickest with the Bible."[32]

While the party politicos under Taggart labored over the
mechanics of a presidential election at Hoffman House headquarters in New York, Parker issued a series of policy statements
and accusations from the seclusion of Rosemount. Parker hit
Roosevelt and the Republicans hard on the tariff issue, explaining the traditional Democratic argument: "The beneficiaries,
having induced the Government to shut out foreign competition
form Trusts and Combinations to stifle domestic competition. Not
all the Trusts and combines are founded on the tariff, but most
of them are. Their continued existence and their mode of self-
perpetuation lead to the belief that the country is no longer
governed by principles but by interests." Then, going straight to
the heart of matters for the mass of Democratic voters, Parker said,
"It is true, as all know, that excessive tariff rates have caused serious injury to the great body of the people. It has increased the cost
of living and added to the price of nearly everything that the
people must buy."[33] The amount of business money flowing
to the Republicans disturbed and frustrated the Democratic
nominee. He was very direct in his criticism on this point: "Political
contributions by corporations and trusts mean corruption. They
cannot be honest. Merely business interests are moved by merely

business considerations. A corporation will subscribe to a political party, only because the corporation expects that party, through its control of public officers, executive or legislative, to do something for the benefit of the corporation, or to refrain from doing something to its injury."[34]

Parker, with his scholarly study of the United States Constitution, believed that under Roosevelt the executive branch of government had usurped powers of the legislative and judicial branches. In thinly veiled words that left little doubt what he really meant, Parker claimed, "Under Republican administration this rule has been disregarded. One of the branches of the national government has on occasion gone beyond its authority, and usurped functions withheld from it by the Constitution."[35] He charged the Roosevelt administration with being fiscally extravagant, pointing out that seven years ago under a Democratic president the federal budget was $366 million, but now it had ballooned to $582 million. Even deducting $50 million for Panama Canal rights and expenses, that still left a bloated budget of $532 million.[36] Parker believed the acquisition and development of the Panama Canal as well as the fiscal questions were examples of an executive branch overstepping its proper boundaries.

Parker, Taggart, and the Democrats also opposed the Republicans on American policy toward the Philippines. The Philippines, acquired from Spain under President McKinley as a result of the Spanish-American War of 1898, was the site of a strong native movement for independence led by Emilio Aguinaldo, which directed its force against the Americans after they replaced the Spanish. Acquiring the Philippines and suppressing the insurgency movement caused a vigorous debate over imperialism in the United States at the turn of the century. Parker promised independence to the islands as soon as the Filipinos were prepared and ready for it. Citing the example of George Washington and the colonists in the American Revolution, Parker pledged himself to self-determination for the Philippines. He charged that the islands had already cost $650 million and 200,000 lives beyond the original $20 million the United States paid Spain for them at the conclusion of the war. "Our duty to the Filipinos," Parker stated, "demands a promise of independence. But if it did not, our own interest demands that we be relieved of the Filipinos just as soon as they are reasonably prepared for self-government. A colony-holding nation is ever subject to expensive wars with other nations and with its colonies. This necessitates strong garrisons and powerful navies, and draws heavily upon the treasury. And history records no instance of a nation receiving from her colonies anything like an adequate return for the blood and treasure spent."[37] Taggart, too, had committed himself on this issue. "I think that the government could have idealized itself to the world by saying to the Cubans and the Filipinos that we would help them form a stable government, set them straight and then withdraw, retaining a coaling station or something like that. Instead, they put themselves on the plane of European imperialists and grabbed the Philippines in toto as a good thing. Now that we are in for it and have to make a showing, I am in favor of going ahead and forcing the natives to surrender but it is too bad that our soldiers should have to be way off there fighting in such a country."[38] The issue of imperialism for the Democrats in 1904 combined conviction and political expediency, the best of all possible worlds in politics.

The rival Republican National Committee had its headquarters in 1904 at Madison Avenue and 23rd Street in Manhattan, just blocks away from Democratic headquarters. The importance that both parties attached to New York can be seen in the fact that their national committees were located there rather than in Washington. The chairman of the Republican National Committee was George B. Cortelyou, the secretary of commerce and labor.[39] The Democrats tried to make "Cortelyouism" a central issue of the campaign, charging that as secretary of commerce and labor he had information about corporations that could be used to get them to contribute to the Republican cause. Indeed, the Republican war chest reached a total of $2,195,000, about four times that of the Democrats. Aside from Thomas Fortune Ryan's contribution of $250,000 and Henry G. Davis's $185,000, the remaining gifts to the Democrats probably did not total $500,000. The Democrats took every opportunity to portray a cozy relationship between Cortelyou and the Republicans and the business community that reeked of impropriety. Roosevelt, for his part, had had enough of this partisan assault on his chairman. In a letter to Cortelyou in early October marked "Important and Confidential," the president wrote, "The editorials in the *Times* and *World* and Brooklyn *Eagle* show that there is to be a concerted attack made upon you. I should think it a disadvantage to remain on the defensive as regards the National ticket any more than as regards the State ticket; and I should have the most savage counterattack possible made upon Taggart, Belmont, Sheehan, McCarren [Patrick H. McCarren was the Tammany leader of Brooklyn], and Parker."[40] Roosevelt's fighting spirit was clearly aroused and, to be sure, he had no use for Parker's national chairman by the end of the autumn campaign. "Above all," he wrote Cortelyou in early November in a letter stamped "Personal," "it should be pointed out that when he chose Tom Taggart as chairman of the National Committee he deliberately and avowedly chose a man whose only conception of running a campaign was to run it by the brutal use of money."[41]

Finally the presidential campaign of 1904 drew to a close, and all the key players awaited the decision of the American electorate. The main cast of characters had a decidedly Hoosier flavor with Taggart managing the Democratic campaign and Charles W. Fairbanks, wealthy senator from Indiana and a Taggart political opponent, as the Republican vice presidential nominee. For Taggart the final days of the campaign were difficult indeed. The eastern crowd at the Democratic National Committee, never fond of Taggart, tried to wrest control from him and take over the operation in the campaign's critical last days. In disgust over the continuing intraparty fighting and bickering, Taggart packed up and returned home to Indianapolis in late October, managing the remainder of the presidential campaign from the top floor of the Grand Hotel.[42] Despite all the Democratic infighting, the Democratic National Committee painted a pretty picture of imminent victory in its preelection prediction of results. Parker and Davis would win the election, the Democrats claimed, with a total of 248 electoral votes, 9 more than necessary. Confidently it was predicted that the ticket would carry the South (151 electoral votes), New York (39), Indiana (15), New Jersey (12), Maryland (8), West Virginia (7), Washington (5), Colorado (5), Montana (3), and Nevada (3). Many in the country and in the press, *Harper's Weekly* for example, were skeptical about the Democratic claim.[43] It was difficult to believe that the Parker-Davis ticket could prevent the incumbent president from gaining a full four-year term in his own right. The outcome on election day more than justified the skepticism. Roosevelt won 336 electoral votes to Parker's 140, and the president carried the popular vote by a tally of 7,628,785 (56.4 percent) to 5,084,442 (37.6 percent). The only states that fell into the Democratic column in 1904 were the eleven states of the Confederacy and Kentucky and Maryland from the border states. Parker's New York, Davis's West Virginia, and Taggart's Indiana all went to Roosevelt. The Republicans dominated the 59th Congress by a 57 to 33 margin in the Senate and 250 to 136 margin in the House of Representatives. The balance in the Senate was unchanged, but the Democrats lost 42 seats in the House. The American people had spoken, giving Roosevelt and the Republican party a resounding mandate to govern.

Parker mixed bitterness with graciousness in his remarks after the election. "Our thanks," he said, "are due to the members of the National Committee and to the Executive Committee in charge of the campaign for most unselfish, capable and brilliant party service. All that it was possible for men to do they did, but our difficulty was beyond the reach of party managers." He did not mention Taggart by name and went on to condemn the "vicious tariff circle" and the illegal trust and corporate contributions given to the Republicans. "Before long," Parker predicted, "the people will realize that the tariff-fed trusts and illegal combinations are absorbing the wealth of the nation. Then they will wish to throw off these leeches, but the Republican party will not aid them to do it, for its leaders appreciate too well the uses to which the moneys of the trusts can be put in political campaigns."[44] The sting of defeat penetrated the refined confines of Rosemount and was felt by the distinguished New York jurist.

There is no record that Taggart was bitter about the campaign experience of 1904. Frustrated, yes, but not bitter. It was not his nature or personality to be so. Surely the fact that politics was his avocation and not his vocation made a great deal of difference in this regard, too. The exposure and contacts that came with being national chairman, in fact, were a boost to both Taggart's business and political careers. He used this experience to cultivate political friendships all around the country that solidified his role as a power broker in the national party, while shamelessly promoting his French Lick Springs Hotel at every opportunity. Taggart even distributed brochures about French Lick and Pluto water at the Democratic convention in St. Louis, for which at least one New York reporter condemned him. But people began to take notice of Taggart and his spa, and soon a group as diverse as New York politicians to scions of the wealthy were visiting the hotel in southern Indiana.[45] The expansion projects then began in earnest and the French Lick Springs Hotel and Pluto water were off and running to profitable futures.

Shortly after the election, on the Sunday before Christmas, there was an accusation in the press against him that riled Taggart. The *New York Sun* published a five-column article about his mismanagement of the presidential campaign, alleging that Taggart secured a total of $35,000 from the Democratic National Committee to support the *Indianapolis Sentinel*, the city's Democratic paper that he controlled and in which he had a creditor interest. The *Sun* charged that Taggart received $10,000 before the convention for his support of Parker, and, later, after he became chairman, he demanded $50,000 more. The group allegedly met him halfway at $25,000, making a grand total of $35,000 for the *Sentinel*. In addition, the New York paper contended that Taggart sought money for his hotel bills and for election expenses in Indiana. When asked to respond, he said, "There is a sequel to that story. I may have something more to say later on. But I will say this now: There was never any such a meeting as that described at which I am represented as asking for $50,000 for the Sentinel."[46] The following April the *Sun* finally retracted its December charges against Taggart, admitting that his support for Parker before the convention had not been won by money for the *Sentinel*. It now reported that the Democratic campaign managers did spend several thousand dollars to keep the *Sentinel* afloat, but that Taggart had only a small creditor interest in the paper and that he never demanded money from the executive committee of the Democratic National Committee. Also, the *Sun* corrected itself again by stating that the national chairman was a financially solvent person rather than the "financially broken man" as reported in its December piece. After several months of challenge to his integrity, Taggart was now vindicated.[47]

Thus an important phase in Taggart's life both ended and began with the close of the presidential race in 1904. The campaign, indeed, was over, but Taggart's role as a national figure in the Democratic party had just begun. He would remain national chairman for the next four years, and he was the undisputed boss of the Democratic machine in Indiana. His hotel at French Lick would become internationally known, highly successful, and a center of national Democratic politics. But Taggart soon found that power and controversy are forever friends.

CHAPTER SIX

A Decade of Power
and Controversy, 1906–1916

I n the ten-year period 1906–16 Taggart consolidated and
exercised political power on the state and national levels
and achieved great success in business with the expansion of his French Lick Springs resort. His family, too,
expanded with the marriages of his daughters Nora and
Emily and the births of the first four of his nine grandchildren.
Indeed, these were years of change and achievement, but power
and success also brought controversy.

In Taggart's trinity of priorities—family, French Lick, and politics—family always came first. So it was with joy that the Taggarts
greeted the marriage of their daughter Nora to David Laurance
Chambers on 26 April 1910. After attending the Benjamin
Harrison Public School and graduating from Shortridge High
School, where she was an editor of the highly regarded *Echo*
newspaper, Nora left Indianapolis to attend college at Vassar,
graduating in 1903. That same year Chambers came to
Indianapolis to work for the publishing firm of Bobbs-Merrill. He
was born in 1879 and hailed from Washington, D.C., where his
father had been an attorney for the government. Chambers had
a distinguished academic career at Princeton where he was a
member of Phi Beta Kappa and was salutatorian of the class of
1900. The next year he earned a master's degree in English as a
Charles Scribner Fellow. During his long career with Bobbs-
Merrill, Chambers became vice president in 1921, editor in 1925,
president in 1935, and chairman of the board in 1953, achieving
an eminent place in the nation's publishing circles.[1] This first wedding of a Taggart child took place in the Taggart home on North

Capitol Avenue. As an orchestra played the wedding march the bridal party entered the central hall of the house where the ceremony was conducted by the groom's brother, the Reverend Tileston Chambers of Saratoga, New York. After the service a wedding supper was served at tables situated throughout the home. Prominent guests included Gov. and Mrs. Thomas R. Marshall, former Vice President and Mrs. Charles W. Fairbanks, and Mr. and Mrs. Meredith Nicholson, the well-known Hoosier writer.[2] This union gave Tom and Eva Taggart their first grandchild on 29 March 1911, when Evelyn Chambers was born. Soon two more grandchildren arrived, David Laurance, Jr., on 14 November 1912 and Judith Nora on 24 March 1914.

The next Taggart marriage was 8 July 1914 when youngest child Emily Letitia married William Richardson Sinclair. Emily, like Nora, graduated from Shortridge High School and then completed her education at a finishing school for young women. Sinclair, commonly referred to as Dick, was born in Belfast, northern Ireland, in 1884 to a prominent business family there. He attended St. Andrews School in Scotland, Rugby School in England, and did a year's work in chemistry and bacteriology at Queens College, Belfast. He began his career in 1903 with his family's meatpacking firm, J. and T. Sinclair and Company Ltd. He came to Indianapolis in 1906 to work for Kingan and Company Ltd., a British-owned meatpacking firm. Sinclair rose to vice president in 1920, treasurer in 1930, and president and chairman of the board in 1936. Sinclair also sat on the boards of the Pennsylvania Railroad, Federal Reserve Bank of Chicago, and the Chicago Board of Trade.[3] This second wedding was special in that it was the first formal function in the Taggarts' new home at 1331 North Delaware Street. The Right Reverend Joseph M. Francis of All Saints Episcopal Cathedral, bishop of Indianapolis, read the Episcopal wedding service. A wedding supper followed with tables set out in the garden amid masses of pink hydrangeas, bay trees, fountains, and oriental lanterns. Afterwards there was dancing in the white pergola built off the sunroom into the garden. Honeymoon plans were for the couple to sail from New York to England and Ireland where they would tour and be the guests of Sinclair relatives.[4] A little over a year later the fourth Taggart grandchild arrived with the birth of Dora Lucy Sinclair on 30 July 1915. Much to his delight and joy, Tom Taggart's family circle was growing ever larger.

Politically, Taggart was clearly the Democratic boss of Indiana. To be sure, there were challenges to Taggart's rule, some successful and some not, and constant party infighting, but he still stood as the single most powerful force to be dealt with in Hoosier Democratic politics. Louis Ludlow summarized nicely when he wrote, "Any political 'Who's Who' of the last third of a century would be incomplete that failed to assign a place of honor to Thomas Taggart. His was the master mind that wrought brilliant and bewildering achievements in political legerdemain. He was a veritable genius in the art of handling men. A more companionable and likable person never lived. He had a way of spreading sunshine and gladness that was peculiarly his own, and no one ever came into contact with him without being affected by the warmth of his genial Irish nature. He won by kindness."[5]

A storm of controversy over gambling at French Lick Springs struck the state and the nation in 1906. The bitter debate had its roots in two sources: the election in 1904 of Republican J. Frank Hanly as governor and William Randolph Hearst. Hanly was a strict moralist, guided by his own lights, and was dead set against the consumption of alcoholic beverages and gambling. Hanly intended to fight and oppose these vices with the full force of government. His inauguration in January 1905 spelled certain trouble for Taggart and his relatively new enterprise in Orange County. Hearst harbored a deep grudge against the Hoosier Democratic boss for opposing his drive for the party's presidential nomination in 1904. The embittered Hearst packed enough financial and media clout to wreak a serious revenge upon Taggart, and he chose French Lick as his target.

Taggart's term as national chairman of the Democratic party extended through the next national convention in 1908, for which he would be responsible. In his capacity as party chairman he had appointed a seven-person subcommittee to assist the congressional campaign committee in raising funds for the off-year elections in 1906. Taggart made his move, apparently, because the regular congressional campaign committee was not doing well with its fund-raising; however, he did not consult the committee regarding the formation of his new subcommittee. This maneuvering was all part of the intrigue of national party politics. Hearst, still a Democratic congressman, blasted Taggart's committee as controlled by the corporations and charged that the chairman himself was owned by the trusts and Wall Street. In an editorial in his papers he wrote, "They would not be of any more value in collecting honest campaign funds than the gentlemen of the congressional committee, and the Democracy don't want, or ought not to want, any dishonest campaign funds. . . . I am opposed to corporation control in politics . . . it is very foolish to allow this trust-owned advisory committee to come in." Then, Hearst zeroed in for his attack on French Lick, charging that Taggart maintained "an institution for the revival of inebriates and a gambling house for their spoliation." Hearst's editorial was published nationwide, and Taggart defended himself by claiming that Hearst was engaging in a personal attack on him.[6]

Taggart had no way of knowing that the campaign against him had only just begun. Within two weeks Hearst unleashed a blistering attack on gambling at French Lick. Under big, bold headlines that read "Tom Taggart Conducts Greatest Gambling Hall in America" and "Men, Women and Children Play for High Stakes, Night and Day, at French Lick Springs Hotel Casino," the Hearst papers revealed that their publisher recently had sent an investigative writer, Evelyn Campbell, to the Springs valley, and she had witnessed wide-open gambling at both the French Lick and West Baden hotel casinos. "There is a Monte Carlo in the United States," she wrote. "It is at the French Lick Hotel club house, French Lick Springs, Ind., owned by Thomas Taggart, chairman of the Democratic National Committee. . . . I saw all kinds of gambling—faro, roulette, poker, Klondike, 'the ponies,' books on the races, slot machines, etc. I saw men and women gambling."

She continued with a discussion of how the gambling took place so openly. "There is no fear of the law at French Lick Springs. Why should there be?" she asked. "Tom Taggart is the over lord. He owns the hotel, the spacious grounds around it, the clubhouse in which the gambling is going on. Gambling at French Lick Springs is undisturbed by law. Any guest of the French Lick Hotel or of the West Baden or other hotels may gamble there if they have the card of admission, which it is a mere formality for the hotel guest to obtain." Getting to the heart of the gambling arrangement in the valley, Campbell alleged that "Ed Ballard, a gambler, born and raised in West Baden, is the gentleman who pulls the very luscious chestnuts out of the fire for Mr. Taggart. Mr. Ballard pays Mr. Taggart $50,000 a year for the gambling privilege at French Lick Hotel. Fifteen years ago he was working for $6 a week. Now he is reputed to be worth $200,000." The Hearst investigator did everything possible to paint the Springs valley as a den of iniquity and vice, reporting that at least six men a season committed suicide because of losses at the French Lick Springs Casino. Campbell further charged that "West Baden and French Lick Springs is a foul stream, the banks of which are lined with suicides, murders, divorces, feuds, broken and blasted homes and lost and ruined souls. It has become the mecca of corrupt and vicious politicians, who flack [sic] there to gamble and concoct laws, measures, schemes and plans to pillage and plunder a long-suffering public." Hearst clearly was pulling out all the stops as he avenged himself. To bolster the veracity of her allegations, Campbell gave a complete description of the gaming rooms in the casino building that stood only yards from Taggart's hotel. There were just two rooms for gambling, a reception room and an inner room where the tables were set up. The decoration in both rooms was, to say the least, elegant. The reception area had expensive carpets on the floor and velvet-covered chairs and divans. The long, narrow inner room had mirrored walls and electric lights, heavy velvet Brussels carpets, nine tables at which one could buy chips, six for roulette, one for Klondike, one for faro, and one for Bookmakers' Ponies (if the ball on the wheel landed on the space marked "ponies" you won five dollars on a quarter bet), and gaming tables lining the walls. Campbell noted that all of the chips bore Taggart's Pluto trademark.

One supposes that all of this came as a surprise to Governor Hanly who had moved against gambling in the valley the previous autumn and reportedly thought it was extinct. When the Hearst-Campbell story broke, the governor declined comment other than to say, "Whatever bitterness there may be between Mr. Hearst and Mr. Taggart is none of my affair." Anyone who knew anything about Hanly did not believe that for a minute.[7]

On Tuesday, 3 July 1906, the state of Indiana raided the hotel casinos at French Lick and West Baden. His personal zeal on the matter aside, the governor had little choice but to raid the valley after the nationwide Hearst allegations. The state's haul from the French Lick casino included nineteen slot machines, four roulette tables, two poker tables, two Klondike tables, one faro table, the famous French Lick Bookmakers' Club wheel, complete paraphernalia for making books on horse races, and many bushels of chips, cards, dice, and "membership" cards. When the officers of the state asked Taggart for teams of horses to help move the gambling equipment out, he smiled and replied that he was busy putting up hay.[8]

The state of Indiana brought suit against Taggart and Lee Sinclair to revoke their hotel companies' charters and place the French Lick and West Baden properties in receivership. The state also sought injunctions against gambling at both places. Taggart, for his part, responded with a burst of righteous indignation over the whole affair. He stated that the building was owned by the French Lick Springs Company, was completely disconnected from the hotel, and that it was leased to a party to use for billiards and bowling. Furthermore, the lease had a strong clause against gambling. To express his outrage over this illegal gambling on his hotel property, Taggart sued the lessee for possession of the building on grounds of breach of contract. "The French Lick Springs Hotel Company has not, and will not, tolerate gambling in any form on its premises," he declared in a statement on the matter. "There has been no raid, nor attempted raid, upon the French Lick Springs Hotel, nor has such a thing been thought of, save by Mr. Hearst and his correspondents," Taggart asserted. The national chairman described Hearst as a "personal enemy" and claimed that he was publishing "vindictive and libelous falsehoods."

Despite Taggart's protestations of innocence in the gambling controversy, cries arose, especially from his political opponents, for his resignation of the party chairmanship. He would have none of it. "The proposition that I should resign is preposterous. It deserves and will receive no attention." But, smelling the scent of blood, many in the party and the press persisted. The *New York World*, a conservative Democratic paper, called on him to resign, "Mr. Taggart should never have been made chairman of the national committee. He owed his election to a superstition that he was the boss of Indiana, a Napoleonic organizer and a politician of indescribable popularity." It then cited the large plurality by which Roosevelt had carried Indiana over Parker in 1904. Clearly, Taggart was now paying the price for Parker's victory over Hearst for the presidential nomination and his subsequent landslide defeat at the hands of Roosevelt.

Neither Taggart nor Sinclair was ready for the trial on the scheduled date of 5 July, so it was continued until 13 July. The state did seat four witnesses on the former date: Robert D. Macken of Indianapolis, R. Harry Miller of Fairmount, James H. Manion of Indianapolis, and J. M. Fletcher of Winchester. Governor Hanly had dispatched all four to the Springs valley the year before to gamble in the casinos and, thus, provided evidence for the state's earlier move against gambling in the area.

Naturally the valley was aflutter over this latest, and most serious, attempt to impose a different moral code on the Orange County communities. Eleven casino managers and workers were arrested this time, and gossip placed local boy Ed Ballard at the center of it all. Ballard was generally credited with owning the leases to the casinos at the two hotel properties, but on paper the French Lick lease was held by Robert M. Colglazier and the West

Baden lease by Thomas G. Derry. In spite of his success up to this point Ballard was now experiencing rough times with his casino businesses. Gov. Jefferson Davis of Arkansas had just closed down Ballard's Arkansas Club at Hot Springs, and Hearst's crusade had resulted in closing his casino in Santa Barbara, California, as well. Ballard also had a casino in Los Angeles and was reportedly interested in setting up business in eastern resort areas. The Springs valley raid could not have come at a worse time for the likable, big-hearted Ballard.[9]

At the time of the gambling controversy Taggart had owned the French Lick Springs Hotel for five years. Although many improvements had already been made to the property by the summer of 1906, it was a far cry from what it would become in later years. Press accounts of the trial described a large hotel, furnished cottages for rent, houses, a pavilion, a casino (or clubhouse), a park, golf links, and tennis courts. The casino at the center of the controversy was a two-story frame building that measured one hundred feet wide and one hundred seventy-five feet in length. It stood one hundred sixty feet from the main hotel building and was connected to it by walks and bridges. The casino had easy access to the walk to the famous Pluto Spring. The gambling club was on the second floor while billiard tables, bowling alleys, and slot machines were on the first floor. The hotel dominated the town of French Lick, which had a population of about one thousand at this time. Taggart had just begun realizing his vision for the property, and now the state wanted to take it away.[10]

The mid-July trial took place in the Orange County court of Judge Thomas B. Buskirk, a Taggart political associate. The judge joined the cases by the state against the two hotel companies. Taggart was represented by John W. Kern, Bernard Korbly, and Alonso G. Smith, all of Indianapolis. They were joined by Perry McCart of Paoli and M. B. Hottle of Salem. Taggart had chosen a trial over signing an iron-bound agreement against gambling, contending that he had nothing to compromise and he had tried to suppress gambling in French Lick. The state called six principal witnesses during the trial, including Evelyn Campbell, no doubt to Hearst's great satisfaction. To the surprise of no one who was familiar with the politics of Orange County or the shrewdness of Taggart, Buskirk ruled in favor of the defendants. The judge denied the state's quest for a temporary receiver and temporary injunction against gambling at the resorts, citing the facts that the casinos had been raided before this suit was filed and that the defendants had sued the lessees for possession of the premises.[11]

Taggart won the case, but his reputation was damaged. The calls for his resignation as Democratic national chairman continued, but with his usual determination he refused these demands and vowed to complete his term, and the national committee supported him. However, he let it be known that he might not seek another term as chairman because of his rapidly increasing business interests. An *Indianapolis Star* article noted that he also had interests in railroads and a pleasure resort in Mississippi as well as the hotel in French Lick. This gesture would have to pacify his vocal detractors because it was all Taggart would give. One of his attorneys in the gambling case, former attorney general Alonso Smith, returned to Indianapolis from French Lick and stated to the press, "Mr. Taggart will not resign from the national chairmanship. There is no reason why he should resign. He has done nothing to bring about his resignation, and no good Democrat will ask him to resign. He has been perfectly vindicated by Judge Buskirk's decision."[12] Not everyone agreed, of course, notably the *Indianapolis News*. The *News* stated that "the people who have been fighting this great battle [moral awakening and respect for the law] will not be likely to have much confidence in a party that is led and managed by a man who has, for years, permitted gambling openly and publicly with his own knowledge on the property controlled by him, and who has drawn large revenues from the gambling business."[13] On the question of how much money Taggart may have received over the years from gambling revenues, one is faced with a vague and uncertain guessing game. If the reported amount of approximately $50,000 per year for the gambling privilege at French Lick is anywhere near the correct amount, and there is no verification of that figure because any transactions were most assuredly in cash, then Taggart would have pocketed well over one million dollars during his ownership of the hotel. That amount would be several times higher in today's money and, obviously, it would have been exempt from any kind of taxation. There was no question about it, gambling could be a very lucrative business.

Governor Hanly must have been disappointed in the outcome of the Taggart trial in Paoli, the Orange County seat, but he did have some success in battling gambling corruption in state government. The state auditor, it turned out, lost great sums of money gambling at French Lick and turned to embezzling state funds to replace his losses. This situation brought to light a host of financial problems in the administration. In the end, Hanly successfully prosecuted the auditor for embezzlement, and the governor also removed the attorney general and secretary of state from office. A decade later Hanly transferred his crusading zeal to the national level when he became the Prohibition candidate for president in 1916.[14]

Late in August 1906 the lingering intraparty bitterness from the Democratic divisions of 1904 and the fallout from the gambling trial of the previous month were apparent when William Jennings Bryan arrived in New York City from Europe to a big reception, including a parade and speech at Madison Square Garden. Over one hundred thousand people lined four miles of streets in

Thomas Taggart attends a gathering on Decoration Day, 30 May 1907, at the residence of Vice President Charles W. Fairbanks, 1522 N. Meridian Street. President Theodore Roosevelt was the honored guest. Taggart is standing behind the president, third person to the left.

Manhattan to welcome Bryan home. But the New York reception committee completely snubbed Taggart, not inviting him or the Democratic National Committee to the festivities. So, determined as ever, the chairman gathered the members of the national committee and they went as a body to the Battery to greet the two-time presidential nominee. Despite this very public snub, which must have had the approval of Bryan himself, Taggart, years later, professed a "strong and affectionate regard for Bryan." Such was his ability to rise above the incivilities of politics.[15]

Throughout 1907 and the first half of 1908 Taggart held on to the national chairmanship in spite of his opponents. Taggart's primary responsibility was to make arrangements for the Democratic National Convention in the summer of 1908, and his term as party leader then would come to an end with the close of the convention. But first there was the matter of the 1908 Democratic State Convention in Indiana. The Democrats assembled at Tomlinson Hall in downtown Indianapolis in March to transact party business, especially the nomination of a gubernatorial candidate to face the Republicans in the fall. Taggart controlled the state convention that year in the sense that he exercised veto control over the nominee chosen to run for governor, and the presiding officers and important committee people were allied with Taggart so he could dictate the flow of business at the convention. Had he been able to dictate the nominee outright, it would have been his longtime friend Samuel M. Ralston, whom he had been promoting for the state ticket's top spot. However, when rumors swept the floor that Ralston was also the favorite of the brewery interests, it became clear to Taggart and other Ralston supporters that they could not put their man over the top. After leading L. Ert Slack and Thomas R. Marshall on the first ballot, Ralston fell into second place behind Slack by the fourth ballot. That was the clarion call for Taggart to flex his political muscle and demonstrate his considerable power. The Taggart circle strongly opposed Slack because he was a supporter of the temperance movement. Taggart did have close connections to the brewery interests, most notably to Crawford Fairbanks of Terre Haute, therefore he cast a disapproving eye toward the streak of puritanism threading its way through the nation's political fabric. So Taggart ordered a twenty-minute delay in the proceedings and passed the word down the line that Ralston's supporters were to switch to Marshall. Ralston withdrew after the fourth ballot, and, predictably, Marshall won the Democratic nomination for governor on the fifth ballot. Marshall, a Columbia City attorney who had never run for office before, was a compromise candidate acceptable to the Taggart machine. The balloting, however, did not go off mechanically or without emotion. The balloting session was nothing short of raucous and lasted for a long twelve hours. The convention chairman had to call policemen to the floor to restore order during the gubernatorial voting after the sergeant at arms and his assistants failed to do so. At one point a rabid anti-Taggart delegate was hustled off the floor by police only to be brought back shortly thereafter by Taggart himself. To be sure, Hoosiers took their politics seriously, and emotions often reached a fever pitch on the floor of each party's state convention.[16]

After the state convention adjourned the thirty people elected as national convention delegates convened in the bar at the Grand Hotel and reelected Taggart as national committeeman from Indiana. The vote was twenty-four for Taggart, two against (the first district was anti-Taggart), two abstentions, and two votes for W. B. Westlake. This vote for national committeeman was perhaps the best evidence that Taggart was still in control of the state party. After the controversy of the gambling trial two years earlier, his opponents sensed political vulnerability in 1908 and mounted the most bitter fight against him to date. But he had whipped his enemies and proved that he remained the boss of the Indiana Democracy.[17]

The next challenges of the year were to conduct a successful Democratic National Convention in Denver, get something for Indiana on the national ticket, and complete his term as party chairman with grace and dignity. All three objectives were met successfully. The national convention nominated William Jennings Bryan for a third run for the presidency. While Taggart and

Chairman Thomas Taggart and Democratic national committeemen on donkeys at the Democratic National Convention in Denver in 1908. William Jennings Bryan was nominated for the presidency for a third time.

Bryan came from different factions of the party, the former was a loyal soldier and backed the Democratic nominee. Bryan then engineered the selection of Norman Mack of Buffalo, New York, as Taggart's successor at the helm of the party.[18] To show their appreciation for Taggart's work for the party as chairman and for his genial personality, Democratic leaders secretly tied a donkey with "the largest ears, most determined disposition, and loudest hee-haw" to his bed in his room on the ninth floor of the Brown Palace Hotel. It was the kind of humorous and lighthearted gesture that Taggart thoroughly enjoyed.[19]

With the presidential nomination going to the Great Commoner once again, Taggart concentrated his time and energy on winning the second spot on the ticket for John W. Kern. The friendship between Taggart and Kern, both personal and political, was genuine and long-standing. Taggart picked Kern to serve as city attorney in Taggart's second and third municipal administrations and secured for him the Democratic gubernatorial nominations in 1900 and 1904, both races Kern later lost in the fall. Kern, in turn, represented Taggart in 1905 in criminal libel proceedings against newspapers over his management of the Parker presidential campaign, legal action that never had to be taken because of retractions, and in all litigation brought by Governor Hanly to annul the charter of the French Lick Springs Hotel Company. Now the Hoosier boss wanted the vice presidential nomination for Kern, and he got it. This was a great political opportunity for Kern and a vindication of sorts for Taggart.[20]

Much as Taggart may have wished it, William Randolph Hearst simply would not go away. Not getting very far within the Democratic party four years earlier, Hearst now formed a third party, the Independence League. He was the temporary chairman of the new party's convention in Chicago in late July where he addressed those assembled, "The Democratic vanguard is the Falstaff army . . . offered by such soldiers of fortune as Sullivan, Hopkins, Murphy, McClellan, Tom Taggart, the roulette gambler, Tom Ryan, the Wall Street gambler, and Belmont, the race track gambler."[21] The convention of the new third party chose Thomas L. Hisgen, an oil dealer from Springfield, Massachusetts, to run for president and John Temple Graves, a feature writer for the Hearst papers from Georgia, for vice president. Hisgen's qualification to run for the presidency apparently was the fact that his family had stood up to Standard Oil in selling axle grease and oil, something Hearst admired. In any case, because Hisgen had been born in Indiana he opened his campaign in Indianapolis accompanied by Hearst. Hearst used good political humor when he declared, "the Republican Party has exchanged its principles for Mr. Morgan's bank checks, and the Democratic Party has cashed its principles for Tom Taggart's blue chips."[22]

The elections of 1908 brought mixed results for the Democrats. It came as no surprise to Taggart that the Republican nominee for president, William Howard Taft, defeated Bryan rather handily. After all, Taggart had been through this twice before with the Nebraskan. The final tally was 7,677,544 to 6,405,707. Much to

Taggart's delight, of course, the Independence League ticket received a negligible vote. Its 83,628 votes reportedly cost Hearst $300,000.[23] In Indiana the Bryan-Kern ticket went down by the narrow plurality of 10,700 votes. But Marshall defeated Republican congressman James Eli Watson of Rushville by 15,000 votes for the governorship. Watson, who was a member of the GOP's conservative Fairbanks wing, would be a future candidate against Taggart himself for the United States Senate in 1916 and again in 1920. To add to this good news for the Hoosier Democrats, Benjamin Franklin Shively was elected to the United States Senate by a joint session of the General Assembly in January 1909. Taggart's success in Indiana in 1908 gained wide attention because conservative Democrats across the nation voted Republican to defeat Bryan and hurt most Democratic candidates in the process.[24]

The presidential election and the party chairmanship behind him, in 1909 Taggart turned his attention mainly to the hotel business and Indiana politics, in addition to his duties as national committeeman from the state. The next big political battle was to be in 1910 when Indiana would select a United States senator. But, in a personal way, the year dawned ominously.

Taggart loved hunting fowl. Late in January 1910, accompanied by Joseph E. Bell and W. H. Norton, his private secretary, Taggart went quail hunting near Fayette, Mississippi, about twenty-three miles northeast of Natchez. On the afternoon of Friday, 21 January, Norton, from forty yards away, fired his gun in Taggart's direction and accidentally hit him in the right side of the face, shoulder, and chest. Approximately forty-two pieces of bird shot were removed from his shoulder and chest and more than a dozen from his face. The shot punctured his face about the right eye, and the doctors in Natchez wanted to remove his eye then and there. Taggart adamantly refused, instead wiring his son Tom to have Dr. Frank A. Morrison of Indianapolis, an eye specialist, go to Louisville to meet his train for an immediate examination. Dr. R. C. French of Natchez accompanied Taggart and the other two men on the train home. Ever his upbeat self, Taggart sent a telegram to the *Indianapolis Star,* "You are aware I was accidentally shot yesterday. No one was to blame. Am feeling well. Think there is a chance to save my eye. Will arrive Indianapolis Sunday forenoon." Tom left French Lick and met his father's train in Louisville and then they brought him to Indianapolis for an X-ray examination in Doctor Morrison's office by Dr. A. M. Cole. Before the X-ray, however, they paused for lunch at Taggart's home. The exam confirmed that Taggart had a very close call. While there was no bird shot in the vital part of his eye, the X-ray showed that one piece had come within 1/32 of an inch of the vital part and that another had passed through the outer coating of the eye. Ultimately he was able to keep his right eye, his sight was restored, and Taggart undoubtedly counted himself a fortunate man indeed.[25]

Weeks later Governor Marshall and Taggart crossed swords at the state Democratic convention in 1910 over the procedures to be followed in selecting the party's United States Senate nominee. Marshall, a favorite of many progressive Hoosier Democrats, had not been altogether friendly toward the party's boss and his supporters who made up the Taggart machine. While Taggart engineered Marshall's selection as a compromise gubernatorial nominee in 1908 and his subsequent election to office that November, Marshall also knew that Taggart's first choice had been Taggart's friend and ally Sam Ralston. The governor, too, cast a disapproving eye on the philosophy and practices of political bossism and machines, favoring instead a more open process. Interestingly, and ironically, their clash at the convention in 1910 came when the governor wanted the small group of delegates to the state convention themselves to choose the senatorial nominee while Taggart wanted a statewide primary to do so. Taggart proposed that the primary be held after the November elections but, of course, before the state legislature made the final selection when it convened in January. Taggart probably supported this plan because he could influence the outcome through his control of the statewide precinct apparatus and because the cost of a statewide campaign would be prohibitive for most contenders. Thus, the primary process strengthened the hand of the boss.

Marshall's plan, however, was adopted by thirty votes, prompting
Taggart to rise and declare, "The Taggart machine has been sent
to the scrap-heap." As a result of this political victory Marshall solidified his progressive image in the public mind.[26]

Much was made of the suggestion by the Indianapolis press that
the nomination of John W. Kern for the Senate in 1910 by the state
convention defeated Taggart's aspirations for the seat. Nothing
could be further from the truth since there is no evidence whatsoever to suggest a breach between Taggart and Kern. Similarly,
there is no evidence that Taggart sought the Senate nod in 1910.
Once his procedural plan, about which he did care, went down
to defeat, the convention moved forward to name a nominee.
Taggart allowed his name to be presented to the gathering as a tactical maneuver to hold the Marion County bloc together until they
saw which way the political winds were blowing. He was a master
at this sort of thing. Taggart said his friends knew he did not want
the nomination for himself, which is believable in view of his large
expansion of his hotel in French Lick that year with the building
of the main wing. Marion County did indeed hold solid for him,
casting 177 of its 183 votes for Taggart on the first ballot. But there
was clearly little support for his nomination outside the county,
which further showed that he was not actively pursuing the seat.
Then Taggart threw all 183 votes from Marion County to Kern on
the second ballot to create the momentum needed to win. Kern
was nominated on the fourth round of voting.[27] Taggart and
Kern had been close for years, and the party boss felt that the loyal
Kern, who had endured defeats for governor in both 1900 and
1904 and for vice president in 1908, certainly deserved the Senate
nomination. To that end Taggart put his organization to work by
electing enough Democrats to the legislature to ensure Kern's victory. Kern defeated Albert J. Beveridge, the progressive Republican
incumbent, and headed for Washington.[28]

Jacob Piatt Dunn, the Indianapolis historian, wrote of Taggart
in 1910, "He is now understood to be quite wealthy, and it may be
noted that his money was not made from politics."[29] Taggart was
a wealthy man with a profitable hotel business, but Dunn missed

the mark in saying politics had nothing to do with it. While there is no evidence or suggestion that he ever diverted public funds illegally to his personal use, Taggart did indeed profit from the lucrative Marion County auditor's post, from his contacts and profile in the national party to promote French Lick Springs, and from the official blind or winking eye toward gambling in the Springs valley. In many respects, then, he did profit greatly from his political involvement. But Taggart himself perpetuated the idea that politics brought him no financial reward, saying in 1912, "Politics has never brought me any money. I was drawn into it by force of circumstances and the interest has been so strong that I have never been able to forsake it. But I have adhered jealously to my hotel business, and it is to that that I owe my income—not to politics." Recognizing the uncertainties of the political life, he warned against making a career in politics. "I would never advise a man to enter the arena of politics as a profession. I have a son who asked me to let him follow in my footsteps when he had finished his college education, but I urged him to take charge of my hotel at the French Lick Springs rather than adopt the course for which he yearned. I am glad to say that he did what I advised."[30] To be sure, this was good fatherly advice.

The Democratic party met in Baltimore in June 1912 to choose its presidential nominee after losing the last four national elections. This presidential nomination contest boiled down to a fight between James Beauchamp (Champ) Clark of Missouri and Woodrow Wilson, the progressive governor of New Jersey who earlier had been president of Princeton University. Taggart went to Baltimore supporting Champ Clark, but his primary objective was to name Governor Marshall the party's nominee for vice president. Taggart and Marshall had sparred over Hoosier political matters during the governor's four-year term, but the boss, in his own unique way, felt a loyalty to Marshall.

The key to securing the second spot on the ticket was to influence the selection of the presidential nominee. To that end Taggart lined up the Illinois, New York, and Kentucky delegations along with Indiana's to refrain from supporting Wilson. Indiana's thirty votes were cast for Marshall on the first twenty-seven ballots. Then, on the twenty-eighth ballot, seeing no further hope for Clark and with A. Mitchell Palmer of Pennsylvania rejecting overtures from Taggart, Charles F. Murphy of Tammany Hall, and Roger C. Sullivan of Illinois, Taggart signaled his move by swinging twenty-nine Hoosier votes to Wilson on 1 July. This move is credited with breaking the convention's deadlock, and Wilson was nominated the next day on the forty-sixth ballot. In the process, of course, the vice presidential nomination went to Indiana.[31] William F. McCombs, Wilson's manager who was elected party chairman in 1912, later sat in the lobby of the French Lick Springs Hotel, pointed toward Taggart's office, and said that Taggart was responsible for Wilson's nomination.[32] William Gibbs McAdoo, Wilson's son-in-law and secretary of the treasury, also recalled, "My acquaintance with him [Taggart] began in the 1912 convention, when he came at an opportune moment to the support of Woodrow Wilson, and that led to a warm friendship which existed until the day of his death."[33]

Following Wilson's nomination Taggart attended a conference with the bosses and managers to settle upon a vice presidential choice. He was told that either Senator Kern or Senator Shively was acceptable, thus opening up a seat for Taggart in the Senate, "but I replied to the proposition that I was not a candidate for any office and that I wanted to see Marshall nominated for the vice-presidency." Actually, McCombs had made an earlier deal with Taggart in which Marshall's vice presidential nomination was promised in exchange for Indiana's votes for Wilson. Wilson, who wanted Oscar W. Underwood of Alabama as his running mate, was unaware of the Taggart-McCombs deal. Luckily for McCombs, Underwood refused to consider the second spot on the ticket. Even though Marshall was opposed by William Jennings Bryan and several Wilson managers as too reactionary, Taggart secured the nomination for the Hoosier governor as he had for Kern four years earlier. Marshall, of course, went on to serve eight years as vice president under Wilson.[34] Finally, at the Baltimore convention Marshall admitted that he had not seen Taggart in a true light up to this time. After seeing Taggart stand by him when even his friends were ready to desert him, Marshall now felt that Taggart might be a political boss, but he was the right kind of boss.[35]

Theodore Roosevelt, who split the Republican party with his Progressive (Bull Moose) candidacy in 1912, did not quite agree. His regard for Taggart had not changed since 1904. In response to suggestions that he align with the Wilson Democrats in 1912, Roosevelt wrote, "I cannot personally support the ticket and Platform of the Baltimore convention and I do not think that the Progressives should do so. I see no advantage in changing Penrose, Barnes and Gugenheim for Murphy, Taggart, and Sullivan."[36] And the Republican-controlled *Indianapolis News* agreed with Roosevelt. "Mr. Taggart has come to be a national representative of a system of politics which, since the nomination of Governor Wilson, is very much out of fashion. He is, therefore, a misfit and a misrepresentative." This kind of political commentary, of course, did not bother Taggart and, interestingly, probably did not now bother his wife much either. A bit surprisingly, Eva Taggart revealed a different side of her political self during the convention in Baltimore. To a reporter she said, "I love politics. If I were a man, I would be in the thick of political life if I could. Meeting people and working for the good of the country and all that appeals to me. And if I can't be in politics I am glad my husband is. I have almost as much of the fun and excitement as he does." Eva's role in her husband's political decisions may have been greater than is commonly supposed for a political wife of the period.[37]

In the second week of July 1912 Taggart executed another one of his brilliant political maneuvers. He abruptly resigned his post as national committeeman, to which he had been reelected earlier in the year at the state convention, in a letter to his friend and now state chairman Bernard Korbly. He stated that his decision was final, thus the state committee would have to fill the vacancy. Neither Senator Kern nor Senator Shively believed the report of Taggart's resignation until he confirmed it. They knew he had met with Woodrow Wilson at Sea Girt, New Jersey, after the convention and pronounced himself pleased with the nominee. Taggart confirmed his resignation in an interview with a correspondent from the *Indianapolis Star.* "I wish you would say for me in this connection," Taggart stated, "that I had no other reason for resigning than that I did not desire the place again. When I was elected last March I was not a candidate and did not want to be re-elected, and when I was chosen after twice declining, I reserved the right to resign after the national convention." He felt the party faced bright prospects for the autumn campaign. "I leave the national committee with a State House full of Democrats, with twelve, and soon-to-be thirteen, Democratic members of the House, two Democratic United States Senators and a Vice President of the United States to the credit of the Indiana Democracy. I include a Vice President, because Governor Marshall is as good as elected right now," Taggart declared. After citing his successes, he issued something of a challenge, "I only hope my successor will leave as many Democrats in office as I am leaving." He promised his support for the party, saying, "I will do all that lies within my power as an individual for the success of the Democratic ticket."[38]

Chairman Korbly, with the support of the state committee, refused to accept Taggart's resignation from his position, but Taggart did not budge. What was Taggart up to in this episode? While any answer is speculative, Taggart seemed sure of a Democratic victory in November and wanted Wilson and Marshall to go on record that he should remain on the national committee. Consequently, upon their election in the fall his hand would be strengthened to handle patronage in Indiana after the long federal drought. Taggart knew that both Wilson and Marshall would have preferred someone else before the convention, but would they now reciprocate for Taggart's support in Baltimore? Marshall lunched with Taggart and stated that he would be pleased if Taggart remained. Then a petition urging him to continue came from leading Indiana Democrats. Finally, the state committee voted unanimously, likely with Wilson's approval, for Taggart to stay as national committeeman. With everyone acknowledging his supremacy in the Hoosier Democracy, Taggart "relented" and agreed to continue. "While it was my desire to retire as national committeeman I could not refuse the request of my many Democratic friends to stay on the job and help to win a splendid victory in November," he stated. And to Chairman Korbly, "What you boys have done is mighty kind. I want to resign, but if you have made it unanimous I will stick."[39] Taggart won.

At the time all this was going on, Taggart had gone down to Washington from Hyannis Port, Massachusetts, where he now vacationed, to testify before the Senate Campaign Expenditure Committee that was investigating the 1904 campaign. Taggart testified that he burned his book of contributions and expenditures for the Parker campaign just before the 1908 Denver convention because he considered it a "dead matter." He had turned over other Democratic National Committee records to his successor. When asked if he ever figured up receipts and expenditures, Taggart said, "When we got through it was not worth while." George Foster Peabody was treasurer of the national committee in 1904 and resigned immediately after the campaign to be succeeded by August Belmont. In response to questioning Taggart answered, "I do not know whether Mr. Peabody was disgusted or not." Taggart estimated that twenty to thirty people solicited funds for the ticket in 1904, but his memory began to fail when his own contributions were questioned. "I suppose you were a contributor?" asked one senator. "I expect I was. Whatever it was, I contributed to the Indiana state committee," Taggart answered. "How much did you contribute?" "I can not recall definitely," replied Taggart. "Well, approximately?" the senator persisted. "I supose [sic] I would be safe in saying $1,000," he responded. Burned records and a foggy memory can be part and parcel of the political experience.[40]

Late in the 1912 campaign Roosevelt's Progressive National Committee (PNC) circulated a piece of material called the *Progressive Bulletin* that charged Taggart was the proprietor of a gambling establishment. Taggart was angry that the gambling talk had resurfaced and demanded retractions from the Progressive National Committee, the *Chicago Tribune,* and other papers. The

Indianapolis Star did not print the article, but it did carry a cartoon that gave it credence. Taggart demanded that the *Star* publish the truth, "Your editors know that I am not the proprietor of a gambling establishment at French Lick Springs, and have no connection directly or remotely with such an establishment. They know that the charges made against me in the Irwin article are cruel and malicious libels."[41] Not getting the retractions he wanted, Taggart filed a libel suit against Joseph M. Dixon, former senator from Montana, and Will Irwin, editor of the progressive publication. Dixon claimed he knew nothing about the article before publication, and Irwin insisted he simply edited another writer's story. Bainbridge Colby, later secretary of state in Woodrow Wilson's administration, represented Dixon and Irwin while the New York City firm of Nicoll, Anable, Lindsay and Fuller represented Taggart. The libel suit was dropped in late summer 1914 after apologetic letters were sent to Taggart from Dixon, Irwin, and the Colby firm.[42]

Wilson, the intellectual progressive, and Marshall, the Hoosier pragmatic progressive, went on to victory in November 1912, defeating incumbent Republican president William Howard Taft and the Bull Moose candidacy of Roosevelt. Clearly, the split in Republican ranks allowed Wilson to slip into the White House with a minority of the popular vote. Nevertheless, it was a victory, and the Democrats were ecstatic over their first presidential triumph in twenty years. Taggart's power and stature in the state and national parties were enhanced. He and his wife attended the Wilson inauguration in Washington on 4 March 1913 and the subsequent luncheon in honor of the new president.

The year 1913 was one of change for the Taggarts in their personal lives. Eva spent most of her time at their apartment in the French Lick Springs Hotel and devoted much of her time to their grandchild, two-year-old Evelyn Chambers, who visited often and was the real ruler of the house. Eva took long walks in the countryside at French Lick and expressed her love for the southern Indiana landscape, "It is the loveliest place in the world to me. I never tire of the wonderful scenery, the beautiful hills that are to be found in the southern part of the state. I have never been

Indiana State Library

Thomas Taggart in 1913.

able to decide whether I like the country better in the winter or the summer. In fact, all seasons are lovely and I like equally well the changes that each brings in scenery."[43] Besides her love for Orange County, one other reason Eva probably spent a good amount of time in French Lick in 1913 was that the Taggarts had sold their home in Indianapolis on North Capitol Avenue and were living in an apartment in a building at 1240 North Broadway Street while a new family home was being built.[44] Then, as now, the experience of being uprooted and temporarily housed was not an altogether pleasant one.

Taggart built his new mansion in Indianapolis at 1331 North Delaware Street, diagonally across the street from the late President Benjamin Harrison's residence, in one of the city's finest neighborhoods. The architect was Frederick Wallick who later built homes for some of Indianapolis's most prominent people: "Westerley" for George Henry Alexander Clowes of Eli Lilly and

Company in 1925; "Lanesend" for Nicholas H. Noyes, also of Lilly, in 1928; and "Walden" for Frederic M. Ayres, Sr., of the department store family. Lucy Taggart, who had an interest in Italian architecture and whose artistic pursuits had taken her to Italy several times, made a major contribution to the house's style and design. Most accounts described the house as having an Italian interior and a Georgian exterior. *House Beautiful* in June 1920 added a third element, American Colonial, when it named "1331" as one of the three best houses in Indianapolis. According to the magazine this building stood on Delaware Street "preaching the gospel of beautified utility." The Taggarts moved into their new home just before New Year's Day 1914.[45]

The three-story brick house had an entryway, living room, dining room, reception room, sunroom, kitchen, and servants' apartments on the ground floor; four bedroom suites with bathrooms, a dressing room for Mrs. Taggart, and accommodations for servants on the second floor; while the third floor consisted of an apartment and studio for Lucy. The Italian style was readily evident in the living room where the walls were covered with tapestry and the beamed ceiling was painted with Italian designs in gold and deep colors. The interior doors from the living room to the dining room and to the entryway were exact copies of doors in Italy, carved, solid wood and painted mostly gold. There was an antique Italian secretary and a high Italian fireplace in the living room. The entryway featured a winding, Italian-design staircase with an iron balustrade that descended from the second floor. The dining room, painted in plain oyster white, was formal and had no buffet or serving table. Its windows were covered with chintz draperies and the dining room table chairs were of Chinese design, upholstered in gold cloth with brightly colored Chinese motifs. The reception room was furnished with beautifully painted furniture, and heavy tapestry hangings were at the long windows. The sunroom, to the back of the house, had floor-to-ceiling windows on two sides overlooking the garden. The room was furnished with an ivory yellow table, which appeared to be one but could be separated into six little tea tables with chairs upholstered in a floral fabric. Lucy's studio on the top floor received plenty of northern light, and her work space was decorated with wonderful rugs, tapestries, and old pieces of copper, china, and bronze that she had bought in Europe. The Taggart daughters named the room in the basement "The Grill" because it was like a modern grillroom. There was a buffet, high Waddel benches, and chairs of Flemish oak covered in brightly colored tapestry. The Taggarts' home was beautiful, of modest proportions, and tastefully decorated. Its construction cemented the Taggarts' social standing in the Indianapolis community.[46]

"It's all news to me," said Senator Shively about reports in early 1914 that Taggart might be a candidate for his seat in the Senate. "I don't know anything about it, except what I have seen in the newspapers. I have no comment to make." The reports of his possible candidacy seem not to have been trial balloons because within hours Taggart issued a statement exploding the boom started for him. "Since I left the office of mayor of Indianapolis I never have been a candidate for any public office," he declared. "I have no aspirations at the present time to become a candidate for the office of United States senator or for any other political office." Gov. Samuel M. Ralston, whom the party organization elected in 1912, state auditor William Hunter O'Brien, Sr., party chairman Bernard Korbly, and Indianapolis mayor Joseph E. Bell all denied taking part in meetings at the statehouse, which had been reported recently in a series of stories, to push Taggart's candidacy. Taggart's statement cited Shively's support for Wilson's tariff and currency measures and urged that he be returned to the Senate to "help carry out the program of progressive legislation which President Wilson has in mind." However, Taggart, just back home from a hunting trip to Mississippi, must have been flattered by the speculation as well as the scores of letters and telegrams of support.[47]

In 1914 Taggart remained president of the Denison Hotel Company in Indianapolis, long after he had sold the Grand Hotel. And, of course, there was French Lick. His other investments ranged far and wide, such as his interest in the development of a

Indiana State Library

The Taggart mansion at 1331 N. Delaware Street, in one of the most fashionable neighborhoods in Indianapolis.

modern highway system that would be good for economic development, including the budding automobile industry in Indiana. Carl G. Fisher, a partner in the Indianapolis Motor Speedway, and Taggart were the original delegates appointed from Indiana to the Dixie Highway Association. This group met for the first time in 1914 in Chattanooga, Tennessee, to push the development of the Dixie Highway from Detroit to Homestead, Florida. Taggart was a friend and adviser to several of the men who helped make Indianapolis second only to Detroit as an automotive center. Fisher was the leading developer of Miami Beach, while Taggart made many investments in Florida. The *Miami Herald* later ran a story that said, "Since the early days of Florida, Mr. Taggart has been a frequent visitor and has always kept in close association with the development of Miami and other Florida cities through his generous investments in Florida enterprises." Taggart proved important to the highway program by getting legislation through the General Assembly to build roads connecting Indianapolis to other cities in the state as well as to Chicago, Louisville, and Cincinnati.[48]

The next year, 1915, brought another firestorm of charges, accusations, and controversy Taggart's way. Undoubtedly it was one of the most challenging years that he ever faced. On 15 February the *Indianapolis News* ran an editorial claiming that Taggart controlled the Indiana state legislature, both houses of which were Democratic. Louis Howland, editor of the *News,* charged that "up to the present time no man who has followed the proceedings of the present legislature can for a moment doubt that it is held in the hollow of Tom Taggart's hand." The editorial was based in part on a speech that state senator John F. Adams gave on the floor in which he charged that "higher ups" were trying to control the vote on a bill to reduce the number of game wardens in Indiana. State senator Otis L. Ballou said there was an attempt to discipline him when he voted against Mayor Bell's finance board bill that would have expanded Bell's authority and which Taggart favored. Taggart sent a letter to the state senate after these accusations and asked for an investigation, writing, "I felt that if I had the influence I would like to know it, or to have the public to know it, and if I did not have it, I would like to know by what authority The Indianapolis News made the statement." He denied doing anything to discipline Ballou for voting against the Bell finance bill. Richard Smith, managing editor of the *News,* responded, "The acquaintance I have had with Indiana politics for ten years, the general report, the general understanding in regard to Mr. Taggart's position in the Democratic power, of his power—all a thousand and one incidents that are reported to me constantly by our men—more than I can remember—all those things are taken into consideration and come forward when a senator gets up and speaks as Mr. Adams spoke in the senate. That, of course, did not appear as a novel thing. It was not an isolated case. Mr. Taggart has been heard of before."

The state senate not only agreed to investigate the charges against Taggart, but it also decided to investigate attempts by the *News* to control the General Assembly. The first session of the committee came on 18 February under the chairmanship of state senator Frederick Van Nuys, later a Democratic United States senator from Indiana. Taggart denied to the committee that he dictated to the legislature and testified that he did not even know about the game warden bill. Other witnesses before the committee included Howland, Richard Smith, and Ellis Searles, all of the *News*, as well as Van Nuys, state senator Adams, and Secretary of State Homer L. Cook. Howland spoke most convincingly about Taggart's role in the political life of the Hoosier state, "When you talk about the control of the senate or the control of anything else, I don't think anybody is fool enough to think that Mr. Taggart takes senators by the back of their necks and tells them what to do, but he has been for years a most powerful man in the political life of Indiana and he is ranked all over the country as one of the great political leaders of a political organization, a man of great power, and when I spoke about his controlling the legislature in that way there was no suggestion whatever of corruption on his part or any-thing of that sort, but through his influence with men that he has been associated with in politics, I would say today—whether that editorial is too strong or not—that he is the most powerful man in Indiana today, in Democratic politics, which are related to legislation." Howland summarized by saying, "He stands all over the country in a class with men of the same ability and capacity and power as Sullivan, in Illinois, and Murphy, in New York, and I really thought that, eliminating any implication or suggestion of cor-ruption, the editorial was rather a tribute to his power than an indictment of his character." The editor of the *News* cited the recent defeat of the direct primary bill as an example of Taggart's power. Changing his position of five years earlier, the Democratic leader had spoken out against the bill and, subsequently, the measure was difficult to get out of committee, delayed, and finally defeated. Both houses were controlled by the Democrats and the last state party convention endorsed the direct primary, but the measure went down anyway. The responsibility for the defeat of that bill was laid squarely at Taggart's feet.[49]

Several days later, after all the testimony had been given, and, to no one's surprise, the senate investigating committee found no evidence to support the charge that Taggart controlled the state legislature. Somehow, with Democrats controlling the committee three to two, the decision was anticlimactic.[50]

For Taggart the senate inquiry was just the beginning of the controversy centering on him in 1915. There was more trouble to come, such as a Marion County (Indianapolis) grand jury probe against Taggart and others focusing on alleged election frauds committed in November 1914 during the off-year elections. The investigation lasted five months, cost over four million dollars, and involved 1,837 witnesses. To be sure, Taggart's opponents were determined to nail him this time. In late June Taggart, along with his friend Mayor Joseph E. Bell and 126 others, was formally indicted for election fraud. The prosecutor had invested much time and resources in this inquiry, obviously encouraged by recent indictments and convictions for election fraud in Terre Haute. Interestingly, the federal grand jury that returned indictments in Terre Haute also had investigated the election fraud allegations in Indianapolis. The federal grand jury, however, returned no indictments for the cases in the capital city. The Marion County grand jury, on the other hand, accused these politically important men of conspiring to have their party subordinates commit unlawful acts, including marked ballots, stuffed ballot boxes, voter coercion, intimidation and assaults, false registry, votes traded, ignorant voters cheated, police at polls acting as partisans, and tampered voting machines. There were forty-eight counts, in total, that were combined into one charge—conspiracy to commit a felony. Taggart lashed out at the prosecutors and stated emphatically that the allegations were not true. He accused the probers of being hypocrites and political "strikers" and pointed out that a recent federal grand jury had not indicted anyone.[51] Despite his protestations of innocence Taggart knew this was serious business and that his political enemies were intent on bringing him down. True to form, he provided his own bail and raised $200,000 in bail money for forty-seven other indicted men who were also citizens of Indianapolis.[52]

Prosecuting Attorney Alvah J. Rucker, a Republican, brought Mayor Bell to trial first in October 1915, and, in the process, the prosecutor learned a little lesson in the ways of hardball politics. All of a sudden witnesses started denying their previous testimony on the stand or did not give certain testimony at all. One case in point involved Paul Hagen, who was secretary of the Home Brewing Company of Indianapolis. Hagen told the grand jury that he had contributed $750 in cash to Taggart for the county Democratic party in October 1914 at the Denison Hotel. This contribution did not appear in any of the party finance reports required by law, thus raising charges of a political "slush fund." However, when he took the stand at Mayor Bell's trial, Hagen denied completely his previous testimony. Prosecutor Rucker could not build a winning case under such circumstances, and the mayor's trial ended with an acquittal. Several days later, in late October, the prosecutor admitted he lacked enough evidence to convict Taggart, and all charges were dropped when Judge William H. Eichhorn sustained Rucker's motion to dismiss.[53]

Alas, the companion of power is very often controversy. And, indeed, Taggart felt the white heat of the print media's fire throughout his years of power and influence. His power, however, was great in 1915: there was a president in the White House whom he had helped nominate and elect; Vice President Marshall held the nation's second most important post almost completely because of him; John W. Kern, who owed him much in his career, sat in the Senate and Benjamin Franklin Shively, a Democrat, held the other seat; his longtime pal Sam Ralston was in the governor's mansion; the General Assembly bent to his will; and his associate Joseph Bell was mayor of Indianapolis. Taggart sat at the controls of a well-oiled political machine and directed much of the state's destiny during this period. His correspondence with Ralston reveals an active involvement in patronage and other decisions across the state.[54] Given his degree of influence, the opposition press targeted him for some of its most withering fire. But, after this difficult and challenging year Taggart emerged in 1916 with a most cherished political prize, appointment to a seat in the United States Senate by his friend Governor Ralston.

CHAPTER SEVEN

The United States Senate

Hyannis Port, Massachusetts, was a special place for the Taggart family. "Hyannis Port was, and still is, a very important part of my life. I loved being there," Letitia Sinclair Mumford, a granddaughter, reminisced about the meaning of "the Port" to her. "I feel that Grandfather was responsible for giving us that gift, our love for the Cape, and it has carried on down with family still living there." Hyannis Port, Mumford continued, is a "second home, a place to renew family relationships and family love."[1] Thomas Taggart began taking his family to New England to vacation before the turn of the century. According to press reports, he first tried the Maine coast but found the waters too cold and so decided to try Cape Cod farther south. The best estimate is that Tom and Eva Taggart first stayed in Hyannis Port about 1907.[2] The area was very much to their liking so the Taggarts began to lease a house in the quaint little village during the summers.

The Hyannis Land Company, founded in 1872, was a syndicate of men from Framingham, Worcester, and Boston who bought the waterfront property from Dunbars Point to the eastern end of Craigville Beach for $100,000 and developed the area around Hyannis Port.[3] The village had long attracted well-known summer visitors to the Cape's southern shore: Andrew Carnegie in 1883; Gen. Lucien Fairfield, Civil War general and governor of Wisconsin, in 1888; Mark Hanna, prominent Republican political leader, before 1896; and President Grover Cleveland in July 1896.[4] If one did not have a cottage, there was the option of staying at the Port View Hotel, a three-story wooden building of rather flimsy construction. Unfortunately the hotel burned on

Amyvale, the main house in the Taggart family compound in Hyannis Port, Massachusetts, built in 1915–16. It was named after Taggart's ancestral village in Ireland. Daughter Emily Taggart Sinclair's summerhouse, built in the early 1920s, is to the right.

Labor Day evening in 1909, and the Hyannis Land Company went bankrupt.[5]

Taggart had been coming to Hyannis Port long enough to realize that the property on which the Port View had stood, on a point of land overlooking the harbor, was a choice residential location. Through a series of real estate transactions, the first of which was recorded in September 1912, Taggart consolidated three properties into one four-acre estate. One parcel was sold to him by Wendell Hinckley, the Hyannis stage driver who was described locally as a quaint character.[6] Taggart's estate had a beautiful, spacious setting with spectacular harbor and ocean views.

One part of the old hotel was left standing and was soon moved to one corner of the property and became a Taggart family cottage. After construction of the main house, the cottage was given to daughter Nora and her growing family and was named Overflow Cottage. Nearby in another building was a garage, laundry, and a studio for Lucy. The main house, a rambling white clapboard structure with pillared porticos on front and back, was apparently built in 1915–16 when records show a significant jump in the property's tax assessment. The two-story house was the most impressive residence in Hyannis Port. The house had two wings built in a wide V formation with both wings meeting at the porticos and center hall. Amyvale—the house was named after Taggart's birthplace in Ireland—was tastefully decorated, always mindful, however, of the attractiveness of summerhouse simplicity. One entered the center hall of the house through a brick-floored portico. On both sides of the center hall, facing the water, were glass-enclosed sun parlors. One served as an informal sitting room and the other had a large telescope set up through which Taggart watched ocean traffic on Nantucket Sound and where he could pick out the islands of Martha's Vineyard and Nantucket on clear days. On one side of the center hall was a long living room and on the other was the dining room with colonial-style cupboards that held old-fashioned china. Beyond the dining room were the kitchen, children's dining area, and the butler's pantry. Upstairs, which was reached by a stairway that ascended from the center hall, were the bedroom suites. There were personal touches throughout the house, such as Taggart's extensive collection of model ships of every description. A fighting frigate, Lucy's favorite and the prize of the collection, came from Alexander Drake of New York, a famous collector of model ships. The ship models were in the living room, center hall, and other rooms of the house. They were framed on the walls and sat on the mantelpiece and atop bookshelves. There were paintings, including Lucy's painting of a Gloucester fisherman wharf side, Charles Hawthorne's por-trait of granddaughter Evelyn Chambers, and a painting of daugh-ter Nora. Eva's airy, rose-colored bedroom overlooking the harbor was covered with framed and unframed pictures of her husband, children, and grandchildren. On the lawn by the water a croquet court was laid out and on the other side, where the Port View Hotel had been, was a tennis court.

In the early 1920s Taggart added a third story and widow's walk to the main house so that his daughter Lucy could have a top-notch studio in Hyannis Port. However, Lucy's principal summerhome soon would be up the coast in exclusive Eastern Point, near

Indiana State Library

Lucy M. Taggart in Paris, 1908.

Gloucester, where there was an active community of artists. Friend and well-known painter Cecilia Beaux introduced Lucy to the Gloucester area in 1922. Nevertheless, she was a frequent visitor to the Cape. Also in the early 1920s Taggart built a large clapboard cottage on his estate for daughter Emily and her family, thus creating a family compound in Hyannis Port. In 1928 Mr. and Mrs. Joseph P. Kennedy purchased the Malcom cottage adjacent to the Taggart property, which they had rented since 1925, and began to establish themselves in the village.[7]

The Taggart children knew summers in Hyannis Port only as adults, but the grandchildren grew up with "the Port" as a regular part of their summer existence. The over twenty-hour journey by rail from Indianapolis to the Cape was a memorable

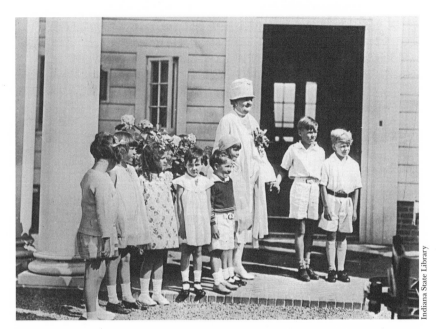

Mrs. Thomas Taggart with her grandchildren on the front portico of the main house in the family compound in Hyannis Port, Massachusetts.

experience for everyone. Grandchildren remembered their parents' challenge of getting children, governesses, servants, birdcages, and all sorts of things plus baggage on the train in time. In fact, two grandchildren recalled how their grandfather once held the connecting train from Boston to the Cape until all his family and their belongings were on board.[8] Tom and Eva, no doubt, enjoyed very much the relaxation and the family time together that Amyvale provided in their busy lives. Eva and her daughters and their children would usually be in Hyannis Port for the entire summer. Her son and sons-in-law would come out for a couple of weeks or so as work permitted. Taggart himself would arrive and depart according to his ever-changing schedule. One summer ritual, however, was traditional among the Taggarts: everyone tried to be at the family compound in Hyannis Port for Eva's birthday on 5 August. Entertainments on the Cape were many for the children and grandchildren—swimming, sunbathing, golf, tennis, crabbing, and boating on the *EVAT,* the family cabin cruiser named after the matriarch. The senior Taggarts, however, did not swim but enjoyed other activities, especially motoring about the Cape and exploring the area.[9] Friends from Indiana visited, the Sam Ralstons in particular. The Taggarts sometimes chartered a private yacht for their guests and cruised the New England coast, putting in at places like Newport, Rhode Island, along the way.[10] Hyannis Port was, in its special way, a place to escape the heavy pressures of business and politics and to renew old ties of family and friendship.

As the spring of 1916 neared, Taggart had no way of knowing that a major change in his life was about to take place. In mid-March one of Indiana's incumbent Democratic senators, Benjamin Franklin Shively, died. Governor Ralston, after consultation and deliberation, appointed fifty-nine-year-old Taggart to the seat. The immigrant boy from Ireland would now sit in the United States Senate, sometimes referred to as the most exclusive club in the world.

Taggart was in French Lick when news of his appointment reached him. He took the early train to Indianapolis on 20 March, arriving at 11 A.M., and went directly to the Denison Hotel. (Taggart was president of the Denison Hotel Company.) At the Denison he huddled in Room 27 with Joseph L. Reiley, secretary of the state public service commission and a Taggart appointee, and Dale J. Crittenberger, a close political friend. During their short conference Reiley presented Taggart with his commission for the Senate from the governor. Although Taggart commented publicly that he did not know if he would be a candidate for the seat in a special November election, speculation in the Hoosier capital had him pitted against likely Republican candidate James E. Watson.[11] Part of Taggart's statement upon appointment read:

> I deeply appreciate the honor done me by Governor Ralston in appointing me to the senate. I am not unmindful of the great responsibilities going with this exalted position.

However, it will be my utmost endeavor to discharge, at all times, the duties devolving upon me as a senator honestly and faithfully always keeping uppermost in mind the welfare of Indiana and its people whom I love so well. I deem it a high honor to accept this appointment from our splendid and universally beloved Governor Ralston, who has contributed so much to the progress and civic uplift of our state. I will support our great president and his administration in every way I can, and sincerely hope I may, in some manner at least, be of aid to him and his policies.[12]

Taggart wrote to Ralston on the same day, using the letterhead of The New Denison Hotel Company, "In the performance of my official duties it will be my aim and desire to help further and maintain the honest and progressive administration which you, as Governor, have given and now are giving the people of this State, and also, in my humble way, to assist our President, Woodrow Wilson, in a continuance of the splendid administration which he is giving to this Nation."[13] And then off to Washington went the newly appointed Senator Taggart.

Governor Ralston's office, of course, was flooded with letters regarding his appointment of Taggart to the Senate seat. Most were supportive of the choice. E. P. Honan of Rensselaer wrote, "Accept my sincere thanks. You have recognized in my judgment the most self sacrificing Democrat our state has ever produced. Long live Senator Taggart."[14] The Democratic press, naturally, hailed the selection. Typical of their response was an editorial in the *Indiana Daily Times* on 21 March: "In view of the intelligence and progressive-mindedness shown in his advocacy of numerous good laws in Indiana, it is reasonable to hope and expect that Taggart will apply to the performance of senatorial duties a clarity of thought and a nationalism of view that may give both Taggart himself, and his state, a forward position in national affairs."[15] Some worried that he might not accept the appointment and run in November for the right to complete the remainder of the unexpired term because of his heavy business commitments. The

Washington Democrat spoke for many, "It was feared that the magnitude and importance of his business interests in Indiana might prevent him from assuming public duties so important and which will be certain to consume so much of his time."[16] Vice President Thomas R. Marshall, who owed his position to Taggart, delivered a curious comment of praise at the time of appointment. After describing the new senator as a "charming" and "agreeable" man, Marshall evaluated his speaking ability, "He is not an orator. He will not be able to discuss questions as did Senator Shively, but he can vote as straight a Democratic vote."[17] Faint praise, to be sure.

There were those people, papers, and organizations, of course, who criticized Ralston's decision, some more strongly than others. The *Indianapolis News* found the appointment difficult to accept and stated that everyone, but especially Democrats, should regret it, "for it is a terrible descent from such men as Hendricks, McDonald, Voorhees, Turpie and Shively to Taggart. We think that this would be admitted even by the new senator. It is doubtful whether he has any illusions about himself. Unless he has he must know that he has few qualifications for the high station to which he has been called by Governor Ralston. . . . Mr. Taggart has realized his ambition."[18] This attack by the *News*, over qualifications rather than differences in political philosophy, must have stung the man who lacked even a high school education. But others were much rougher in their commentary. Not surprisingly, the Prohibition National Committee blasted his selection. "Friends of gamblers, manipulators of purchasable voters, blatant protector of vice and prostitution in the Hoosier capital during two shameless terms of office and old style boss in every sense of the word, and finally lucky evader of indictment for election frauds in the grand jury cases before the Federal Court last year, Tom Taggart is happy in his 'vindication' as the latest chosen representative of the Hoosier State at the Federal Capitol." The Prohibitionists took a final hit by referring to Taggart as "Indiana's most notorious liquor boss."[19] Similarly, Pastor Oscar Reed McKay of the First Baptist Church in Bluffton took the governor to task over Taggart's reported links to gambling. "I know perfectly that Mr. Taggart has side stepped all responsibillity [*sic*] for the gambling at French Lick but his connection with it is too close to deceive people of discriminating minds and who have not received Mr. Taggart's political favors." Pastor McKay vigorously protested the appointment of "a man whose name smells of the gaming table."[20] The people with evangelical rather than liturgical religious backgrounds found his easygoing and flexible approach to issues involving their strict ideas of morality unacceptable, even sinful. Taggart found himself in the center of such evangelical-liturgical political and cultural conflicts throughout his career. Finally, *The Outlook,* a weekly newsmagazine published in New York, took a dim view of his elevation to the Senate. "Few men have been so powerful in the Democratic party as Taggart. . . . If he has any convictions on great National questions, they are not generally known," the reporter wrote. The article cited his problems with gambling at French Lick and the recent election fraud indictments and pointed out that Taggart, Charles F. Murphy of New York, and Roger C. Sullivan of Illinois secured the 1912 nomination for Wilson and thus got the spoils. "The nomination of Mr. Taggart to the Senate is but one illustration of the hold which machine oligarchy has upon the party," it said. "With all due allowance for the bitterness of politics in Indiana, there can be no doubt that Taggart has represented a discreditable type of politics."[21]

Taggart had been through it all before. There was nothing new in this latest series of attacks so it was all really rather routine criticism. "I THOUGHT I WOULD INFORM YOU," he wired Ralston from Washington, "THAT I REALLY LIKE MY JOB WASHINGTON IS A BEAUTIFUL CITY AND EVERYBODY IS VERY KIND AND COURTEOUS REGARDS TO MRS. RALSTON."[22] Taggart, indeed, was a man proud to be sitting on the floor of the Senate, and no amount of criticism could ruin that.

The swearing in of Taggart as United States senator was very much a Hoosier affair. Shortly after noon on 27 March Sen. John W. Kern announced Taggart's presence to the Senate. Taggart, who had been sitting next to Kern, then rose and the two made their way to the platform for the short ceremony. This was the dignified body's first item of business for the day. Seated above the floor in the gallery row reserved for the vice president were Mrs. Taggart, Mrs. Marshall, Miss Lucy Taggart, and a family friend, Miss Helen Rockwood of Indianapolis. Vice President Marshall administered the oath of office to Taggart after which the new senator signed the book for the occasion. Afterwards, the Marshalls, who had entertained the Taggarts the previous evening at their apartment in the Willard Hotel, hosted a luncheon in the Capitol for the Taggarts, Miss Rockwood, and Senator Kern. Then, after lunch, Taggart received visitors and floral tributes in the committee on pensions room. His first official action was to appoint Byford E. Long, who had served Shively as well, as his private secretary and committee clerk.[23] An exhilarating and exhausting day, 27 March 1916 was a landmark date in the story of Tom Taggart. A seat in the United States Senate not only allowed him to participate in the political decisions of the day, but it also bestowed a legitimacy and respectability that he was driven to seek throughout his life.

With Taggart installed in the Senate in Washington, the question now was whether or not he would be named by the April state convention to be the Democratic candidate in the fall election to complete the remainder of the unexpired term. If nominated, would he accept the honor? A. C. Sallee, secretary of the state Democratic committee and an old Taggart aide and loyalist, wrote Taggart on 31 March, "Democrats are talking of starting a movement over the state to have the convention nominate you unanimously whether you like it or not—and it looks like they are going to make some headway."[24] Not every Democrat was behind Taggart, however. Many in the Hoosier Democracy felt that the nomination for the special election should go to Ralston, who was completing his final year as governor, and state law at the time prohibited him from seeking a second consecutive term. Lew M. O'Bannon, prominent Democrat from Corydon, wired the governor on 1 April, "I HOPE YOU WILL ENTER THE RACE OR ALLOW THE USE OF YOUR NAME FOR UNITED STATES

SENATOR I THINK THE PARTY EXPECTS IT AND WOULD BE PLEASED TO HAVE YOU ON THE TICKET."[25] Taggart himself joined those pushing the governor when he announced he would not seek the Senate nomination in April and came out for Ralston.[26] As usual, Taggart only wanted the position if support was unanimous, thus strengthening his hand. On 5 April Bernard Korbly, state chairman and longtime political ally, notified Taggart that he had been chosen temporary chairman of the state convention and would deliver the gathering's keynote address. Korbly also pleaded with Taggart to accept the Senate nomination, "It appears you will be nominated by the convention in spite of your expressed wish not to be. I don't see how you can refuse to accept nomination. If you love the old democratic party and want it to succeed next fall, for God sake don't say you will not take the nomination if it is tendered to you by the convention."[27] Taggart did accept the nomination on 26 April from the Democratic delegates gathered from across the state. At the same time he retired from the post of national committeeman after sixteen years of service. The platform passed by the convention pointed to progressive reforms by the Democratic party at the federal level, such as a banking law, the popular election of senators, liberal pensions, extension of parcel post, perfecting postal savings banks, the income tax, and the strengthening of the Sherman Antitrust Act. On the state level the platform emphasized such things as workmen's compensation, vocational education, the public service commission, the primary election law, payment of state debts, anti–loan shark laws, provision for a state fire marshal, the inheritance tax law, and the antilobby law.[28]

Taggart addressed the issue of his ability to serve Indiana in the Senate during his acceptance speech to the Democratic state convention. "As you well know," he said, "I have never pretended to be either an orator or a statesman, and at the time of my declaration that I would not accept this nomination, I felt that these qualifications were both desirable and necessary in a United States senator. Becoming better acquainted with the situation, however, it is no reflection upon the able men in the Senate to say that there appears to be room in that distinguished body for plain, every-day, business men—men who are not only familiar and in touch with large business affairs, but who understand from actual and constant contact and dealings with those people who do not possess great individual fortunes, but who make for general prosperity and who have the last word in the shaping of all our social and governmental policies—the smaller business man, the farmer, the mechanic and the laborer."[29] After just a few weeks on the job in Washington, a full measure of confidence clearly had returned to Taggart.

Once he was back in the District of Columbia, living at the New Willard Hotel[30] and working hard at his Senate duties, Taggart still maintained a steady contact with the state committee in Indianapolis and focused his considerable energy on the campaign as well as the legislative business at hand. Even before the state convention took place he requested from the state committee the primary vote in 1916 for president, vice president, senator, and governor and the numbers for the same offices in the 1912 general election.[31] In May he wired for a list of all precinct committeemen and vice committeemen from across the state. In the same telegram he wanted a report on the 18–19 May meeting in Indianapolis of all ninety-two county chairmen and secretaries.[32] In July Taggart requested an updated list of precinct committeemen and county chairmen in the state and sent each one a letter, explaining that "I am doing this in order to get in touch with the organization throughout the State."[33] Organization. Communication. Taggart's vaunted political machine needed constant maintenance and the master mechanic was ever vigilant. His attention or lack of attention to the organization, he felt, could spell the difference between victory and defeat. By August he indicated that he was now receiving reports from across the state, some bad and others good, and that the bad ones came invariably from areas where the organization had not yet started.[34] There was a two-way relationship between Taggart's Washington office and the state committee at 147 East Market Street in Indianapolis.[35] In late May Korbly asked Taggart to send him the names of all Hoosiers who worked for the federal government in Washington along with their Indiana and Washington addresses. Taggart's office obliged with lists of Hoosier employees in executive departments and federal commissions.[36] Additionally the state committee suggested that Taggart write to every farmer in Marion County and supplied him with the name, address, and amount of acreage for every farmer in the county. Clearly no Hoosier stone would be left unturned in the search for Democratic votes.[37]

It was apparent by late summer that a major problem for the Democratic ticket in Indiana would be the defection of German Democrats to the Republicans. While Homer L. Cook, Indiana secretary of state, felt that things were getting better among Germans in Marion County, even though conceding that "I am afraid that conditions are too bad yet," one leader in the Indianapolis Chamber of Commerce saw no hope and reported that Germans were absolutely opposed to Woodrow Wilson. John Barnett (a leader in the Indianapolis Chamber of Commerce) wrote Taggart, "Not only against him [Wilson] but so much so that I am sure they cannot be turned back. . . . The thing to do is figure up the number of German Democratic votes in Indiana that are against us, and figure to make them up elsewhere." There was no question that President Wilson's policies toward Germany were alienating a large segment of the traditional Democratic vote in Indiana, and that meant trouble for Taggart and the entire ticket. As an overture to the German vote, Taggart lodged a protest with the State Department when the British blacklisted the New York agents of the Oliver Chilled Steel Plow Company of South Bend for allegedly helping the Germans break the blockade of the continent. Taggart redoubled his campaign efforts, asking Korbly for absentee ballot applications for Hoosiers in Washington and pledging to hunt down every Hoosier in town and getting him to go home to vote, if possible. He sent Korbly a list of Democrats from around the state who precinct committeemen said would not vote for Wilson. Taggart asked the state chairman to take up the problem with his respective county chairmen.

Secretary of State Cook sent Taggart a list of secretaries of factories that contained about fifteen thousand names and a list of all attorneys in Indiana. There was much work to be done if Taggart was to prevail in November.[38]

The problems of organizing the campaign persisted as the so-called greatest deliberative body in the world inched toward adjournment in early September. There was the question of why 106 blacks, a traditionally Republican constituency, from Henderson, Kentucky, had arrived in Indianapolis in the last thirty to sixty days. Taggart wanted to know who sent them and for whom they worked.[39] Taggart was concerned about the Lake County organization's inability to get itself together, and Korbly proposed a meeting between the Lake County organization and prominent Democrats to iron things out.[40] Finally, there was the considerable business of arranging Vice President Marshall's second notification at Tomlinson Hall in Indianapolis on 14 September. Evans Woollen was chairman of the event and state senator Van Nuys was secretary of the General Arrangements Committee. Korbly wanted Taggart to use his influence to get national chairman Vance McCormick and members of the Democratic National Committee to attend. "We are very anxious to have you back in Indiana," Korbly wrote to Taggart. "It seems that everybody from every quarter is clamoring for you."[41] Korbly, stating that "conditions are good. We are working hard and getting results," made a plea for funds from anyone in Washington for Marshall's notification. Taggart responded in his typical fashion, "Mark me down for a hundred or more if necessary to make the notification meeting a success."[42] Taggart was especially eager for the state party to publicize among the working people in Indianapolis the fact that Sen. Lawrence Sherman of Illinois, who was to make the notification speech in Indianapolis for Republican vice presidential nominee Charles W. Fairbanks on 31 August, had referred to Samuel Gompers as a public nuisance on the floor of the Senate.[43]

From Room 337 of the Senate Office Building, Taggart set his course in the Senate. He believed that a senator was essentially a member of the National Board of Directors and, thus, had an obligation to speak and be heard. This, of course, flew in the face of historical precedent whereby freshmen senators were to sit silently and observe the proceedings. Taggart would have none of that and spoke out forcefully during his months in the Senate, especially on the issue of wasteful government spending.[44] In a humorous vein, that was not the only precedent he broke. In late July he took his new bird dog onto the floor of the Senate, reportedly the first time such a thing had ever happened![45]

One of his first senatorial decisions involved committee assignments. In the end Taggart chose to chair the Committee on Forest Reservations and the Protection of Game. Among this committee's nine members were such prominent senators as Benjamin R. Tillman of South Carolina and Gilbert M. Hitchcock and George W. Norris of Nebraska. Byford E. Long, Taggart's private secretary, also served as committee clerk. Presumably Taggart's love of animals, hunting, and the out-of-doors prompted his selection of this committee chairmanship. The record shows, however, no legislative activity by this committee during Taggart's several months as chairman. In fact, the Committee on Forest Reservations and the Protection of Game seems to have existed largely to provide its chairman office space. The Senate abolished this committee in 1921 as part of an effort to streamline its operations. Taggart also sat on the Census, Corporations Organized in the District of Columbia, Interoceanic Canals, Pacific Railroads, Patents, Pensions, and Territories committees.[46]

Taggart made a reputation for himself as an opponent of wasteful and unnecessary government spending during his short tenure in the Senate. Unquestionably, he brought a businessman's approach to his review of federal legislation. In late May he attacked the river and harbor appropriation bill of $40,899,935. He pointed out that river transportation had declined in the last twenty-five years while the government spent over $800 million on it. The rivers could not compete with the railroads and, too, Taggart was concerned that there be enough money for war preparedness. Thus he proposed cutting the appropriation by fifteen to twenty million dollars. "Although a new Member of this body," Taggart declared, "I refuse to send or be a party to sending the Treasury of the United States to the 'scrap heap' so that every little river from Raccoon Creek, New Jersey, to Kissimmee River, Florida, shall be improved; and unless a large number of these seemingly useless items are eliminated from this bill I shall be compelled to vote against it." As a "business proposition," he could not support the bill.[47] Several days later Taggart offered an amendment to the river and harbor bill. According to his measure only appropriations for maintenance and partially completed projects would be available unconditionally. The secretary of war would have to determine what other projects would promote, or were essential to, interstate or foreign commerce.[48] The audacity of a rookie senator to propose such a thing and to speak out like that must have raised more than a few eyebrows.

Taggart took a special interest in Indiana's proposed system of state parks. Richard Lieber had been appointed chairman of the Committee on the Indiana State Centennial Memorial that planned to mark the state's one hundredth anniversary with the creation of a state park system. A campaign was started to buy the property that became Turkey Run State Park, but in the meantime the site of McCormick's Creek State Park was purchased. According to Lieber, the father of the state park system, both Senators Taggart and Kern encouraged the effort as it began in the spring of 1916.[49] Also, on the federal level, Taggart pushed the idea of creating a national park in the dunes region along Lake Michigan in northwestern Indiana. To that end he submitted a resolution in 1916 asking that the secretary of the interior study the feasibility of establishing a national park in the Indiana dunes and report back to Congress. After hearings were conducted in Chicago in the autumn of 1916, a report favorable to the idea was sent to Congress. Since Taggart lost his election in 1916 and nothing was done about the findings of the report, the Indiana Dunes National Lakeshore would have to wait several decades before it was established.[50]

Mexican-American relations and the prospect of war between the two neighboring countries dominated part of the news in 1916. On 9 March Francisco "Pancho" Villa, a rebel general battling Mexico's president Venustiano Carranza, crossed the border and attacked and burned the town of Columbus, New Mexico, killing nineteen American citizens in the process. President Wilson sent Gen. John J. Pershing in pursuit of Villa, but he soon found himself three hundred miles into Mexico without apprehending Villa. Carranza demanded Pershing's withdrawal from Mexican soil after fighting broke out between Mexican troops and the Americans at Parral on 12 April. Wilson responded with a stinging rebuke to the Mexicans and mobilized most of the National Guard and sent it to the border. Another armed clash occurred on 21 June at Carrizal in northern Mexico, after which Taggart offered to resign from the Senate, organize and equip a regiment to fight in Mexico, and to pay for it all himself. Letters from men all over the state poured in to Taggart's office offering to serve in his regiment should war break out with Mexico. Fortunately the two nations pulled back from the brink of war and settled their differences peacefully.[51]

During the first several days of July Taggart got away from the heat, humidity, and pressure of Washington by escaping to his new summerhouse and the Cape breezes in Hyannis Port. His daughters and grandchildren were there, but his sons-in-law, Laurance Chambers and Dick Sinclair, were staying together and were hard at work back in Indianapolis. Chambers wrote his father-in-law, "I am living with Dick at his house these days, and it is very pleasant up on Thirty-second Street. All the same I am desperately lonely without Nora and the babies."[52] Five days later another letter from Chambers to Taggart ended with, "Give my love to all the dear folks at Hyannisport. I wish I were there!"[53] Before summer's end the two men would get to "the Port" to spend a couple of weeks or so relaxing with their young families.

On 12 August Taggart, back in Washington, cemented his reputation as an opponent of the government's wasteful spending when he delivered a speech to the Senate entitled

"Government Should Practice Same Kind of Economy that a Good Business Man Would Follow." "I wonder what would happen to each Senator and to each Member of the House if he spent or appropriated money in his private affairs as he spends it in public affairs?," Taggart asked. "I wonder how long it would be until we would all find ourselves in a court of bankruptcy? On the other hand, I wonder what would happen to the country if every Member of the Senate and House would make up his mind in the direction of the rigid economy, and fearlessly cut off every useless dollar of appropriations? I wonder if the taxpayers of the Nation would rise up and revolt against Congress if such a thing should happen? I favor a liberal but businesslike economy."[54] To indicate their displeasure at such brashness and stinging criticism from a freshman, many veteran senators left their seats when he gave this speech.[55] But Taggart's words came from the heart and genuinely reflected his political philosophy and, certainly, they were well received back in conservative Indiana, if not on the floor of the Senate. The *South Bend News-Times,* never a supporter of his, now suddenly detected the quality of statesmanship in Senator Taggart. Not only did the paper laud his speech on government economy in general, but it also pointed out that he called Sen. Nelson W. Aldrich's estimate of government waste of $300 million per year too conservative.[56] Even the *Indianapolis News,* his old nemesis, spoke out in his favor when Taggart voted against free seed distribution for members of Congress, a perk that cost taxpayers an estimated $252,540 annually. "Mr. Taggart has rashly invaded the holy of holies. The new senator from Indiana is a very bad boy," the paper observed.[57]

Taggart also declared for a tariff commission, woman's suffrage, federal aid to state roads, the merchant marine, developing trade with South America, flood control on inland rivers, a government nitrate plant, war preparedness, and a bond issue to help pay for preparedness in mid-August.[58] Taggart toed the traditional party line on issues such as the tariff, supported the Progressives on items such as a government-owned nitrate plant, was squarely behind Wilson on military preparedness, and pushed pet projects such as federal assistance to states in developing a network of highways. In a speech in the Senate entitled "Wealth Must Bear Its Just Proportion of the Burden of Taxation," Taggart emphasized the responsibility wealthy people had to support their government through taxation, especially at a time when preparedness efforts would require more money. "No objection can be made to any plan which causes wealth to bear its just proportion in meeting national expenditures. Wealth should shoulder its responsibility in contributing its fullest share in the general scheme of taxation for the support of the Government," contended the wealthy Taggart. He specifically endorsed the income tax law during the campaign of 1916,[59] which to him was a matter of fairness and civic responsibility. Thus, given the opportunity to demonstrate his convictions in a legislative forum, the boss of the Democratic machine in Indiana proved he was a loyal supporter of Wilson's progressive administration.

The Senate session continued until early September, and Taggart wanted very much to get some rest at the Cape before returning to Indiana for the autumn campaign. "As you know," he wrote Korbly from Washington on 3 September, "I have been here pretty constantly since I was appointed, and feel that I ought to be at home helping you with the organization, but I do want to go to Hyannisport for a few days as soon as Congress adjourns and return home in time to be with you for the notification meeting on the 14th."[60]

Now the time had come for some good old Hoosier politicking for which the state is famous. Taggart left Byford E. Long in charge of his Senate office until Long himself returned to Indianapolis on 6 October.[61] Taggart campaigned across the length and breadth of the Hoosier state, speaking to people from as many of the state's 3,151 precincts and 1,016 townships as possible.[62] Senator Taggart, the candidate, was the same self-effacing person as always. To Willis Thompson, who was writing much of the Democratic campaign material in 1916, he wrote, "the name of Thomas Taggart for U.S. Senator has been mentioned very often. I wish from now until the close of the campaign you would refer to my running mate the Hon. John Worth Kern just as often as you do myself."[63] Senator Kern, challenged by Republican Harry S. New, also was lauded by former Secretary of State William Jennings Bryan in *The Commoner*, along with all the other Democratic candidates for the Senate in 1916, except for one, Taggart.[64] This snub was part of a long-standing pattern of treatment of Taggart by Bryan. Still, after Taggart's loyalty to Bryan through three presidential campaigns, this unkind treatment must have hurt.

The Republicans nominated James E. Watson in 1916 to oppose Taggart for the Senate. Former congressman and unsuccessful Republican nominee for governor against Marshall in 1908, Watson was a formidable opponent. Louis Ludlow, journalist and later a Democratic congressman, observed Watson at rural campaign stops and reported he had no equal as a spellbinder. As he cranked up the emotion of his political appeal, Watson would remove his collar, then his coat, and finally his vest.[65] Even though Watson's speaking ability on the stump was most effective, the Republican party still had to formulate an alternative policy vision to that of Wilson and Taggart. The *Indianapolis Star* summed up the challenge to the Republicans on its editorial page, "For some time past the basis of that party policy hereabouts has been confined to a specific and localized hostility to Thomas Taggart. There has been no positive or constructive effort whatever, but merely the exploitation of venom toward Mr. Taggart and his friends."[66] For Republicans, Taggart was the Democratic party in Indiana and, like a lightning rod, he drew their wrath and criticism.

A highlight of the autumn Democratic campaign in Indiana came on 12 October when President and Mrs. Wilson visited Indianapolis to help Hoosiers celebrate the centennial of Indiana's statehood. And, of course, it would be helpful politically to visit a crucial swing state that had two native sons, Thomas R. Marshall and Charles W. Fairbanks, opposing one another for vice president on their respective tickets. Wilson wanted to blunt any impact Fairbanks's selection by Charles Evans Hughes as his running mate may have had in the state, and he certainly needed both Taggart and Kern back in the Senate to complete his progressive agenda. To celebrate the visit of the presidential couple, Governor and Mrs. Ralston hosted a luncheon in the Riley Room of the Claypool Hotel for the Wilsons and one hundred guests. The room, decorated in red, white, and blue, had a large oval table in its center at which were seated Mrs. Wilson, Mrs. Ralston, Mrs. Taggart, Mrs. Kern, and other prominent women. There was a long table along the wall with Governor Ralston to the left of the president and Taggart on his right. Others at the head table were United States district attorney L. Ert Slack, Mayor Joseph E. Bell, Charles A. Bookwalter, Caleb S. Denny, Elwood Haynes, John H. Holliday, Carl G. Fisher, and Dr. I. S. Harold. Taggart, convivial as usual, left his seat at the main table several times to greet people. Meredith Nicholson, noted writer and party activist, was invited to the main table at the close of the luncheon for a warm greeting from Wilson. The presidential party then proceeded to Monument Circle where they reviewed the "Centennial Highway Day" parade. Governor Ralston was a prominent advocate of the good roads movement and, according to some, had been converted during a summer vacation at Taggart's Hyannis Port home when he traveled over the smooth roads of Massachusetts. Ralston had appointed Taggart chairman of the state highway commission in 1914 to study road conditions in Indiana and had also appointed him to the Dixie Highway Association, along with Carl G. Fisher, to plan that interstate road link.[67] Then, as now, the appearance of the president of the United States gives a tremendous boost to that party's state campaign by raising morale throughout the organization. The Hoosier Democracy was grateful for Wilson's help.

Taggart, nearing his sixtieth birthday in November, vigorously crisscrossed Indiana during the fall campaign. The major focus and challenge of his effort, aside from winning the Senate seat, was to defend President Wilson and his policies of the previous four years to Hoosier voters. Since Wilson was a minority president who owed his election mainly to the split in Republican ranks in 1912, the challenge was great in 1916 to fashion a majority vote for him in Indiana in the face of a reunited Republican party. Social justice leader William Bauchop Wilson, having completed a campaign tour for the president from Pennsylvania to California in mid-October, predicted Taggart's efforts would be rewarded with a return to the Senate. Taggart's campaign appearance at the Memorial Opera House in Valparaiso on 21 October was typical of his campaign. In his speech he launched into a spirited defense of Wilson, his administration, and its policies. Taggart praised the eight-hour day, criticized Republican candidate Charles Evans Hughes, and made sarcastic comments about Theodore Roosevelt. There was frequent and prolonged applause throughout and he was cheered at the end while a band in the balcony played George Frederick Handel's "See the Conquering Hero Comes." Then, as in a whirlwind, Taggart was off for his next stop in Gary. Taggart was so effective in defending Wilson's progressive agenda that there was a "New and Taggart" slogan making the rounds among Progressive party members that worried Kern and Watson.[68]

Taggart, Kern, and Wilson all were narrowly defeated in Indiana at the hands of their Republican challengers on 7 November. Hughes edged out the president by just under seven thousand votes in the state in a hard-fought race, but Wilson held on to the presidency by eking out a victory nationwide. Taggart lost to Watson and Kern lost to New by almost identical margins of just under twelve thousand votes. The Hoosier electorate had spoken, however narrowly, and now both $7,500-per-year Senate seats from Indiana would go over to the Republicans.[69] In retrospect, this would be a significant loss to Wilson during his fight with the Senate over the League of Nations after World War I. In addition to losing two votes in the Senate, Kern had been that body's majority leader. Claude G. Bowers, private secretary to and biographer of Kern, called the election of 1916 "a cross between a comedy and a tragedy." Bowers blamed the defeat on poor morale and poor organization. Others have pointed to additional factors such as German Americans voting in large numbers against the Democrats after the outbreak of war in Europe, former Progressives returning to the GOP fold, and the corruption charges against the Democrats in Terre Haute and Indianapolis the previous year. Also, in the week before the election the *Union Labor Bulletin*, statewide organ for the American Federation of Labor, denounced Taggart for using nonunion workers in the construction of the French Lick Springs Hotel and endorsed his opponent.[70] All things considered, the Hoosier Democracy performed quite well in the November election. But performing well and winning are two entirely different things in politics, and on 4 December 1916, after just over eight months in office, Taggart retired from the Senate.[71] Taggart's return to private life, however, still meant a lot of politics as well as overseeing his extensive investments and business holdings.

Taggart found himself in the midst of some controversy again early in 1917. The state legislature convened, as usual, in January, and the difficult issue of prohibition surfaced as a focus of debate. It was common knowledge that Taggart long had been associated with the brewery interests in Indiana. Democratic state senators David F. Culbertson, the floor leader, and Walter S. Chambers huddled with Taggart at the Denison Hotel to reach some agreement on this sticky question. Although Taggart had been associated for years in both the hotel business and politics with Crawford Fairbanks, owner of the Terre Haute Brewing Company, Fairbanks turned against him in the 1916 campaign and threw the brewery interests to the Republicans. As a bit of political payback Taggart dropped his opposition to prohibition, the state went dry, and Fairbanks was put out of business. Thus, Culbertson and Chambers returned to the Democratic Senate caucus at the Claypool Hotel to report that Taggart intimated he favored a state constitutional convention on the matter and that he would keep out of the liquor issue in the legislature.[72] Prohibition was one of the period's most controversial issues, to say the least, and this would not be the last time that Taggart was in the middle of the fray over it. However, one must note his political "flexibility" in handling the issue. He was not so flexible though when he thought his image had been tarnished, and he was ever vigilant about detecting any slight to his character in the nation's press. George Creel, Wilson's chairman of the Committee on Public Information during World War I, wrote an article entitled "The Next Four Years" for *Everybody's Magazine* in February 1917. The cartoonist for the article, Rollin Kirby, drew a picture of Taggart with Charles F. Murphy and Roger C. Sullivan that triggered Taggart's defensiveness. To Sam Ralston he wrote, "On page 131 you will find a picture of your distinguished friends, Charlie Murphy, Roger Sullivan and myself. I do not know that there is anything in the article that is libelous, but I do not like the looks of the picture. Tell me whether or not, in your judgment, you consider the article defamatory."[73] The gambling trial in 1906, the election fraud indictment in 1915, and the narrow Senate loss in 1916 all combined to heighten Taggart's sensitivity about such matters. The advent of American participation in World War I on 6 April, however, changed everyone's focus, including Taggart's.

Taggart clearly felt a patriotic duty to aid the American war effort in 1917. When the federal government asked the states to form councils to help coordinate the total war effort, Gov. James P. Goodrich, a Republican, named Taggart to Indiana's eighteen-member State Council of Defense on 19 May. Will H. Hays served as the first chairman, and other members included former vice president Charles W. Fairbanks, humorist George Ade, and Charles Fox, president of the Indiana State Federation of Labor.[74] These councils played an important role in coordinating the war effort on the domestic front, and Taggart's membership on Indiana's council allowed him an opportunity to make a meaningful contribution to the cause. He had been a champion of war preparedness during his short tenure in the Senate the previous year, so he especially welcomed this appointment. Taggart also accepted membership on the reception committee to look after the speakers at the State Wide War Conference in Indianapolis on 13–14 December. There was one disturbing note, however, to his acceptance. "I shall be glad to be with you on those dates," he wrote just days before the conference, "if I am feeling well enough, but at present I am not feeling extra well."[75] Taggart also accepted a role on the State Advisory Committee in the statewide War Savings campaign in early 1918. Having just celebrated his sixty-first birthday in November 1917, this was the first sign that he was beginning to experience health problems. Concerns over ill health, however, were overshadowed by the birth of his fifth grandchild to daughter Emily Sinclair on 19 November. Much to his delight and joy, his second male grandchild was named Thomas Taggart Sinclair.

The off-year congressional elections were held in 1918, and Taggart spoke forcefully about the need to focus on victory in a nonpartisan way. "This is no time for politics," he declared while visiting Washington. "If I had my way, I should nominate and elect the best men to Congress, regardless of their politics. We need in Congress the best men. . . . I would rather vote for the election of a Republican whom I knew to be all right than to vote for a Democrat whom I knew to be all wrong."[76] Unexpected, if not unusual, words from the veteran Democratic party boss and kingmaker of the Hoosier state. Taggart continued to keep in close touch with national politics and maintained a friendly relationship with President Wilson, even gifting him with French Lick's most famous product. On 27 April the president wrote Taggart, "My dear Senator: It was very kind of you to send us the case of Pluto water which has been received, and Mrs. Wilson joins me in sending our sincerest thanks. Cordially and sincerely yours, Woodrow Wilson."[77] Pluto had now been promoted from the spring house to the White House.

Apparently health problems continued to plague Taggart as January 1919 found him at the Breakers Hotel in Palm Beach with his wife and daughters Nora and Irene. Taggart always bounced back from these bouts of illness, and he wrote Sam Ralston on 22 January that he was feeling "pretty well."[78] In early August Taggart asked Frederick Van Nuys, the Democratic state chairman, to invite all the members of the state committee and their wives, the Ralstons, and a few other friends to spend the weekend of 7–10 August with him at the French Lick Springs Hotel.

Taggart never took his finger off the state's political pulse, and he was most generous in using the hotel as a gathering place for politicians. Taggart's offer of the weekend prompted Van Nuys to comment in his invitations, "The hospitality of our genial host is proverbial."[79]

The year 1919 also brought the joyous news of the birth of another grandchild, the Taggarts' sixth. This third child born to Dick and Emily Sinclair on 22 May was christened Elizabeth Richardson Sinclair. And more happy family news came in late summer when daughter Irene became their third child to marry. Irene wed William Jackson Young, a dermatologist from Louisville who was a staff physician at the French Lick Springs Hotel, on 10 September at the main house in the family compound in Hyannis Port. Following the family's long Episcopal tradition, the Reverend Oscar Fitzland Moore, rector of St. Mary's Episcopal Church in Barnstable, performed the service. Tom and Eva Taggart served as witnesses for the nuptials. With daughters Nora, Emily, and Irene married and with Lucy pursuing her artistic career rather than a family one, the Taggarts had only one potential wedding remaining, that of their thirty-three-year-old son Tom.[80]

Apathy and a sense of defeatism pervaded the Indiana Democratic party as 1920 began, but that attitude started to change in February as petitions circulated throughout the state urging Taggart to oppose Senator Watson once again for his former seat. On 2 March Howe Landers, Taggart's representative and an Indianapolis attorney, filed a petition of candidacy with one thousand names on it in the secretary of state's office. Morale soared at the prospect of having Taggart on the ticket with Dr. Carleton B. McCulloch, whom Taggart and Ralston had endorsed for governor in the upcoming May primary. McCulloch was a son of well-known Oscar Carleton McCulloch, pastor of Plymouth Congregational Church in Indianapolis and a strong proponent of the Social Gospel in the late nineteenth century. Many Democrats also felt that Republican Governor Goodrich had created so much discontent in the GOP that they now had a chance to capture the statehouse.[81] One week later, however, on

9 March, Taggart sent a letter of withdrawal from the Senate race to A. C. Sallee, the state chairman, citing ill health and lack of physical strength as the reasons for getting out. The press noted that his health had not been good for some time and that Mrs. Taggart objected to his being in the race given his physical state. Since he was the only senatorial candidate in the Democratic primary, the state committee now had to find a replacement. Vice President Marshall flatly refused the honor, so the Democrats were in something of a mess.[82]

The Hoosier Democracy wanted and needed Taggart on the ticket in 1920, so negotiators began to work something out. In the meantime three men declared themselves for the Democratic Senate nomination: Samuel M. Foster, a manufacturer from Fort Wayne, who was considered the favorite; Bernard Shively of Marion, a state senator; and John C. Snyder, supreme scribe of the Tribe of Ben Hur, a fraternal organization and insurance company based in Crawfordsville. On 27 March the state committee met at the Denison Hotel in Indianapolis and elected Benjamin Bosse, two-term mayor of Evansville and chairman of the First District, as its chairman. Bosse succeeded A. C. Sallee, who had been chairman only since the first of the year when Frederick Van Nuys resigned to become United States district attorney. The state committee voted unanimously to request Taggart to rejoin the state ticket, and the three contenders agreed to step aside. Bosse put in a long distance call to Taggart in French Lick to convey the sentiment of the state Democratic organization and after hearing Bosse's plea, Taggart agreed to reenter the Senate race and "make the fight of his life." Part of the deal was a clear-cut plan to organize the state for the autumn campaign. Bosse planned to divide Indiana into six districts with two paid managers, a man and a woman, at each headquarters. Women, about to be given the vote for the first time in 1920, were being integrated into the mechanics of the political process. The state committee and the managers were to meet together monthly and act as a clearinghouse for the six headquarters. This was the kind of plan that Taggart liked and felt could lead to victory.[83]

The primary campaigns for both Senate nominations in 1920 were uneventful. Neither Taggart nor Senator Watson had any opposition. Taggart did run newspaper advertisements before the primary election, and one in particular provides a source of amusement. Taggart is pictured in the center of the ad with an 1887 picture of the French Lick Springs Hotel above him and a 1920 photo of the hotel below. The text reads, "The above illustrates the remarkable evolution of the French Lick Springs institution under the supervision of Thomas Taggart, which stands today as a monument to his inventive genius and executive ability." The amusing aspect was that the supposed 1887 picture of the hotel was actually a sketch of the original circa 1845 building at the French Lick site, which did indeed make the development of the hotel property even more dramatic.[84] Voters in Indiana's 3,387 precincts trooped to the polls on 4 May and dutifully sent Taggart and Watson into combat against one another for the second time in four years. The Democrats also chose McCulloch to run for governor while the Republicans selected Warren T. McCray for that office. The fate of both parties depended upon national trends of postwar voter sentiment and the selection of presidential nominees.[85]

By this time Taggart had long played a major role in nominating presidential candidates at Democratic national conventions. Shortly after the primary he told the *Indianapolis Star* that Charles F. Murphy, the boss of Tammany Hall and his longtime friend, had recently spent several days with him at French Lick and that they had discussed the presidential nomination. Taggart stated his support for Vice President Marshall, even though Marshall repeatedly said that he was not interested. Although it was not widely known in the country at the time, Mrs. Wilson had been running the country since Wilson suffered a stroke in October 1919, and Marshall had consistently refused all suggestions that he should act in the president's place. Taggart reported that Murphy expressed admiration for Marshall, said he had made good, and that he would not be objectionable as president.[86] On the same day that the *Star* reported its conversation with Taggart, 10 May, the *News* carried a story saying that the *New York Sun* and *New York Herald* were reporting a deal between the two bosses that would swing the New York delegation at the summer convention to Marshall after the first ballot. Tammany reportedly liked Marshall because of his opposition to the League of Nations and to the Volstead Act (prohibition). Those close to Marshall denied these allegations and Marshall himself said, "It is all bosh." Marshall then gave his own summary of Taggart. "I am going to be frank about this matter. I think Tom Taggart made a good, clean, competent senator. He is a business man and believes in business methods and if we had had him here during the war, he would have done a great deal to see that things were run on a business basis. He is not in politics for money. He likes to boss and name candidates and all that, but he is not a candidate for office for the money he will get out of it. I can say that without hesitation. But as far as politics goes, we have never played the same game and I have never followed his leadership. I do not believe in the kind of politics that he believes in."[87] Many in the party were offended by the vice president's remarks. The Democratic *Indianapolis Times* published an editorial "Marshall Belittles Taggart" and stated that as a candidate for the Senate Taggart was "entitled to some respect even from so highly cultured a political aspirant as Thomas Riley Marshall, the vice president of the United States. . . . It is very obvious that Mr. Marshall has never followed the leadership of Mr. Taggart. Had he done so the democratic party of Indiana would not now be so demoralized." It went on to criticize Marshall's handling of patronage while governor and vice president, pointing out that he essentially ignored the party in the patronage process.[88] Clearly Taggart was the epitome of a machine boss while Marshall advocated reforms that opened up the electoral process, so differences between the two were inevitable. Although differences are natural in politics or in any human endeavor, Marshall's assessment of Taggart seemed to lack tact and grace, especially since Taggart had put Marshall in the nation's second most powerful position. Marshall, indeed, came off the worse for his remarks. Taggart, surely somewhat offended, dropped all further efforts to nominate Marshall for the presidency.

The Democratic state convention convened in mid-May with Vice President Marshall giving the keynote address to the party faithful. In his comments he expressed the hope that President Wilson and the Senate, over which Marshall presided, would come to some agreement over the League of Nations issue. There was much speculation that Marshall opposed the League, but in his speech he vaguely stated that he favored a League. In precisely what form or with what reservations he did not say. He declared that he would not read anyone out of the Democratic party over the League and that he expected the same treatment. Despite his earlier comments about Taggart, Marshall endorsed him for the Senate, saying that the country needed him. The press noted that there was more applause from the delegates than usual for this endorsement. The platform adopted by the convention demanded ratification of the League of Nations as presented by President Wilson, favored women's suffrage, supported more pay for teachers, and called for repeal of the primary election except for selection of party convention delegates and an optional primary law for town, city, and county offices. The thorny issue of prohibition was never mentioned.

Taggart delivered his acceptance speech to the convention on 20 May and provided a comprehensive summary of his views on most of the major issues of the day. He called Wilson the "greatest man of his generation" and criticized Indiana's two Republican senators for not giving the president any credit or honor. This followed with a pledge, if he were elected, to support the president of any party in the field of foreign policy. "President Wilson, my fellow-citizens, has made it possible for a wonderful service to be rendered the world," Taggart said. "He has made it possible to reduce to a minimum, through the League of Nations, the possibility of war, and I am not in favor of increasing the possibility of war by weakening the League through reservations." Everyone was aware that the issue of Ireland, her freedom from British control, and the League had driven many Irish Catholic Democrats into the opposition camp. Taggart tackled that sensitive topic in a most effective way. "And just here, pardon me for touching on a point in a sense personal—through my veins there courses the warm blood of an Irish ancestry, and in my heart there is an undying love for old Ireland," he began. "As God is my judge, I have asked Him a thousand times to bless Ireland, the land of my birth, by liberating her. I have read and studied as carefully as I have been capable of doing the president's interpretation of the league covenant as it bears upon Ireland. And I say to my Irish friends that I never spoke more sincerely in my life on any subject than I do when I say that if this country joins the allied nations under the league covenant it will be in a much better position to help Ireland than it now is or will be if it remains out of the league. This is an additional reason for my being for the league of nations."

Taggart's sense of fair play and empathy for the less fortunate most likely stemmed from his own childhood and upbringing. "Democrat as I am, I am not, if elected, going to the Senate to serve partisan purpose, but to serve my state and the American people to the best of my ability. I shall go there to play no favorites but to do what I believe to be just and right. I shall insist that women be recognized as having every right that men have, and one right men do not have—the right to be protected by man. I shall treat as fairly the poor man as I do the rich man and guard as sacredly the constitutional rights of the colored man as I do the similar rights of the white man." While Taggart expressed concern for women, the poor, and blacks, his thinking was framed by the period of time in which he lived.

The Red Scare and the fear of Bolshevism fueled many a political discussion in America in 1920. Reeling from the Russian Revolution of 1917, postwar economic dislocation and strikes, and a rash of radical bombings, American voters were concerned about the relationship between labor and capital and the perceived threat of Bolshevism. "I believe in capital and I believe in labor," Taggart declared. "But I sometimes think there are times when they are both open to criticism for not being more appreciative of the relation that should exist between them. I want to see capital make a fair profit and be safeguarded in its property rights and with equal zeal do I want to see labor have a fair wage—a wage sufficiently large to give a competence on which to live and to educate children without experiencing a sense of humiliation, and to lay aside, by observing the prudent rules of life, something for a rainy day. Until this condition can be brought about Bolshevism will increase and law and order will be threatened and you will agree with me that the red flag must never have a place in our sky." His remarks, perhaps surprising to his detractors who considered him reactionary, revealed an insight into the fundamental causes of social unrest and political instability.

As was the case during his brief Senate term in 1916, Taggart was especially concerned about the federal budget and taxation. Very critical of the federal government's budgetary procedures, he declared that he was "in favor of the closest scrutiny in every department for which appropriations are asked. I am strongly in favor of a budget system properly organized and directed by the most competent men with authority to investigate the requests of the various departments and make suggestions to the proper committees before any appropriations are made." He complained that the government was unbusinesslike in its fiscal methods. "Up to and including the present time it is and has been the custom to make the appropriations first and then find out on what course congress can levy a tax to get the money with which to meet these appropriations. It has not been unusual in the present congress for millions of dollars to be appropriated for various purposes without even a roll call and without even a quorum being present. Can you imagine the directors of any private concern acting on this basis?," he asked. He stated that the American people were "entitled to a rest from the heavy burden of taxation" caused by the Great War. In one of his most quotable lines Taggart declared, "People cannot be made prosperous by taxation—be it either direct or indirect." As for the excess profits tax, it "should be removed at once, but as I see it at the present time there will be little reduction in taxes unless the question of retrenchment and economy in every department is given serious consideration and practical methods of business put in operation at once." Understandably, this issue of government efficiency was close to his heart, and with this eloquent and detailed address to the state convention Taggart began his second campaign for the United States Senate.[89]

Taggart wasted no time in going on the attack after the Democratic state convention, meeting with party organization leaders, along with the other state candidates, at the Denison Hotel where he gave a vigorous talk that emphasized the need for efficient organization down to the smallest precinct. He pledged again to give every ounce of his energy to the campaign.[90] The Democratic strategy in Indiana was to focus the entire campaign on Taggart and his assault on Watson. Taggart's candidacy was reportedly so crucial to Democratic chances that he had agreed to run only after a trip to Washington and a conference with an unknown politico. Basically, though, it was through Taggart that the Democrats hoped to carry Indiana,[91] and he was happy to lead the charge. On 18 June, the day the GOP national ticket of Warren G. Harding and Calvin Coolidge was chosen, Taggart attacked the Republican plank on the League of Nations as "retroactive, cowardly and pussyfooting." The *New York Evening Post* speculated that Taggart had anticipated a straddling Republican plank on the issue and had, therefore, spoken so firmly on the issue at the state convention so he could inject the League into the fall Senate campaign.[92]

The national Democratic party now faced the considerable challenge of nominating a presidential candidate who could mount a competitive campaign against the Republicans. Wilson insisted on making the presidential race a "solemn referendum" on the League of Nations, but the American people showed every sign of wanting to forget foreign policy and World War I. Thus came Senator Harding's ringing campaign call for a return to "normalcy." There was much behind-the-scenes political maneuvering before the Democratic National Convention convened in San Francisco late in June. Taggart, of course, was a fixture at these quadrennial proceedings. In mid-June, on their way from New York

Gov. Alfred E. Smith on horseback at the French Lick Springs Hotel. Thomas Taggart is in the background. Smith and Tammany boss Charles F. Murphy stopped in French Lick in June 1920 en route to the Democratic National Convention in San Francisco.

to San Francisco, New York governor Alfred E. Smith and Tammany boss Charles F. Murphy stopped in French Lick to huddle with Taggart and discuss the nominating contest about to take place. The coming struggle seemed to be shaping up between the progressive governor of Ohio, James M. Cox, and the former secretary of the treasury, William Gibbs McAdoo, dubbed the "Crown Prince" because he was Woodrow Wilson's son-in-law. Reportedly Cox's name figured prominently in the conference at French Lick, and Taggart declared the Ohio governor satisfactory to him. Taggart was personally friendly to United States Attorney General A. Mitchell Palmer, another name mentioned as a possible contender, but he kept himself free of all alliances. One thing was quite evident at this point: Taggart was no longer pushing Marshall for the presidency.[93]

The special train carrying the Indiana delegation to the San Francisco convention pulled out of Indianapolis in the early afternoon on Saturday, 19 June. The excited delegates were taking the scenic, leisurely route to California with stops ranging from one to eighteen hours in length, for sightseeing at Denver, Colorado Springs, Royal Gorge, Tennessee Pass, Salt Lake City, Los Angeles, and the redwood forests. The delegation would take a week getting there, arriving in San Francisco the following Saturday, 26 June. There were sixty rooms and a reception room reserved for the delegation at the Manx Hotel, which was within walking distance of the convention hall. Another thirty-five rooms were held at the Oakland Hotel for Hoosiers who were not delegates. The Indiana delegates, as usual, elected Taggart chairman, Bowman Elder of Indianapolis as secretary, and Charles J. Murphy of the capital city as treasurer.[94] The Hoosier Democracy had thirty votes at the convention, composed of twenty-six district delegates from the thirteen congressional districts and four at-large. The four at-large delegates were Taggart, Sam Ralston, Vice President Marshall, and Mrs. Alice Foster McCulloch of Fort Wayne.[95]

All of the mounting suspense over the Democratic presidential nomination peaked on the convention floor when balloting for the top spot on the national ticket began. The contest quickly boiled down to the expected face-off between Cox and McAdoo. The Hoosier delegation fell into a consistent pattern of voting nineteen votes for Cox and eleven for McAdoo on the early ballots. After the twenty-sixth ballot, with still no candidate chosen, Taggart caucused the delegation and swung Indiana to McAdoo, saying McAdoo would be very helpful to Taggart in his Senate race. So, Indiana now voted twenty-nine to one for McAdoo. There was strong Cox support among the Indiana delegates and, therefore, much reported disappointment over Taggart's move. But the delegates, clearly, with one exception, were obedient to Taggart's wishes. The McAdoo boom failed to take hold and, after the thirty-eighth ballot, the Hoosiers reverted to their earlier nineteen-to-eleven split for Cox.[96] The convention eventually chose Cox to be the party's standard-bearer and Wilson's young assistant secretary of the navy, Franklin D. Roosevelt, to be Cox's running mate. Because of the meeting in French Lick of Taggart, Murphy, and Al Smith before the convention, opponents charged that the

Roger C. Sullivan ready for campaign tour.

national Democratic ticket carried the label "Made in French Lick."[97] What most people did not know was that Taggart played a role in making Roosevelt the vice presidential nominee at the convention. According to Walter D. Myers, an Indianapolis attorney who was a Taggart associate and a casual acquaintance of Roosevelt's, Roosevelt came to Myers in San Francisco and asked for Taggart's help in securing the nomination. Taggart agreed and went to work contacting Governor Cox and many others on Roosevelt's behalf. Consequently, the three men already nominated at the time for the second spot withdrew, and Roosevelt got the convention's nod without opposition. Myers gave one of Roosevelt's seconding speeches and was Indiana's member of the vice presidential notification committee.[98]

Once the convention was over and the delegates were back home again in Indiana, Taggart demonstrated his proverbial hospitality and generosity to his fellow Democrats by hosting four hundred party leaders and candidates as weekend guests at the French Lick Springs Hotel in late July. The thirteen candidates for Congress were there, no Democrat now represented Indiana in the House, and all thirteen pledged to keep mum on the hot topic of prohibition in the coming campaign.[99] Despite Taggart's advertising and entertaining related to the Senate race, his pre- and post-primary race financial reports filed with the secretary of the Senate showed zero expenditures. Senator Watson on the other hand reported $1,958.56 in expenses by early August.[100] All that now remained before the traditional Labor Day campaign kickoff were the notification ceremonies for Cox in Dayton on 7 August and for Roosevelt two days later at his family estate in Hyde Park, New York.

Toward the end of August Hoosier author Meredith Nicholson, summering at Northport Point on Michigan's scenic Leelanau Peninsula, issued a strong statement of support for Taggart. He cited Taggart's qualities of industry, integrity, persistence, and intelligence and his career as a successful, efficient businessman. Nicholson described the party boss as public spirited and stated that "his brief service in the United States senate was in all ways dignified and worthy of the best traditions of the state. On the occasions that he spoke he talked common sense in the plain language of a straight-thinking man." Taggart, Nicholson wrote, was free of bigotry and intolerance and "his capacity for friendship is extraordinary; he is a friend and lover of mankind. Having risen from the lowest round of the ladder he thinks of the other fellow. No other citizen of Indiana at any period has enjoyed the friendship of so many people of all classes and creeds as Thomas Taggart." According to Nicholson, Watson, however, was a member of the Republican "Old Guard" and hostile to the progressive spirit. The author charged that the domination of the Republican party by the Watson crowd posed a menace to American security, prosperity, and peace. Nicholson, known as an independent Democrat, summarized eloquently the feelings and thoughts of Taggart supporters across the state.[101] Equally vocal, however, were those who considered Taggart the epitome of everything that was wrong with the American political process. And so the battle was on.

Prohibition and the League of Nations were the two issues that dominated the senatorial campaign. Much as the Democrats may have wished it, the subject of prohibition would not go away. The Anti-Saloon League had been helping Watson, whose campaign managers circulated rumors throughout the state that Taggart in fact represented the liquor interests and would undermine the enforcement of prohibition should he be elected. In response to this whispering campaign, Taggart announced that he would support enforcement of the Volstead Act as it currently stood.[102] So, when Governor Cox proposed to advocate 2.75 percent beer, Taggart wired his disapproval and urged him to say he would veto any change to the Volstead Act. When 179 ladies from Crawfordsville wrote asking about his stand on prohibition, Taggart responded with an emphatic "yes" that as a senator he would work for the effective enforcement of prohibition. But he added that the paramount issue of the campaign was the League of Nations rather than prohibition. "Not only America, but the leading countries across the seas, are expecting the women of the United States to support with a fine intelligence the league of nations, an issue of world-wide importance, having for its object peaceful homes rather than battlefields for our boys," Taggart wrote the Montgomery County women.[103] Clearly the strategy was to blunt the prohibition issue among women, who were voting for the first time, by pledging strict enforcement and diverting their attention to the League of Nations. On 14 September the *Indianapolis News* quoted him on the League, "Why have our churches been sending out missionaries to foreign countries all these years? That is being done to teach the brotherhood of man. The mothers of this nation were willing to give their sons to a noble cause during the war, and now that the war is over there should be a league of nations so that future wars can be prevented."[104]

For his part Senator Watson had voted twice for the League of Nations with reservations that President Wilson adamantly rejected.

The Senate, Watson contended, saved the independence of the United States in its actions on the League. Watson had chaired the resolutions committee at the 1920 Republican National Convention in Chicago and said the platform did not endorse the League with reservations because the party did not want to bind Harding amidst changing diplomatic conditions.[105] Watson also favored a separate peace with Germany, a stance many viewed as pandering to the substantial German-American vote in Indiana.[106]

With the arrival of autumn, the campaign was off and running. Efforts were made to whip up enthusiasm for Taggart's candidacy, including distribution of this campaign song by Roy L. Burtch, titled "Taggart, We Want a Man Like You for Senator":

Some men have made a history, That has been handed down. The business man we sing about, Sure he's of great renown. He made a splendid mayor three times, In the capitol of our state. On his good judgment you can bank, He's right up to date.

A Senator should know his biz, To push important things. Tom Taggart's prov'd what he can do, In business he's a king. All parties they will vote for him, Because he's on the square. With honor he will fill the place, You hear ev'rywhere.

CHORUS
Tom Taggart is his name, A business man of fame. Senator will be his place, He is sure to win the race, His friends will stick like glue, They know what he can do. Taggart, Taggart we want a man like you. We want "Taggart"—the man we know is true.[107]

Taggart began his speaking tour of the state's thirteen congressional districts in late September, accompanied by state chairman Benjamin Bosse. Given his rather frail health at almost age sixty-four, Taggart maintained a strenuous and demanding schedule. As one example, he campaigned in Lake County in northwestern Indiana on 14 October and spoke in two towns in Lawrence County in southern Indiana the following day. One

Indiana State Library

Thomas Taggart and one of his two namesake grandsons, Thomas Taggart Young, son of Irene Taggart Young and Dr. William J. Young.

joyous event that helped lighten the stress of his heavy schedule was the birth of his seventh grandchild, to daughter Irene, on the day he was campaigning in Lake County. Irene and Dr. Young named their son Thomas Taggart Young. This birth was especially good news because tiny granddaughter Elizabeth Sinclair died in 1920 of pneumonia.[108] At about this time Taggart wrote the chairman of the local Democratic committee in Jeffersonville with this assessment of the political situation in the state, "Conditions throughout the state are looking better every day. Governor Cox is making a wonderful campaign and is having good meetings wherever he goes. If we all keep up our good work, am sure we will come out winners in November."[109] Taggart believed in fighting the good fight right up to the end.

The results on 2 November crushed any Democratic hope of victory. Hoosiers, along with the rest of the American people, repudiated the Wilson administration and the League of Nations in favor of a return to Senator Harding's promised "normalcy." The Republican ticket buried Cox and Roosevelt by a popular vote of 16,152,200 (61 percent) to 9,147,353 (34.6 percent) and by 404 to 127 in the electoral college. This was the worst showing ever of any Democratic presidential candidate in the popular vote. Until 1920 that dubious distinction had belonged to Judge Parker in 1904. In Indiana Cox received 511,364 votes to Harding's 696,370. The razor-thin margin of the 1916 presidential race in the state was but a faint memory now. The state Democratic ticket could not survive the powerful Republican tide flooding the state and nation. Senator Watson retained his seat over Taggart by a vote of 681,854 (57 percent) to 514,191 (43 percent). Warren T. McCray defeated Dr. Carleton B. McCulloch for governor by a margin of 683,253 to 515,253.[110] Taggart took the defeat with his customary grace, wiring Watson that "the best qualified man won." Senator Watson wrote that his elation over winning reelection was dampened only by the fact that he defeated Taggart. As for the president-elect, he and Taggart were fast friends from Senate days, and the Hoosier boss visited Harding in the White House whenever he was in Washington, usually stopping by for lunch and a chat.[111] The Republican ascendancy in national politics began with the election of 1920, but Taggart would spend the rest of his days working hard for the party of Jefferson and Jackson.

CHAPTER EIGHT

The Final Years

The beautiful roses and sweetpeas brought me such a charming greeting from you and are still lovely and fresh," Florence Kling Harding wrote to Taggart from the White House a month after her husband's inauguration. "I shall look forward to welcoming you sometime in our new home, and with warmest thanks for your kind thought, and regards in which Mr. Harding joins me."[1] Taggart, of course, did not let politics interfere with friendship, so, in a bipartisan spirit, he visited the Hardings frequently. Upon receipt of a box of Pluto golf balls, the president wrote Taggart, "It is exceedingly good of you to remember me in this way and I want you to know of my appreciation." The hallmark of the Harding candidacy in 1920 was a withdrawal from the government's policy of progressive activism over the previous twenty years. The weary nation, with its idealism spent in the ravages of World War I, responded enthusiastically to Harding's call for "normalcy." And, all the better, the distinguished Ohioan looked every inch a president. Unfortunately, that was as far as Harding's leadership skills went. During his short tenure as president, corruption plagued his administration, particularly the Teapot Dome scandal that broke in the autumn of 1923.[2] Suddenly, however, before Teapot Dome was public knowledge, the congenial president died in August 1923 after a trip to Alaska. The Taggarts were moved, as was the nation, by Harding's shocking death in office and sent Mrs. Harding their condolences. The Taggarts received Florence Harding's letter thanking them for their expression of sympathy in Gloucester, Massachusetts, where daughter Lucy summered.

Family wedding reception for Tom and Adele Taggart at 1331 N. Delaware Street in
Indianapolis.

Taggart followed up with a $500 gift to the Harding Memorial
Association in the spring of 1924.[3]

Following the Senate campaign of 1920 life for the Taggarts
returned to some of its ritual rhythms. Autumn, winter, and
spring were spent mostly in Indiana, with the couple spending
more and more time in French Lick in their later years. An
annual trip to Florida in the winter was also part of the family routine in this final decade of Taggart's life. Summers were spent in
Hyannis Port with children and grandchildren, with the number
of the latter continuing to grow. The summer of 1922 was significant for the Taggarts personally because of the marriage of their
only son and the birth of their eighth grandchild. Just shy of his
thirty-sixth birthday, young Tom married Adele Wilson Pringle on
8 June 1922 in his parents' apartment in the French Lick Springs
Hotel.[4] Adele and Tom took up residence in an apartment in the
hotel that was just below the elder Taggarts' apartment and connected to it by a bright red, curving iron staircase. This apartment
in the deluxe wing of the hotel is now known as the Governor's
Suite. On 28 July the family celebrated the birth of Dick and Emily
Sinclair's fourth child, Emily Letitia. A year later, on 5 August 1923,

on Eva Taggart's birthday, Adele Taggart gave birth to a daughter, who was named Eva after her paternal grandmother. This ninth and last grandchild was the only grandchild to bear the surname Taggart, and then only until marriage.

The political pace began to quicken in 1923 as the next presidential election year neared. In 1922 Taggart's longtime friend and ally Samuel M. Ralston won a Senate seat over Republican Albert J. Beveridge, who had defeated Sen. Harry S. New in the Republican primary. Taggart had thrown the full weight of the Democratic organization behind Ralston's candidacy and pledged in a letter to Ralston from Boston in mid-September that "when I return I will be ready to enter the war and enlist until the seventh of November."[5] Taggart turned his attention increasingly toward partisan concerns, except for service on the Lincoln Memorial Commission, to which Republican governor Warren T. McCray appointed him in a nonpartisan spirit on 5 May 1923.[6] Prohibition was an issue that dogged the Democratic party across the nation. How could the party, with its wet ethnics and dry Solid South, address this difficult issue and maintain any semblance of unity for victory in 1924? To Claude G. Bowers, at the *Fort Wayne Journal-Gazette*, Taggart wrote on 25 June, "It seems to me that the Democrats would be foolish to insert a wet platform, because it would be the only subject heard of or discussed during the campaign, and would be simply pouring water on the Republican wheels." In any case, Taggart felt the American people were not yet ready for a reversal on prohibition. Always mixing hospitality and politics, he added, "I have often invited you to French Lick. Why dont [*sic*] you pack the Madam up and come over for a little vacation. Will guarantee you a good time if you can regulate the weather."[7] The question of prohibition continued to prey on Democratic minds throughout the remainder of 1923. Late in the year Taggart met with leading Democratic bosses Charles F. Murphy of Tammany Hall, George Brennan, Roger C. Sullivan's successor in Illinois, and Col. James M. Guffey of Pennsylvania at French Lick to discuss the upcoming platform and presidential nomination. In regard to prohibition Taggart campaigned for a

Thomas Taggart and Charles F. Murphy, boss of New York City's Tammany Hall, confer at French Lick.

dry plank at the meeting, no doubt out of political expediency rather than conviction, while Murphy and Guffey wanted to take a wet stand. Murphy also pressed his case to excommunicate William Randolph Hearst from the Democratic party for recently opposing Tammany's slate of candidates, but the others were wary, from experience, of taking on Hearst and his media empire.[8] As for who the next Democratic nominee would be, one can reasonably assume that Taggart made a strong argument for Senator Ralston, whom he wanted to put in the White House in 1924.

The early autumn of 1923 marked a time of worrisome health problems for Taggart. While at his summerhome in Hyannis Port in the latter half of September he suffered a severe bout of postnasal hemorrhaging. Dr. E. E. Hawes of Hyannis finally got the hemorrhages under control, drove Taggart, Eva, and Lucy the eighty miles to Boston the next day, and admitted him to Phillips House, a recent addition to Massachusetts General Hospital, where he was placed in a room on the Charles Street side of the eight-story hospital with a view of the Charles River and the city of Cambridge beyond. Even though he had been in poor health, he had never had this kind of medical problem before. Dr. Harold G. Tobey, a nose and throat specialist, was Taggart's physician and declared Taggart would be out of danger in thirty-six hours if his progress continued. While his condition did improve and he returned to Indiana, he was not a well man.[9]

The first three months of 1924 brought renewed concerns about Taggart's health. Because of his poor condition Dr. Carleton B. McCulloch, Taggart's personal physician, advised him to go to The Presbyterian Hospital of the City of Chicago for observation to find out exactly what was wrong. Doctor Sippy supervised the observation procedures and treatment at the hospital, located on the southeast corner of Congress and Wood Streets. Taggart was a patient at Presbyterian Hospital for about four weeks from mid-January to mid-February.[10] As ever, politics were never far from his mind. From his hospital bed he sent a letter to the annual banquet of the Indiana Democratic Editorial Association that was chock-full of political comment and advice. He recommended state senator Walter S. Chambers for state chairman and advised the party always to "organize from the bottom. A good foundation is most important to the structure." Taggart denied working against William Gibbs McAdoo for the presidential nomination but stated his clear support for Senator Ralston. Finally, he suggested that a movement be launched among Hoosiers to build a monument in Indiana to Woodrow Wilson who had died on 3 February.[11] As for his medical situation, Doctor McCulloch had suggested the previous Christmas that Taggart take a trip through the Caribbean for his health, and Taggart now decided to follow that advice. He left Presbyterian Hospital in mid-February and returned home to Indianapolis. Then on 18 February Taggart left for New York City, the point of departure for the cruise, with his wife, Lucy, Nora, the Sinclairs, and maids who would accompany them on the voyage. He felt the cruise, which left New York on 20 February and returned there on 20 March, "will restore me to perfect health." The ship, the *Orca,* owned by The Royal Mail Steam Packet Company, sailed through the Caribbean, along the northern coast of South America, and on to Bermuda during its month-long sojourn.[12] Upon returning, Taggart pronounced the trip "splendid" and said he was feeling much better. As often happened, when the Taggart party was being processed through the Immigration and Inspection Office at the Port of New York he ran into some old Democratic friends who worked there. They asked for his help in improving their salaries, which had not increased in ten years. He dutifully sent the information along to Senator Ralston.[13]

The overriding political goal in 1924 for Taggart, called by his initials "T. T." in the latter part of his life, was to make his friend Samuel Ralston president of the United States. Ralston and Taggart, sixty-eight and sixty-seven years old respectively, had a close personal and political relationship that stretched back over decades and had shared countless experiences as they labored together for the Hoosier Democracy. For all of his recent political success Ralston also had tasted defeat at the polls. Most notably, voters rejected him in 1888 when he ran to represent Boone, Clinton, and Montgomery Counties in the state senate and again in 1896 and 1898 when he ran for secretary of state. In 1908 the delegates from his own party denied him the gubernatorial nomination in favor of Thomas R. Marshall. However, his was the only name presented for nomination for governor four years later in 1912. He won the nod by acclamation and went on to win election that November. Ralston's tenure as governor was marked by such achievements as the founding of Indiana's state park system, a workmen's compensation law, and the primary election legislation. After completing his gubernatorial term Ralston bought a twenty-six-acre estate, named Hoosier Home, on the northwest side of Indianapolis and joined the law firm of Ralston, Gates, Van Nuys and Barnard. Six years later Ralston defeated Albert J. Beveridge for the Senate and began his service in that body on 4 March 1923.[14]

Just days after his return from the Caribbean cruise, Taggart informed Ralston that he was receiving many letters asking for men to go to various states to present Ralston's case for president. His

reply had been that he had not yet secured Ralston's consent to
be a candidate. Taggart also suggested, at the instigation of others, that Ralston investigate carefully the Harding and Coolidge
administrations' interest in leasing two government-built nitrate
plants and a nearly completed hydroelectric facility on the
Tennessee River at Muscle Shoals, Alabama, to Henry Ford.
Progressives, led by Sen. George W. Norris, were making Muscle
Shoals the focal point of a national debate over the government's
role in the electric power industry. Taggart returned to Chicago
for several more days of observation and a checkup by Doctor
Sippy at Presbyterian Hospital. Although Taggart's health seemed
better, he wanted to reduce the amount of powders and medicines
he took. From the hospital he advised Ralston not to make a public
statement on the Ku Klux Klan plank until Ralston returned
home for the primaries and until Ralston's friends could discuss
it. Taggart also recommended Sen. Thomas J. Walsh for chairman
of the national convention's resolutions committee, rather than
as convention chairman, so he could defend the plank on the religious question. He also asked that Walsh and Ralston put together
a plank on religion that the Indiana Democratic convention
could adopt and, thus, harmonize with the national platform.[16]
Taggart knew that the split between the largely rural Protestant
and urban Catholic wings of the party, often related to issues like
the Klan and prohibition, had to be healed if the party were to have
any chance of success. He ventured the prediction, always risky in
politics, that the Iowa and Missouri delegations "eventually will be
ours."[17] A month later, anticipating problems at the national
convention in New York over the questions of prohibition and the
Klan, Taggart wrote Ralston, "I don't want to see a fuss if we can
avoid it, either in the Committee [on Resolutions] or on the
floor of the Convention." On the Hoosier situation, he added,
"Things are getting pretty warm in Indiana and a little bit mixed.
It is hard telling what the outcome will be but we shall do our best
not to lose our heads or do anything that will lose us votes."[18]
Taggart certainly saw the political pitfalls ahead for the party in
1924.

Ralston gave every indication of being a candidate for president of the United States on the eve of the Democratic National Convention in New York. With the usual obligatory self-effacement of all presidential contenders, Ralston nonetheless indicated his availability for the nomination in a letter to Taggart on 19 June. "As I have heretofore told you," he began, "I should be pleased to have the Indiana delegation make an earnest effort to bring about the nomination of some Democrat other than myself for President. If, failing in this, the convention should turn to me, I shall do all in my power to bring success to our party this fall."[19] There was no doubt about Ralston being interested in the White House. The next day, however, he wired Taggart at the Waldorf-Astoria Hotel this unexplained message, "Before making definite statement talk with Judge [Moses B.] Lairy who leaves tomorrow for New York." The telegram was sent from the offices of Ralston, Gates, Lairy, Van Nuys and Barnard in Indianapolis, former state supreme court justice Lairy being a member of Ralston's law firm.[20]

Taggart, once again chairman of the thirty-member Indiana delegation and a delegate at large, devised a strategy for Ralston by which the Hoosier delegates would remain friendly with all other candidates, most importantly William Gibbs McAdoo and Gov. Alfred E. Smith and their backers and would make no alliances whatsoever. Should those two camps deadlock, which seemed likely, then the Hoosiers would invite them both to support Ralston. Upon arriving in New York, Taggart spoke highly of both Smith and McAdoo, and on 21 June he visited McAdoo at the Vanderbilt Hotel and Smith at the Waldorf-Astoria. Taggart also stopped at the headquarters of the other candidates to pay courtesy calls. He squelched rumors that he was anti-McAdoo and ready to join the Smith forces and stated most succinctly, "I am against nobody. I am simply wholeheartedly for Sam Ralston." Taggart refused to attend any conferences on the presidential nomination, even though he was invited to two or three daily. "Just say that we have a boat waiting on the Wabash with Sam Ralston as pilot and we invite all the footsore wayfarers to get aboard,"

Thomas Taggart and son Tom in New York City during the Democratic National Convention of 1924.

Taggart replied to invitations and inquiries. Privately, if pressed to name their second choice after Ralston, the delegation, which included a young Wendell Willkie, actually favored John W. Davis of West Virginia; this despite a reported Taggart-McAdoo agreement, brokered earlier in French Lick, whereby Taggart would urge McAdoo upon the Hoosier delegation as second choice in return for McAdoo not contesting in Indiana.[21]

Taggart always believed that politics and fun went hand in hand. Accordingly, he hosted a banquet for the Indiana Society of New York at the Waldorf-Astoria a few days after he arrived in the city. The "permanent" members of the society in attendance were Will H. Hays, former chairman of the Republican National Committee and now head of the Motion Picture Producers' Corporation of America; Charles C. Pettijohn, a coworker with Hays; Joseph Fanning, a Taggart ally; Leon Bailey, an attorney; and Claude G. Bowers, former editor of the *Fort Wayne Journal-Gazette* and now editorial writer for the *New York World*. The "transients" were the Hoosier delegates and alternates to the convention. In a moving gesture Hays arose at the banquet and said, "I'd like to pay a tribute to Tom Taggart—Tom Taggart of the big heart. We would go a long way before we would find a truer friend than Taggart." The audience responded to these remarks with a standing ovation. Extending his sense of fun a bit further several days later, Taggart promised that if Ralston were nominated he would give the first national papaw banquet in the history of the world out along the Wabash River. He would serve the defeated candidates of both parties, the entire Democratic National Committee, and the newspapermen covering both conventions. No doubt the mention of "Hoosier bananas," which drop off their trees at the first frost, must have seemed exotic indeed, even to New Yorkers.[22]

By the summer of 1924 Taggart was the lone survivor of the Murphy-Sullivan-Taggart triumvirate, and he was not cooperating with the successors of Murphy and Sullivan at the convention. In fact he declared strongly that the old New York-Illinois-Indiana coalition was not at work in 1924. This time Indiana, or Ralston, would take the presidential nomination or nothing. Helping Taggart for the first time as a key cog in a national political operation was his son Tom. When Franklin D. Roosevelt, Smith's campaign manager, said he had a "very satisfactory talk with Taggart," Taggart denied they had had a conference. "If I did," he said on 25 June, "I didn't know it." No alliances, no deals, just Ralston. The Indiana delegation trumpeted Ralston's record of tax reduction while governor, hoping to gain additional support for him. But Taggart was concerned about things moving too fast for Ralston; there was a certain artistry and pacing required in such an endeavor, much like a horse race. "We don't want to work this colt into a lather too soon," Taggart declared. "We just want to have him well curried and walk him around the track a little bit. Let the other managers breeze their colts all they like. We will play the other game." When stories about Ralston's poor health began to circulate early on, his strong backers wanted him to come to New York to disprove the rumors. Taggart flatly refused to bring Ralston to the convention. "Senator Ralston is not coming to the convention," he stated firmly. "He is out home and he is going to remain there."[23] Clearly Taggart ran the show.

The Ku Klux Klan was an explosive, divisive, and destructive issue at the Democratic National Convention of 1924, and Taggart was faced with the challenge of steering Ralston's candidacy through that fractious debate. On the one hand Taggart was encountering difficulty because Ralston was considered by some to be too old and to be a sure loser in Indiana because he was not supported by the Klan. Those familiar with Hoosier politics knew that the Klan was responsible for Ed Jackson being the Republican gubernatorial nominee in 1924 and that he would have considerable Klan support at the polls. This spurred rumors at the convention that Taggart would first go for McAdoo and, if he were eliminated from the running, then all McAdoo votes would go to Ralston.[24] On the other hand Taggart had issued a statement in late June saying Ralston was not a Klan candidate, hoping to allay the fears of the largely Catholic ethnic elements of the party, who had heard the rumor of Ralston's Klan sympathies. One source of the rumor of Ralston's Klan connection was an incident during his gubernatorial days when he appeared sympathetic to the Klan's position in a Klan-inspired fight over parochial schools. Thereafter the Klan embraced him. Another source for the rumor was a newspaper report that the Klan headquarters in Lebanon was named after Ralston. Taggart stated that Ralston wanted a stronger anti-Klan plank in the Indiana Democratic platform than the plank that was adopted. All people, Taggart said, could unite on Ralston, and the senator welcomed the support of those who were pro-Klan and anti-Klan. "The fact that stories are being circulated to the effect that Ralston is to be a Klan candidate shows the extremes to which the friends of the other candidates are going to defeat him," Taggart concluded. The debate over the Klan played itself out most overtly in the resolutions committee that was hammering out a platform.[25] In the end the Democratic convention voted against condemning the Ku Klux Klan by name on a vote of 546.15 to 541.85. The Indiana delegation split 25 to 5 against singling out the Klan, the majority reasoning that the Klan

Indiana State Library

George Brennan, Democratic boss of Illinois, and Thomas Taggart.

plank closely resembled the one adopted by the state Democratic convention.[26] There was speculation at the time that Ralston would suffer because Taggart had not thrown enough votes to Illinois boss George Brennan's position to single out the Klan for condemnation in the platform. Indeed, Taggart broke sharply with the other northern bosses in his moderate and compromising approach to the Klan. Some considered this might possibly be a fatal blow to Ralston's chances.[27]

With its seemingly endless squabbling and quarreling over prohibition and the Klan, the Democratic National Convention of 1924 became an embarrassment to the party of Jefferson and Jackson. The battles over these issues and others were fought first in the resolutions committee, then on the floor in the debate over the platform, and finally in the selection of a presidential candidate. The whole affair played out over three weeks, and 103 ballots were required to settle, at last, on a nominee. One political wag, commenting that the convention would eventually need a sedative, said, "At this moment Old Doctor Taggart will appear with the anaesthetic Ralston, and he may be able to calm them down. Maybe. It isn't certain yet, but Old Doc is an experienced practitioner, and he has his hopes."[28] So he did.

Ralston's law partner and political associate Frederick Van Nuys nominated Ralston in a brief speech. Van Nuys emphasized Ralston's vote-getting ability, citing the fact that Ralston won the Indiana Senate race over Beveridge in 1922 by 50,000 votes while Harding had carried Indiana two years earlier by 185,000 votes. Ralston's record of fiscal efficiency as governor was recalled plus the fact that he left a surplus $5 million in the state treasury after his tenure and no debt for the first time in eighty-two years. By prior agreement, there was only a brief reference to his "excellent physical condition." Taggart made no attempt at a prolonged and boisterous demonstration following Van Nuys's speech but, instead, had Anna Case, an opera singer, take the podium and lead the convention in singing "On the Banks of the Wabash." This rendition of the Indiana state song substituted for the customary seconding speech.

Taggart wanted his dark horse to come out of the gate slowly and carefully so that when the favorites, McAdoo and Smith, deadlocked Ralston would be able to quicken his pace and take the prize. The key to winning the nomination, especially under the circumstances of 1924, was timing, and Taggart was indeed a master of political strategy. When asked what he thought about Ralston's progress the day after Ralston was nominated, Taggart replied, "The Ralston boom is coming along just as we expected it would. We are in no hurry. All through the day while I was sitting in the Garden delegates from other states came to tell me that they were interested in Senator Ralston and would be glad to support him. The same has been true since I returned to the hotel this afternoon. I am just as pleased as can be with developments up to date and I expect that Senator Ralston will be the nominee of the convention." He did encourage the delegates who came to him to fulfill their obligations to other candidates first. The only negative point at this time for the Hoosiers was the continuing report about Ralston's poor state of health. Taggart's reply, "That report is utterly without foundation. Senator Ralston could go out and plow a field and feel none the worst for it."[29]

Taggart owned a race horse named "Senator" that won many races. Explaining his horse's success, Taggart said, "Senator laid back for seven-eighths of a mile and finished first in the stretch, regardless of his position early in the race."[30] The analogy with the Ralston candidacy was clear, and Taggart's instinct told him that Ralston was moving too quickly when he passed John W. Davis during the presidential balloting in early July. Thus, Taggart produced a telegram from Ralston requesting that his name be withdrawn to help the cause of party harmony. Taggart then split Indiana's delegation between Smith and McAdoo and the Hoosiers did not return to Ralston until the eighty-seventh ballot, when the time seemed right.[31]

For whatever reason, political expediency or genuine sincerity, Ralston had wired Taggart three times, on 1, 3, and 4 July, asking that his name be removed from consideration by the convention. The first request related to the bitter battle over the Klan. On 1 July Ralston telegraphed, "I reaffirm my statement often repeated that I do not now have and never have had any relationship with the Ku Klux Klan but in view of the persistent charges that I have some connection with it and in view of the feeling resulting from the controversy over that organization which feeling threatens injury to our party I wish to make whatever contribution I can toward a peaceful solution of the condition now confronting the convention and I therefore desire my name withdrawn from further consideration by the convention." On 3 July Ralston asked Taggart for a second time to remove his name and he did so again on 4 July with this wire, "For the sake of party harmony I forego any personal ambition I may have and request you to withdraw my name from further consideration by the convention." Taggart indeed used Ralston's withdrawal as a temporary tactical maneuver, but returned to him on the later ballot.[32]

After thirteen days of balloting the Democrats could not decide on a nominee. Taggart knew instinctively that the time was now right to go all out for Ralston and bring the nomination home to Indiana. He had an agreement signed by thirty-five senators who would come out for their colleague Ralston, and he "had the pledges of enough delegates that they would shift to Ralston on a certain ballot to have nominated him." Three years later, in an interview at Hyannis Port, Taggart recalled the 1924 convention. "We would have nominated Senator Ralston if he had not withdrawn his name at the last minute. It was as near a certainty as anything in politics can be." Ralston indeed had removed himself, with sincerity, from consideration at the critical moment. Taggart remembered: "Everything was all set and we were getting ready to spring the surprise when, in the very middle of it, I had a personal telephone message from Mr. Ralston asking me to withdraw his name. I pleaded and argued with him and explained the situation, but it didn't do any good. He said that the state of his health forbade it and there was nothing left but to carry out his directions." In retrospect, with Ralston's death in October 1925, Taggart then knew that "Ralston was a sick man at the time. There is no doubt of that."[33]

Ralston's withdrawal at the last minute came as a crushing blow to Taggart. This was to be his crowning achievement in national politics. But it was not meant to be. Louis Ludlow, reporter and later congressman, wrote of Taggart's disappointment. "Smiling and sunny as Taggart usually was, I remember one occasion when I saw him in tears. That was at the 1924 Democratic National Convention, just after he had received a telegram from Samuel M. Ralston in which Mr. Ralston declined to have his name presented for the Presidential nomination."[34]

Ralston agreed with Taggart's assessment that the nomination would have been his for the asking. In a letter to a Missouri supporter on 14 July 1924 Ralston wrote, "I think that the nomination would, undoubtedly, have come to me had I allowed my name to remain before the Convention and, without going into details, I think it will prove to be best both for my party and myself that I withdrew my name from consideration by the Convention."[35] Sen. Byron Patton (Pat) Harrison (D-Mississippi), working with

Taggart in the latter's room at the Waldorf-Astoria, believed Taggart could have orchestrated Ralston's nomination in the twenty-four hours following his withdrawal. Furthermore, Harrison wrote, "If Ralston had only given his word and permitted Taggart and the Ralston managers to proceed, he would have been nominated and I believe elected President of the United States." As it was, Senator Harrison promptly announced to the politicos in Taggart's room that John W. Davis would be the nominee, and the weary delegates agreed on the 103d ballot at 3:25 P.M. on 9 July. Just after the final ballot Taggart dramatically stood on a chair in the center aisle by the Indiana standard, and Chairman Walsh recognized "the gentleman from Indiana" amid silence in Madison Square Garden. Taggart then moved that the convention nominate Davis by acclamation, and the motion was accepted with a roar.[36]

The party chiefs then met with Davis in the third-floor dining room of the Manhattan Club to decide on a running mate for the wealthy nominee, a Wall Street lawyer who had served as ambassador to Great Britain. Surprisingly Taggart offered the name of Thomas R. Marshall, probably as a last-ditch way to help the Indiana Democracy, but the proposal went nowhere because few felt that Marshall would accept it. In the end the party settled on Gov. Charles W. Bryan of Nebraska, brother of William Jennings Bryan, on 10 July. Most believed Bryan would help in the West and with Progressives and, thus, would provide balance to a ticket with the eastern conservative Davis.[37]

The result in November was a devastating defeat for the Democratic party. Davis polled the smallest percentage of votes ever for a Democratic nominee, losing to incumbent President Calvin Coolidge, who had succeeded to the office in August 1923 upon Harding's death, by a vote of 15,725,016 (54.1 percent) to 8,385,586 (28.8 percent). The electoral vote count was a lopsided 382 to 136. Also, Robert M. La Follette, disenchanted with both major party candidates in 1924, put together a progressive third party effort and captured 4,822,856 votes (16.6 percent) and the thirteen electoral votes of his own Wisconsin.

In Indiana Dr. Carleton B. McCulloch lost the governor's race for the second consecutive time. Taggart especially regretted McCulloch's defeat. McCulloch was his personal physician, and Taggart had broken with some of his friends to support McCulloch in 1924. There were eight candidates for the Democratic gubernatorial nomination in the spring, some of them Taggart's friends and political allies over the years, but Taggart endorsed McCulloch over the others. The reason dated back to the campaign of 1920. In that equally difficult year for Democrats, McCulloch had asked Taggart if he expected to be elected to the Senate. Taggart replied that he did not. "Well, I'll be as good a Democrat as you," McCulloch said, and he entered the governor's race.[38] Taggart admired and appreciated that kind of dedication to the party and its organization. Now in 1924 McCulloch lost to Klan-backed Ed Jackson, and the situation for Democrats all across the country was indeed bleak. Torn by internal struggles over prohibition and the Klan and faced with Republican prosperity, election year 1924 proved to be nothing less than a debacle for the Democratic party.

Nagging questions about Ralston's withdrawal from the Democratic nomination race remain despite the explanation that his poor health prevented his accepting the nomination. Ralston's physician, Dr. Sterling Raffin, sternly urged him not to run for president before the convention and yet Ralston allowed a buildup toward nomination anyway. Was Ralston simply indecisive and let events unfold on their own or did Taggart know about Ralston's health and the senator's opposition to the idea and proceed anyway? In a telegram to Taggart on 29 June Ralston thanked Taggart for his "tireless devotion" and reported that Mrs. Ralston considered him a "superb general." In his only mention of health, Ralston wired, "I beg you not to overtax your physical strength. I think more of preservation of your health than I do of the nomination for myself."[39] There was no indication of Ralston's opposition to being nominated at this point. One aspect of the situation was revealed in a telegram from Ralston on 11 July to Taggart in Hyannis Port where he had gone after the convention. "Happy you are in good condition," Ralston cabled. "Ever lastingly indebted to you and yours. Our son is out of danger."[40] Robert K. Murray confirms in his *The 103rd Ballot: Democrats and the Disaster in Madison Square Garden,* as does David Burner in *The Politics of Provincialism: The Democratic Party in Transition, 1918–1932,* that Ralston's son, and also Ralston's wife, were ill at the time. Over five years later, after Taggart's death, A. C. Sallee, a Taggart political functionary, wrote young Tom Taggart regarding Ralston's withdrawal in 1924, "Those of us who know the inside also must realize that there are many things which could not be printed or given to the public."[41] So the mystery of Ralston's sudden exit from the nominating contest in 1924 remains. "The wiliest boss of them all," as Davis's biographer William H. Harbaugh characterized Taggart, had been denied his moment of glory on the national political stage.[42]

The autumn of 1924 brought Taggart's poor health into focus once again. He returned to Boston, where he had been hospitalized a year earlier, for an operation to correct his condition. It has been suggested that he never fully recovered from this surgery in the almost four and a half years left to him.[43] After his operation Taggart spent much of the following winter in Florida where he had become an annual winter visitor. Usually the Taggarts made their Florida vacation headquarters in Palm Beach, frequently staying at the Breakers Hotel since they owned no residence in Florida. There were side trips of varying length down to Miami each year, especially after the Miami Jockey Club was formed. Given his love for horses and horse racing, it was not surprising that one could always find Taggart in the clubhouse at Hialeah.[44] This postoperative trip found him headquartered for a month or so in an eighth-floor apartment at the Flamingo Hotel on Miami Beach. He thoroughly enjoyed the view from his apartment as well as driving around the beach. "I'm just loafing now and playing with my eight grandchildren," Taggart told the Miami press. Commenting on area development and his friend Carl G. Fisher, he said, "And the growth of Miami Beach is even more marvelous to me because I remember so well that many of his friends

Thomas Taggart at the Flamingo Hotel on Miami Beach.

in Indianapolis thought Carl Fisher was crazy or would go broke when he came down here a few years ago to begin this develop-ment."[45] Even in Florida politics were never far from his mind. On 12 March 1925 the *Miami Herald* carried a picture of Taggart meeting several national political figures at the Hotel Pancoast the previous day. Included in the "casual, happenstance" meeting were Norman E. Mack (New York), Homer S. Cummings (Connecticut), Judge Charles D. Lockwood (Connecticut), Edward N. Hurley (Illinois), Dan Mahoney (Ohio), and Taggart.[46] In an article during the 1924 convention that described Taggart as one of the most popular and high-class bosses, the *Washington Herald* hit the nail on the head when it stated that he loved poli-tics as others do baseball or golf. Florida simply represented a change of venue, not a change of interests.[47] The Florida sun must have helped his health somewhat because he wrote Ralston on 24 May that he was feeling well "and I hope that you are feeling much better than you were when I last saw you." He planned to visit the senator the next week. This was the last known piece of correspondence between Taggart and Ralston.[48]

In spite of declining health, Taggart continued to be involved in business and politics as much as possible. Always the entrepreneur looking for a new profitable venture, he decided to join Victor Wenzel in an oil and gas drilling operation in northern Louisiana. Taggart and Wenzel owned properties at the Pine Island Field in Caddo Parish, about twenty-five miles north of Shreveport, where the latter was in charge of drilling the wells in search of oil and gas. Despite his health Taggart took a hands-on approach to this investment and visited his 120-acre lease often in his final three years.[49] He also found time and energy to serve effectively as chairman of the board of the Fletcher American National Bank in Indianapolis and as a member of the board of directors of the Indianapolis Light and Heat Company.[50] Taggart also remained sensitive and defensive about any mention of gambling at his French Lick Springs establishment. When Pulitzer prizewinner Edna Ferber wrote *Show Boat* and included references to West Baden and gambling at Taggart's place, Taggart consulted with his attorneys who threatened a $100,000 libel suit against the publisher, Doubleday, Page and Company, unless references on page 303 to gambling at Taggart's layout were eliminated. The lawyers also demanded that books in stock be changed and all those at retailers be recalled. Over 135,000 copies of the novel had already been sold. A week later the law firm of Greenbaum, Wolff and Ernst reported that Ferber agreed to strike Taggart's name from page 303, leaving the reference to gambling intact. The revised page read: "Next week we'll run down to West Baden. Do us good. . . . In the evening we can take a whirl at Sam Maddock's layout." The fictitious Sam Maddock replaced the real Tom Taggart. Nelson Doubleday, vice president of the company, concurred with the decision, "This business of using true names in fiction is bad stuff. The use of Mr. Taggart's name was purely incidental, and was not essential to the story. Any other name will do just as well, and since Mr. Taggart objected, we were only too glad to make the change." Taggart was certainly not satisfied that the three paragraphs he wanted eliminated were still in the book so his lawyers threatened to proceed with the libel suit. In addition, Frederick Van Nuys, Taggart's legal adviser, said he might sue *Women's Home Companion* and its publisher, Crowell Publishing Company, if the objectionable portions were printed serially. In a moment of lawyerly pique, Van Nuys declared, "It has been proved time and again that Mr. Taggart and the French Lick company have not a penny's interest in gambling either at West Baden or French Lick." Julius C. Ralston, one of the lawyers representing Taggart, stated that a suit was likely because the publisher had not only used Taggart's name in the book but had also released the details of their correspondence to the press. Indianapolis booksellers were quick to take advantage of the publicity and put copies of the book in their downtown display windows. In the end it seems that Taggart had to be content with just the striking of his name from the offensive passage.[51]

Taggart concentrated his last political energies on promoting Evans Woollen, a graduate of Yale University, a railroad attorney, and president of Fletcher Savings and Trust Company in Indianapolis, for president of the United States in 1928. In short, Woollen would be Taggart's replacement for the late Samuel M. Ralston. The first step to the White House came in 1926 when Taggart sponsored Woollen for the Democratic senatorial nomination and the right to oppose Taggart's political nemesis, Sen. James E. Watson. Woollen won the nomination but was defeated in the general election in November. Not deterred by this setback, Taggart continued to promote Woollen for the presidential nomination in 1928. The Indiana Democratic Editorial Association endorsed Woollen for the presidency at its meeting in June 1927 by a unanimous vote. Interviewed in Hyannis Port in July 1927, Taggart said of the Woollen candidacy, "It will be my last fight, but it's going to be a real fight. I believe I have one more fight in my system, one last stand, and, by Jove, I'm going to make it!" Taggart believed that the 1928 convention would be a replay of 1924 with the Smith and McAdoo forces creating a deadlock that would present the opportunity to bring Woollen forward, just as it had for Ralston four years earlier. Regarding Smith, Taggart commented, "I think if Governor Smith were elected he would make a good President. The fact that he is a Catholic doesn't make any difference. I would have no fear that that would influence his actions as President."[52] The Democratic National Convention in Houston in June 1928 was not a replay of 1924 after all. Most important for Woollen, Taggart's doctors forbade him to attend the convention because of his health. He did indeed, however, line up the Hoosier delegation solidly for Woollen, whose name was presented to the gathering. The Democrats, though, turned this time to Smith, thus becoming the first major party to nominate a Roman Catholic for the American presidency. In the aftermath Woollen was not the least bit bitter. In a letter to Taggart on 29 June he wrote, "I was never under any illusion and accordingly there is no slightest disappointment—only pride that my state under your leadership did me the very great honor of presenting me as worthy of consideration."[53]

Tributes came Taggart's way in these last years, and perhaps none was more fitting than the one changing the name of Riverside Park to Tom Taggart Park. The movement to rename the park that he created as mayor started on 10 December 1925 at a birthday dinner for his friend George J. Marott at which Taggart was honored. The following year brought the successful conclusion of this effort by Taggart's many friends in the Indianapolis community and headed by Marott. The Tom Taggart Park Committee then created a fund to erect sixteen bronze markers at the entrances to the park which read, "Tom Taggart Park/In honor of Thomas Taggart, whose vision made possible this park." For a contribution to the fund of one to twenty dollars, a person received a Certificate of Friendship. Tributes to Taggart from famous Hoosiers, a history of the park, and a listing of contributors to the fund were all included in a Book of Friendship presented to him in December 1927.[54] Perhaps Doctor McCulloch, Taggart's friend, physician, and political associate, summarized best the feelings of Taggart's friends when he wrote him on his

Provided by Letitia Sinclair Mumford

Family members celebrate the fiftieth wedding anniversary of Tom and Eva Taggart.
Pictured left to right, back row: Irene Taggart Young, David L. Chambers, Jr.,
Thomas D. Taggart, Adele Taggart, Evelyn Chambers, Nora Taggart Chambers,
D. Laurance Chambers, Dora Sinclair, Judy Chambers, Dr. William J. Young,
William Richardson (Dick) Sinclair, Emily Taggart Sinclair, Lucy Taggart; front row:
Thomas Taggart Young, Letitia Sinclair, Thomas Taggart, Thomas Taggart Sinclair,
Eva Taggart, and granddaughter Eva Taggart.

seventieth birthday in November 1926, "I know of no man I admire more. This is not on account of your many kindnesses to me, but it is because you have all the qualities. I won't enumerate them, but the outstanding three, in taking the measure of a man, are kindliness, courage, and loyalty."[55]

Sunday, 17 June 1928, was an especially important date in the personal lives of the Taggarts, their fiftieth wedding anniversary. The golden anniversary celebration was grand in spite of Taggart's poor health. Friends paid their respects to the couple all day at their home in Indianapolis, and floral tributes filled the house. Appropriately, the family's anniversary dinner featured a large golden wedding cake with fifty candles. Present at the dinner with the Taggarts were their five children with respective spouses and their eight grandchildren. Surrounded by their entire immediate family on this special day, the elder Taggarts felt the warmth and closeness of family love.[56]

Construction started in 1928 on two family residences that Taggart built for children Tom and Lucy. Earlier he had given a home to Nora and built one for Emily in the family compound in Hyannis Port on the Cape. Now he was building a home in French Lick for his only son. Sometime before Taggart had purchased a commanding hilltop site just over two miles from the hotel, where a wooden one hundred-foot observation tower named Mt. Airie stood. The tower was torn down and its timbers were used to build a thoroughbred horse barn on the property. The house, named Mt. Airie, was a brick copy of the family's main house in Hyannis Port. There were two stories plus a full attic, with fold-down stairs leading to the rooftop lantern and widow's walk, and a full basement with an underground tunnel leading to the garage. The first floor included the living room, dining room, den, breakfast room, and kitchen while the second story had four bedroom suites. Hidden stairs from young Tom's bedroom down to the living room below and a hidden door from his bedroom to the roof of a porch, as well as the tunnel, were interesting features of the house, presumably designed to escape kidnappers and any harmful actions by organized crime. The mansion was magnificent and the site spectacular with its landscaped gardens and lawns and views of the southern Indiana countryside stretching away for miles. Taggart never saw his son's Mt. Airie home since it was not completed until September 1929, six months after his death.[57]

The same was true for Lucy's summerhome in gated Eastern Point near Gloucester, Massachusetts. Construction started in 1928 and was completed in midsummer 1929, several months after Taggart's demise. Architect Ralph Adams Cram of Boston designed her house, named "Tower of the Four Winds," in the French farmhouse style. It sat at water's edge overlooking Gloucester harbor, impressive in size with its granite exterior and slate roof. The construction costs alone totaled an estimated $125,000. Noted decorator Henry (Harry) Davis Sleeper of Boston, whose summerhouse "Beauport" sat four doors away from Lucy's, did the interior in his celebrated refined aesthetic taste.[58]

James Philip Fadely

Overflow Cottage, summerhome of Nora and David Laurance Chambers in the family compound in Hyannis Port, as it appears today.

The first signs of Taggart's final illness came during the summer of 1928 in Hyannis Port. Shortly after he returned to Indianapolis in October he entered Methodist Hospital for an operation to correct an acute stomach ailment. While recovering from surgery at Methodist, Gov. Al Smith, the Democratic presidential nominee, paid him a visit on 20 October during a campaign swing through Indiana.[59] From his hospital bed Taggart solicited and received news about the election campaign from people all around the state.[60] His doctors allowed him to go home the day before the election, but he was forbidden to leave his bed to vote on 6 November.[61] Surely it was the first election in which he had not voted in his long career. Taggart's Democrats went down to defeat once again with Smith losing the presidential race to Herbert Hoover. Several days later, on 17 November, Taggart celebrated his seventy-second birthday with his wife and daughters Lucy, Nora, and Emily, enjoying a large birthday cake and reading

The Mt. Airie tower that was torn down to make room for son Thomas D. Taggart's mansion named Mt. Airie near French Lick.

hundreds of congratulatory telegrams. It was felt that his condition was improving slowly under the care of his physician, but, in fact, the improvement was not sustained.[62]

Indiana State Library

Portrait of Thomas Taggart in March 1928.

The end came on the morning of 6 March 1929. Surrounded by members of his family, Taggart slipped away quietly at his home on North Delaware Street. The funeral on Friday, 8 March, was held at the Taggart home. The dining room was converted into a sanctuary with the bier surrounded on all sides by flowers. Friends sat in the living room and entry hall for the private service. Police rerouted traffic at 13th and 16th Streets to keep the

Indiana State Library

Lucy Taggart's summerhouse in exclusive Eastern Point, near Gloucester, Massachusetts.

area quiet for the funeral. There were ten active pallbearers and twenty-seven honorary ones for the brief services. The Right Reverend Joseph M. Francis, bishop of the Episcopal diocese of Indianapolis, conducted the funeral service. He opened by reading from the Book of Common Prayer and then the fifteenth chapter of First Corinthians. In his eulogy the bishop said, "The life of Thomas Taggart was a remarkable one. It was a life with a purpose and a vision. His integrity in public office; his winsome personality; his kindness and helpfulness and generosity, endeared him to a great multitude. A valiant fighter and yet a more valiant loser, who harbored no grudges and bore no malice, he has left behind him a heritage which will endure." Bishop Francis concluded by reading Alfred, Lord Tennyson's poem "Crossing the Bar." Those gathered then proceeded to Crown Hill Cemetery where the bishop conducted the brief Episcopal committal service at the Taggart family plot. At 2 P.M. that day, when the services started at the Taggart home, the Indiana General Assembly met in solemn session to pay their respects to Taggart. Michael E. Foley, an Indianapolis attorney and friend of Taggart,

Indiana State Library

Mt. Airie, the estate of son Tom, near French Lick. The mansion is a brick copy of the family's main house in Hyannis Port and was completed six months after Thomas Taggart's death in 1929.

Indiana State Library

View of the formal gardens at Mt. Airie and the rolling countryside of Orange County.

gave the eulogy in the General Assembly. Flags on public buildings flew at half staff, and Republican governor Harry G. Leslie
asked Richard Lieber, director of the state conservation department, to lower flags in all state parks to honor Taggart as an
ardent supporter of conservation measures. Meanwhile, in French
Lick there were dual services at 2 P.M. for Taggart, one for blacks
at the African Methodist Episcopal Church on Wells Avenue and
one for whites at the French Lick Methodist Episcopal Church.
Also, at 2 P.M. businesses in French Lick closed for one hour so
employees could attend the services, and the powerhouse whis-
tle blew at the same time so all work would cease for three minutes in Taggart's memory.[63]

In his work *Indiana: One Hundred and Fifty Years of American
Development*, Charles Roll wrote of Taggart, "Not through the
power and responsibility of office, but by his personality, his great
influence as a leader of men, and his remarkable ability as an organizer there came to Tom Taggart a power in our American life and
affairs that has been wielded by comparatively few men in the
history of the nation. Few native Americans have made such a figure in politics and affairs as this son of Ireland."[64]

Indeed, Taggart was a dominant force in Hoosier Democratic
politics from the 1890s until his death in 1929. For the first quarter of the twentieth century he was the boss of the Democratic
organization, or machine, in Indiana. Unlike most other bosses
who controlled a particular urban area, Taggart ruled over a
machine that was statewide in scope. As important as Taggart was
to the political life of the state during these years, politics was always
third in his trinity of priorities: family, French Lick, and politics.
He was a man who cherished his wife and six children and found
sustenance and support in them. Given the fickle nature of politics, Taggart placed his means of livelihood, the hotel business and
other enterprises, ahead of all political involvement. As a result he
became a multimillionaire with a lifestyle that included homes in
Indianapolis, French Lick, and Hyannis Port.

In the end, Taggart's wide reputation was a result of his political career. He is known, first and foremost, as the boss of the

Hoosier Democracy, a fact that is indisputably true. There was a drive in Taggart's personality for both financial success and political power, a drive for legitimacy and respectability rooted perhaps in his impoverished family background. His peers were famous machine politicians such as Charles F. Murphy in New York and Roger C. Sullivan and George Brennan in Illinois.[65] With the advent of the progressive period in American history, during which time Taggart exercised his greatest power, the terms "political boss" or "machine politician" assumed pejorative tones in the national vocabulary. This stemmed from the key progressive objectives of opening up the nation's political process and restoring, as they saw it, public control over major segments of American life. Those who disagreed with the progressive line of thinking were then cast in a negative light. The Progressives viewed contemporary politics as an urban struggle between public impulses for "good government" against the corrupt alliance of "machine politicians" and "special interests." To be sure, the scandalous corruption that characterized some of the urban political machines of the period helped frame this progressive viewpoint. Taggart himself benefited from his political influence and connections in the protection of illegal gambling in the Springs valley, and he was not above using the various tricks and devices of electoral politics employed by all sides to sway an election. Taggart's instinct, however, was to provide good government when his people were in power. It should also be noted that the kind of special personal privilege that Taggart exercised was by no means absent in the subsequent political world created by the Progressives. In any case, the reform-bossism synthesis of the Progressives subsequently became the basis of historical analysis in American history until the 1960s, and Taggart, who steadfastly opposed opening up the political process and who believed firmly in the importance of political organization, was viewed as a reactionary by many Progressives and by later students of history.

Taggart, however, was much too complicated to be so easily categorized. Not only was he fairly unusual among bosses in having a statewide organizational constituency, but Taggart can be judged and analyzed differently than most political bosses because, unlike them, he held elective office as auditor of Marion County, mayor of Indianapolis, and United States senator from Indiana. Thus, in addition to leaving a legacy of naming candidates, Taggart left a public record as an elected official that allows insight into his political convictions and policy decisions. Here was a machine boss who sponsored the careers of John W. Kern and Samuel M. Ralston, two respected Hoosier public servants with progressive reputations; secured the vice presidency for the progressive Thomas R. Marshall; played a major role in making Woodrow Wilson the Democratic presidential nominee in 1912; trumpeted progressive achievements such as the federal reserve law, the income tax, the Clayton Act, the child labor law, the eight-hour day, and workmen's compensation. He also provided good government during the years he held public office. Indeed, he proudly declared during the senatorial campaign of 1916 that "the Wilson administration, backed by a democratic senate and congress, accomplished more progressive legislation and reforms demanded by the people than had been brought about in a generation preceding."[66] In Taggart's case, the political boss or the machine politician did not represent the antithesis of the progressive program. In fact, the Taggart machine represented Hoosiers well. Ironically, the argument can be made that Progressives destroyed much of the power of the lower and middle classes, the very people who made up the machine structures, when Progressives attacked all political machines as corrupt and undemocratic. Taggart, convinced of the wisdom and efficacy of the boss-led political organization, coexisted with the progressive movement, supporting parts of its agenda and opposing others. While this interpretation refutes the conventional assumptions, it squares with an insightful appraisal of Taggart by Thomas R. Marshall: "He has believed in the power, efficiency and necessity of organization. I was never able to divorce myself from the idea that the appeal for principles should be made to the individual." Marshall's statement says much about the progressive movement, for at its heart lay an emphasis on individualism. The submersion of the individual in a political organization, which was paramount for Taggart, was anathema to Progressives. This helps explain the gulf that existed between many Progressives and Taggart. Concerning the perception many had of him, Marshall continued, "Few men have been more misinterpreted than he. Power of reputation, or misrepresentation, has undeservedly stricken him down at many times."[67] In the end, Taggart, the Hoosier machine politician who mixed old political methods with new policy objectives, secured an important place in the history of Indiana and, indeed, the nation.

Epilogue

In a clever and shrewd financial move, Taggart distributed the French Lick Springs Hotel Company, real estate, and most of his holdings to family members about ten years before his death, protecting the bulk of his estate from inheritance taxes and leaving his fortune largely intact for his wife and children. So when his will, dated 27 November 1926, was filed for probate in the court of Judge Mahlon E. Bash, it was revealed that his estate consisted of $300,000 in personal property and $1,000 worth of real estate. After a number of relatively small bequests to siblings and employees, the residue was to be divided by law—one-third to his wife and two-thirds to his five surviving children. The estimates of Taggart's actual fortune at the time of his death in 1929 ranged from $7 to $8 million by the *Pittsburgh Press* to $2 million by the *New York Times*. Whatever the correct figure, he was certainly one of the state's wealthier citizens.[1]

To memorialize husband and father, Eva Taggart and her five children donated $58,000 to the Methodist Episcopal Hospital and Deaconess Home in Indianapolis to create the Thomas Taggart Memorial for Children on the fifth floor of the new Julius A. Hanson Unit.[2] Regarding the gift son Tom said, "It is a pleasure to all members of the family of Thomas Taggart that we have found through the Methodist hospital an opportunity to extend to humanity service of a type that was always in his mind."[3] The Taggart floor was dedicated on 30 May 1930, Memorial Day.[4]

Not long after Taggart's death the family found itself embroiled in controversy with its new neighbor in Hyannis Port, Joseph P. Kennedy. In November 1928 the Kennedys became next-door neighbors to the Taggarts, who by that time had been going to

Hyannis Port for over two decades.[5] Because of the angular configuration of the point on which both houses sat along the shore, Kennedy believed that the Taggart pier crossed his right-of-way and filed suit to that effect. The case was unpublished under Massachusetts law, but it is known that a compromise settlement was worked out.[6]

The Kennedy children and the Taggart grandchildren were contemporaries, and there was some interaction between them during summer vacations at "the Port." Thomas Taggart Sinclair dated Kathleen Kennedy, and he horsed around wrestling with Jack while his cousin David Chambers wrestled with Joe, Jr. Chambers remembered that the two sets of boys did not particularly like each other. Chambers also recalled going next door to watch advance movies on a machine called a Vitaphone that cost $15,000. Kennedy purchased a second machine for his house so he would not have to wait while a new reel was put on. Evelyn Chambers Denny, the eldest Taggart grandchild, remembered watching Joe Kennedy and Gloria Swanson through a telescope set up in the Taggart garden when the famous actress visited the Kennedys.[7] Although both were Democratic families of Irish background, the Episcopalian Taggarts and the Roman Catholic Kennedys developed little more than casual summer relationships in Hyannis Port over the years.

A lasting memorial to Taggart was constructed by his friends and the city of Indianapolis in Tom Taggart Park. This memorial was a grand colonnade designed by Indianapolis architects Burns and James and built at a cost of $35,000 during the Great Depression. Episcopal Bishop Joseph M. Francis gave the invocation and benediction for the three hundred people gathered in June 1931 for the colonnade's dedication. Michael E. Foley, a Taggart friend and former member of the board of park commissioners, presided over the ceremonies. George Marott, who was key in naming the park for Taggart, spoke about his friend as did Mayor Reginald H. Sullivan and Gov. Harry G. Leslie. Sullivan told those assembled that "Thomas Taggart was the most charitable man I ever knew. He gained his fame because he was kind enough to forgive and

Indiana State Library

Thomas Taggart Memorial colonnade erected in Riverside Park in Indianapolis in 1931.

to overlook. He never spoke evil of any man." Governor Leslie called for rejoicing in Taggart's memory, saying, "We can hope that this arch will inspire your children and mine to emulate the beautiful deeds that made Mr. Taggart famous."[8]

Young Tom Taggart carried on his father's legacy in many respects. Most important, he operated the French Lick Springs Hotel until selling it in 1946, after forty-five years of Taggart ownership, for a reported $4 million. He also served as Democratic national committeeman from Indiana during the period from 1931 to 1938. Upon his selection as committeeman, he said he was mindful that the honor came to him as a tribute to his father. Young Tom stated that "I hope that I am able to maintain those traditions which surrounded him. . . . It is my heartfelt desire to win and hold the loyalty and support and the respect of every Democrat in our Hoosier state."[9] When he retired from the committee in 1938, the *Indianapolis Star* noted the occasion with a poignant editorial. "The Democratic Party without a Taggart as Indiana mentor is not going to seem the same," the piece began. "The Taggarts, father and son, have been active in the state and national affairs of their party more than a half a century. They became a much-respected institution and it is bound to be a long time before Hoosier politics will seem natural without Taggart leadership."[10] And so it was.

Eight years after the senior Taggart's death, Eva Bryant Taggart died in Indianapolis on 30 July 1937, and her ashes were interred beside her husband in Crown Hill Cemetery. The Taggart children followed, beginning with Tom on 7 January 1949 and then Lucy (1960), Nora (1967), Emily (1969), and Irene (1970), bringing to a close the first two generations of the Taggart family in Indiana and leaving a legacy securely rooted in the pages of Hoosier history.

Notes

Chapter 1

1. *Indianapolis Star,* 11 Oct. 1903.
2. Notes, Evelyn Chambers Denny Papers, Hyannis Port, Mass.; Thomas Taggart Death Certificate, 7 Mar. 1929, Indiana State Board of Health, Indianapolis; Biography Sheets, Miscellaneous Notes File, Thomas Taggart Papers, Indiana Division, Indiana State Library, Indianapolis (hereafter cited as TTP).
3. Notes, Denny Papers. The elder Thomas Taggart's sisters were Sallie Taggart Johnson, Jane Taggart Arthurs, Ann Taggart Mills, and Mary Taggart Watson.
4. Ibid.
5. Notes of Irene Taggart Young, Denny Papers.
6. Rena Niles, "The Taggart Tradition Is to Start at the Bottom," undated newspaper clipping, TTP.
7. Biography Sheets, TTP; notes for *National Cyclopedia of American Biography,* Denny Papers; George Irving Reed, ed., *Encyclopedia of Biography of Indiana,* 2 vols. (Chicago: Century Publishing and Engraving Co., 1899), 2:268. Reed states that the elder Taggart was station agent for the P.C.C. and St. Louis Railway in Xenia and held the position for twenty years. The source cited him as a man of good business qualifications and said he lived continuously in Xenia until his death.
8. *Columbus (Ohio) Dispatch,* 9 Mar. 1929.
9. Reed, ed., *Encyclopedia of Biography of Indiana,* 2:268.
10. *Pictorial and Biographical Memoirs of Indianapolis and Marion County, Indiana* (Chicago: Goodspeed Brothers, 1893), 128–29.
11. *Indianapolis Star,* 27 Feb. 1966.
12. Ibid.
13. John B. Stoll, *History of the Indiana Democracy, 1816–1916* (Indianapolis: Indiana Democratic Publishing Co., 1917), 1034.
14. *New York Herald,* 18 Sept. 1904.
15. Notes for *National Cyclopedia of American Biography,* Denny Papers.
16. *Indianapolis Star,* 11 Oct. 1903.

17. Harold Zink, "Tom Taggart" (unpublished manuscript), 1–3, in possession of Diana Chambers Leslie; Stoll, *History of the Indiana Democracy*, 1035.

18. Citizenship Papers, 1874–1914 File, TTP.

19. *Indianapolis Star*, 11 Oct. 1903.

20. *Fort Wayne Gazette*, 13 July 1925.

21. Reed, ed., *Encyclopedia of Biography of Indiana*, 2:270; Indiana Biography Series (Indiana Division, Indiana State Library), 16:77; DAR Membership Certificate, Denny Papers.

22. Notes and letter from Mrs. Margaret B. Fraser, Denny Papers.

23. Notes, ibid.

24. Marriage information about Edwin Douglass Bryant and Lucy Viola Inscho, Edwin D. Bryant scrapbook, 1859–1905, TTP.

25. Notes, Denny Papers; Frances Shimer College advertisement, TTP.

26. Notes, Denny Papers.

27. Sons of Temperance Membership Certificate for Edwin D. Bryant, Denny Papers; Bryant scrapbook, TTP.

28. Notes taken by a daughter, Denny Papers.

29. Newspaper clipping of wedding of Eva D. Bryant and Thomas Taggart, 17 June 1878, Bryant scrapbook, TTP; newspaper clipping of the wedding, Denny Papers.

30. Notes, Denny Papers.

31. *Indianapolis City Directory, 1888* (Indianapolis: R. L. Polk and Co., 1888).

Chapter 2

1. *Indianapolis Star*, 27 Feb. 1966.

2. John B. Stoll, *History of the Indiana Democracy, 1816–1916* (Indianapolis: Indiana Democratic Publishing Co., 1917), 1035.

3. Harold Zink, "Tom Taggart" (unpublished manuscript), 7, in possession of Diana Chambers Leslie; *Indianapolis News*, 21 Jan. 1966; *Indianapolis City Directory, 1880* (Indianapolis: R. L. Polk and Co., 1880), 84; *Indianapolis City Directory, 1883* (Indianapolis: R. L. Polk and Co., 1883), 72.

4. George Irving Reed, ed., *Encyclopedia of Biography of Indiana*, 2 vols. (Chicago: Century Publishing and Engraving Co., 1899), 2:268–69; *Indianapolis Star*, 27 Feb. 1966.

5. Stoll, *History of the Indiana Democracy*, 1035.

6. Commission of Taggart as Marion County Auditor by Gov. Isaac P. Gray, 13 Nov. 1886, 2 Nov. 1887 File, Thomas Taggart Papers, Indiana Division, Indiana State Library, Indianapolis (hereafter cited as TTP); commission of Taggart as Marion County Auditor by Gov. [Alvin P.] Slim

Hovey, 10 Nov. 1890, 2 Nov. 1891 File, ibid.; "Politics and the Politicians," *The Illustrated Indiana Weekly* 8, no. 18 (9 Sept. 1899): 8.

7. Stoll, *History of the Indiana Democracy,* 1035.

8. Louis Ludlow, *From Cornfield to Press Gallery: Adventures and Reminiscences of a Veteran Washington Correspondent* (Washington, D.C.: W. F. Roberts Co., Inc., 1924), 127–28.

9. *Indianapolis Star,* 11 Oct. 1903; *Time,* 18 Mar. 1929; Richard Walter Haupt, "History of the French Lick Springs Hotel" (M.A. thesis, Indiana University, 1953), 95.

10. Reed, ed., *Encyclopedia of Biography of Indiana,* 2:268; *Indianapolis Star,* 27 Feb. 1966; Biography Sheets, Miscellaneous Notes File, TTP.

11. *Indianapolis Times,* 14 July 1943; Jeannette Covert Nolan, *Hoosier City: The Story of Indianapolis* (New York: Julian Messner, Inc., 1943), 235.

12. Newspaper clipping, 15 Apr. 1888, Edwin D. Bryant scrapbook, 1859–1905, TTP; Clifton J. Phillips, *Indiana in Transition: The Emergence of an Industrial Commonwealth, 1880–1920* (Indianapolis: Indiana Historical Bureau and Indiana Historical Society, 1968), 28–29, 36; Biography Sheets, TTP; Notes for *National Cyclopedia of American Biography,* Evelyn Chambers Denny Papers, Hyannis Port, Mass.

13. Ludlow, *From Cornfield to Press Gallery,* 126–27.

14. *Indianapolis News,* 21 Jan. 1966, 6 Mar. 1929.

15. Thomas Taggart to Samuel M. Ralston, 29 Apr. and 16 May 1892, Box 1, Ralston Correspondence, 1886–Nov. 1912, Jan.–Aug. 1892, Samuel M. Ralston Papers, Lilly Library, Indiana University, Bloomington. The Indiana Democratic State Central Committee had its offices in downtown Indianapolis in rooms 10, 11, and 23 in the Union Block on Maryland Street between the Grand Hotel and the Board of Trade. In 1892 the state central committee, made up of congressional district chairmen, consisted of First District, August Brentano, Evansville; Second District, William M. Moss, Bloomfield; Third District, Melchert Z. Stannard, Jeffersonville; Fourth District, William H. O'Brien, Lawrenceburg; Fifth District, Willis Hickam, Spencer; Sixth District, Charles Buchanan, Union City; Seventh District, Thomas Taggart, Indianapolis; Eighth District, James M. Hoskins, Brazil; Ninth District, David F. Allen, Frankfort; Tenth District, Henry A. Barnhart, Rochester; Eleventh District, Jerome Herff, Peru; Twelfth District, W. W. Rockhill, Fort Wayne; and Thirteenth District, Emmett F. Marshall, South Bend. The officers were Tom Taggart, chairman, Joseph L. Reiley, secretary, and John R. Wilson, treasurer. The latter two men were not district chairs but served as officers. Additionally, the state party had an executive committee composed of active Democrats who were not members of the state central committee. They were Charles L. Jewett, Samuel E. Morss, Charles B. Stuart, Anthony Stevenson, James H. Rice, James Murdock, Henry C. Berghoff,

George W. Geiger, John E. Lamb, James L. Keach, August Kiefer, and Simon P. Sheerin who served as a national committeeman from Indiana. *Pictorial and Biographical Memoirs of Indianapolis and Marion County, Indiana* (Chicago: Goodspeed Brothers, 1893), 128–29.

16. William F. Harrity to Samuel M. Ralston, Sept. 1892, Box 1, Ralston Correspondence, 1886–Nov. 1912, Sept.–Dec. 1892, Ralston Papers; *Indianapolis News*, 10 Oct. 1895.

17. Taggart to Ralston, 9 Aug. 1892, Box 1, Ralston Correspondence, 1886–Nov. 1912, Jan.–Aug. 1892, Ralston Papers; Taggart to Ralston, 10 Sept. 1892, ibid., 1886–Nov. 1912, Sept.–Dec. 1892.

18. Newspaper clipping, 26 Mar. 1892, TTP.

19. Taggart telegram to Ralston, 9 Nov. 1892, Box 1, Ralston Correspondence, 1886–Nov. 1912, Sept.–Dec. 1892, Ralston Papers.

20. Herbert R. Hill, "Lost River Valley Meccas: West Baden and French Lick, A Classic Springs Rivalry," *Outdoor Indiana* 61 (Nov. 1976): 34.

21. A. C. Sallee, "T.T.," unpublished manuscript, Miscellaneous Notes File, TTP.

22. Will Cumback and J. B. Maynard, eds., *Men of Progress, Indiana* (Indianapolis: The Indianapolis Sentinel Co., 1899), 374.

23. *Indianapolis News*, 10 Oct. 1895.

24. Martha Alice Tyner, "Walter Q. Gresham," *Indiana Magazine of History* 29 (Dec. 1933): 328; Matilda Gresham, *Life of Walter Quintin Gresham, 1832–1895*, 2 vols. (Chicago: Rand McNally and Co., 1919), 2:685, 815. For a more recent treatment of Gresham's life see Charles W. Calhoun, *Gilded Age Cato: The Life of Walter Q. Gresham* (Lexington: University Press of Kentucky, 1988).

25. *Indianapolis Sentinel*, 23 Dec. 1895; *Indianapolis Star*, 17 Nov. 1914; *Indianapolis Star*, 11 Oct. 1903.

26. Biography Sheets, TTP; notes for *National Cyclopedia of American Biography*, Denny Papers; files from the Indianapolis Historic Preservation Commission, Indianapolis; *Indianapolis News*, 5 June 1937, 2 Sept. 1926. Family notes indicate that Taggart was proprietor of the Denison Hotel as early as 1893, but other sources refer only to his management of the Denison and to a partnership interest. The exact chronology and nature of Taggart's involvement with the Denison are unclear.

27. Reed, ed., *Encyclopedia of Biography of Indiana*, 2:268; Kate Milner Rabb and William Herschell, eds., *An Account of Indianapolis and Marion County* (Dayton, Ohio: Dayton Historical Publishing Co., 1924), 784–86; Jacob Piatt Dunn, *Greater Indianapolis: The History, the Industries, the Institutions, and the People of a City of Homes*, 2 vols. (Chicago: The Lewis Publishing Co., 1910), 2:1204; Haupt, "History of the French Lick Springs Hotel," 96; *Indianapolis Star*, 27 Feb. 1966.

28. *Indianapolis Star,* 11 Oct. 1903.

29. *New York Herald,* 18 Sept. 1904.

30. Dunn, *Greater Indianapolis,* 2:1204; "Brethren of the Senate: Senator Taggart," *The Indiana Freemason* 68 (Sept. 1970); *Indianapolis Star,* 27 Feb. 1966; *Indianapolis News,* 6 Mar. 1929.

31. Indianapolis newspaper article, 7 Sept. 1900, Thomas Taggart scrapbook, Oct. 1900–Feb. 1901, p. 1, TTP; Indianapolis newspaper article, 14 May 1901, Thomas Taggart scrapbook, 1 May–28 June 1901, p. 15, ibid.; undated Indianapolis newspaper article, ibid.; obituary for Peter H. Pernot, 7 May 1923, Indiana Biography Series, vol. 1, p. 112, Indiana Division, Indiana State Library.

32. *Indianapolis News,* 6 Mar. 1929.

33. Newspaper clipping during Taggart's mayoral administration, Bryant scrapbook, 1859–1905; "Politics and the Politicians," 8; information on the back of a photograph of Taggart residence at Tennessee and St. Clair Streets, TTP.

34. *The Indianapolis Woman* 1, no. 14 (8 Feb. 1896): 3.

35. St. Paul's Protestant Episcopal Church Family Information Record, Denny Papers; confirmation materials provided by Jane E. Darlington, C.G.R.S.

36. Mystic Tie Lodge 398 F. & A.M. Indianapolis article, Miscellaneous Notes File, TTP; "Brethren of the Senate," 34; Reed, ed., *Encyclopedia of Biography of Indiana,* 2:270; "Politics and the Politicians," 8; University Club membership certificate, 1874–1914 File, TTP.

37. Stationery from Edwin Douglass Bryant's store in Indianapolis and notes, Denny Papers.

38. *Indianapolis News,* 28 Dec. 1895.

Chapter 3

1. Scrapbook, Aug. 1895–12 Sept. 1896, Thomas Taggart Papers, Indiana Division, Indiana State Library, Indianapolis (hereafter cited as TTP).

2. *Indianapolis Sentinel,* 10 Oct. 1895.

3. *Indianapolis News,* 10 Oct. 1895; *Indianapolis Star,* 11 Oct. 1903.

4. *Indianapolis Sentinel,* 8 Oct. 1895.

5. *Indianapolis News,* 9 Oct. 1895.

6. Ibid.

7. Ibid., 9, 10 Oct. 1895; *Indianapolis Sentinel,* 11 Oct. 1895.

8. *Indianapolis Sentinel,* 21 Nov. 1895.

9. *Indianapolis News,* 14 Oct. 1895.

10. *Indianapolis Journal,* 12 Oct. 1895.

11. Ibid., 6 Nov. 1895.

12. George Irving Reed, ed., *Encyclopedia of Biography of Indiana*, 2 vols. (Chicago: Century Publishing and Engraving Co., 1899), 2:270. For discussion of the evangelical-liturgical political theory for this period in Indiana see Paul Kleppner, *The Cross of Culture: A Social Analysis of Midwestern Politics, 1850–1900*, 2d ed. (New York: Free Press, 1970); Richard J. Jensen, *The Winning of the Midwest: Social and Political Conflict, 1888–1896* (Chicago: University of Chicago Press, 1971); Philip R. VanderMeer, *The Hoosier Politician: Officeholding and Political Culture in Indiana, 1896–1920* (Urbana: University of Illinois Press, 1985). Kleppner contends that by the mid-1890s, and after the depression of 1893, the Republicans were becoming the party of prosperity and the Democrats of pietism. Jensen identified two primary factors in determining party affiliation: party loyalty and religion combined with ethnic and racial loyalties. Economic and class factors were of secondary importance. Jensen saw a major political shift in the 1890s as William McKinley fashioned a pluralistic Republican party that attracted many former Democrats. VanderMeer found great continuity in Hoosier politics from the Gilded Age through the Progressive Era.

13. *Indianapolis News*, 17 Feb. 1896.

14. *Indianapolis Journal*, 24 June 1896.

15. Jeannette Covert Nolan, *Hoosier City: The Story of Indianapolis* (New York: Julian Messner, Inc., 1943), 229–38, 239–49, 302 (census information).

16. For works on Frederick Law Olmsted see Elizabeth Stevenson, *Park Maker: A Life of Frederick Law Olmsted* (New York: Macmillan Publishing Co., 1977); Melvin Kalfus, *Frederick Law Olmsted: The Passion of a Public Artist* (New York: New York University Press, 1990); Laura Wood Roper, *FLO: A Biography of Frederick Law Olmsted* (Baltimore: The Johns Hopkins University Press, 1973); John Emerson Todd, *Frederick Law Olmsted* (Boston: Twayne Publishers, 1982); Connie J. Zeigler, "Landscape Design," in *The Encyclopedia of Indianapolis*, eds. David J. Bodenhamer and Robert G. Barrows (Bloomington and Indianapolis: Indiana University Press, 1994), 895.

17. Will Cumback and J. B. Maynard, eds., *Men of Progress, Indiana* (Indianapolis: The Indianapolis Sentinel Co., 1899), 375.

18. Nolan, *Hoosier City*, 230–31.

19. Clifton J. Phillips, *Indiana in Transition: The Emergence of an Industrial Commonwealth, 1880–1920* (Indianapolis: Indiana Historical Bureau and Indiana Historical Society, 1968), 383.

20. *Indianapolis Sentinel*, 28 Dec. 1895; *Indianapolis Journal*, 28 Dec. 1895.

21. *Indianapolis Journal*, 1 Jan. 1896.

22. *Indianapolis Sentinel*, 22 May 1896; Indianapolis newspaper article, 4 Sept. 1900, Thomas Taggart scrapbook, Oct. 1900–Feb. 1901, p. 54, TTP.

23. *Indianapolis Sentinel,* 1 July 1896.

24. *Indianapolis News,* 1 July 1896.

25. Alfred M. Glossbrenner, "Tom Taggart Park," *The Shield* 20, no. 1 (1928): 16.

26. Ibid., 19.

27. Ibid., 16.

28. Ibid., 18; *Book of Friendship* (Dec. 1927). This book was compiled by Taggart's friends as a testimonial to his role in the city's parks movement and included a detailed history of his involvement. A copy of it was loaned to the author by Wanda L. Willis.

29. *Indianapolis Star,* 26 Sept. 1957, 27 Feb. 1966; Jonathan L. Birge, "Past Imperfect" (paper read before the Indianapolis Literary Club on 3 Dec. 1969). Birge is a great-grandson of Taggart, and his paper is on file in the Special Collection of the Indianapolis-Marion County Public Library. *Book of Friendship.*

30. *Indianapolis News,* 9 Jan. 1926.

31. Glossbrenner, "Tom Taggart Park," 19; *Book of Friendship.*

32. For a review of the literature on Progressivism see Daniel T. Rodgers, "In Search of Progressivism," *Reviews in American History* 10 (Dec. 1982): 113–32.

33. *New York Times,* 16 Aug. 1925.

34. *Indianapolis Journal,* 31 Oct. 1895.

35. *Indianapolis Sun,* 10 Nov. 1895.

36. *Indianapolis Journal,* 18 Nov. 1895.

37. *The Civil Service Chronicle* 2, no. 35 (Jan. 1896).

38. See Ari Hoogenboom, *Outlawing the Spoils: A History of the Civil Service Reform Movement, 1865–1883* (Urbana: University of Illinois Press, 1961). Matthew Josephson, writing during the Great Depression and under the influence of Karl Marx and Max Weber, argues that the civil service reform movement was a businessman's movement designed to take the reins of government away from the spoilsmen and to make political parties dependent upon business contributions. See Matthew Josephson, *The Politicos, 1865–1896* (New York: Harcourt, Brace and Co., 1938). For a good survey of the civil service see Paul P. Van Riper, *History of the United States Civil Service* (Evanston, Ill.: Row, Peterson and Co., 1958). For a biography of the Hoosier civil service reformer Lucius B. Swift see William Dudley Foulke, *Lucius B. Swift: A Biography,* vol. 9 of Indiana Historical Society *Publications* (Indianapolis: The Bobbs-Merrill Co., 1930).

39. *Indianapolis Sentinel,* 30 Nov. 1895.

40. Cumback and Maynard, eds., *Men of Progress,* 374–75; Reed, ed., *Encyclopedia of Biography of Indiana,* 2:268–69; *Indianapolis Sentinel,* 12 Oct. 1899; *Book of Friendship; Indianapolis Star,* 11 Oct. 1903.

41. *Indianapolis News,* 21 Jan. 1966; Jacob Piatt Dunn, *Greater Indianapolis: The History, the Industries, the Institutions, and the People of a City of Homes,* 2 vols. (Chicago: The Lewis Publishing Co., 1910), 1:422; Reed, ed., *Encyclopedia of Biography of Indiana,* 2:269; Harold Zink, "Tom Taggart" (unpublished manuscript), 14–15.

42. *Indianapolis News,* 7 Nov. 1895; *Indianapolis Sentinel,* 8 Nov. 1895.

43. *Indianapolis Star,* 27 Feb. 1966.

44. *Indianapolis News,* 9 Oct. 1895.

45. Ibid., 11 Dec. 1895.

46. *Indianapolis Journal,* 26 Mar. 1896.

47. *Indianapolis News,* 30 Jan. 1896; *Indianapolis Sun,* 30 Jan. 1896.

48. *Indianapolis News,* 9 Apr. 1896.

49. *Indianapolis Sun,* 14 May 1896.

50. *Indianapolis Sentinel,* 16 May 1896.

51. *Indianapolis Journal,* 3 June 1896.

52. Ibid., 14 July 1896.

53. *Indianapolis Sun,* 9 Sept. 1896.

54. *Indianapolis News,* 11 Sept. 1896.

55. Ibid., 17 Aug. 1896.

56. Ibid., 12 June 1896.

57. *Indianapolis Star,* 7 Mar. 1929.

58. *Indianapolis Journal,* 4 Dec. 1898.

59. *Dixie,* 19 May 1974, p. 9. This source was provided courtesy of Diana Chambers Leslie.

60. *Indianapolis News,* 18 May 1899; Lawrence Jones to Taggart, 14 Jan. 1899, 1874–1914 File, TTP.

61. Maida Goodwin, archives specialist, Smith College, to the author, 1 July 1993.

62. *Indianapolis News,* 28 Jan. 1899.

63. Taggart telegram to Eva B. Taggart, Mobile, Ala., 17 Jan. 1899, and Charles W. Fairbanks telegram to Taggart, Washington, D.C., 16 Jan. 1899, Dated-to-be-filed File, TTP.

64. Taggart telegram to Eva B. Taggart, Mobile, Ala., 18 Jan. 1899, ibid.

65. *Indianapolis Sentinel,* 15 May 1899.

66. Taggart telegram to Eva B. Taggart, Biloxi, Miss., 21 Jan. 1899, Dated-to-be-filed File, TTP.

67. Lucy Taggart telegram to Taggart, 21 Jan. 1899, ibid.

68. Newspaper article of 23 Jan. 1899, provided courtesy of Diana Chambers Leslie.

69. *Indianapolis News,* 28 Jan. 1899.

70. Letter of condolence from Indiana Hotel Keepers' Association, 26 Jan. 1899, TTP.

71. *Indianapolis Sentinel,* 6 Feb. 1899.

72. Ibid., 12 May 1899.

73. *Indianapolis Sentinel,* 13 May 1899.

74. *Indianapolis News,* 18 May 1899.

75. *Dixie,* 19 May 1974, p. 9.

76. *Indianapolis News,* 18 May 1899.

77. Ibid.

78. George Woodland to Taggart, 10 June 1899, 1874–1914 File, TTP.

79. *Indianapolis Sentinel,* 15 May 1899.

80. *Indianapolis News,* 18 May 1899.

81. *Indianapolis Journal,* 23 Aug. 1899.

82. 1899 newspaper article, Evelyn Chambers Denny Papers, Hyannis Port, Mass.

83. Lucy Taggart telegram to Taggart, 11 Oct. 1899, 1874–1914 File, TTP.

Chapter 4

1. *Indianapolis Times,* 29 July 1951.

2. *Indianapolis Star,* 12 June 1966.

3. Ibid.

4. Ibid.; *The Hoosier Waltonian* (fall 1977): 3; Mary Beth Moster, "Whatever Happened to Pluto Water?," *Indianapolis Star Magazine,* 27 July 1975.

5. *Indianapolis Star,* 12 June 1966.

6. Richard Walter Haupt, "History of the French Lick Springs Hotel" (M.A. thesis, Indiana University, 1953), 40–41.

7. *Springs Valley Herald,* 19 Sept. 1957.

8. *Indianapolis Star,* 11 Dec. 1927.

9. Moster, "Whatever Happened to Pluto Water?," 8.

10. Haupt, "History of the French Lick Springs Hotel," 41.

11. *Indianapolis News,* 27 Oct. 1955.

12. *Hoosier Waltonian,* 3.

13. Haupt, "History of the French Lick Springs Hotel," 83, 88–89, 92; Arthur L. Dillard, *Orange County Heritage* (Paoli, Ind.: Stout's Print Shop, 1971), 122; Richard S. Simons, "When Grandpa and Grandma Took the Waters," *Indianapolis Star Magazine,* 9 Aug. 1959; *Springs Valley Herald,* 19 Sept. 1957.

14. Haupt, "History of the French Lick Springs Hotel," 97.

15. Ibid., 98.

16. Articles of Association of the French Lick Springs Hotel Company, 25 June 1901, French Lick Springs Hotel File, Thomas Taggart Papers, Indiana Division, Indiana State Library, Indianapolis (hereafter cited as TTP);

Minutes of French Lick Springs Company, 1874–1914 File, ibid.; Articles of
Association of the French Lick Springs Hotel Company, 19 June 1901, ibid.;
Haupt, "History of the French Lick Springs Hotel," 99–100. Syndicate mem-
bers in attendance at the 27 May meeting were W. W. Hite (president), F. A.
Henry, J. T. Duffy, D. B. Sperry, and John C. Howard (secretary). The seven
incorporating members of the company were Daniel P. Erwin, Indianapolis;
Floyd A. Woods, Indianapolis; Joseph T. Fanning, Indianapolis; Charles
Murdock, Lafayette; Henry A. Hickman, Chicago; Loyal L. Smith, Chicago;
and George W. Kretzinger, Chicago. At the meeting on 26 June in Louisville,
Taggart, Crawford Fairbanks, Charles Murdock, Daniel Erwin, Henry
Hickman, Livingston Dickason, and George Kretzinger were elected direc-
tors of the company. Taggart, Fairbanks, and Dickason replaced Woods,
Fanning, and Smith in the intervening week.

17. "The French Lick Springs of Indiana," *The Hotel Monthly* (ca. 1923),
Miscellaneous Notes File, TTP.

18. Haupt, "History of the French Lick Springs Hotel," 97.

19. John W. O'Malley, S.J., "The Story of the West Baden Springs
Hotel," *Indiana Magazine of History* 54 (Dec. 1958): 371; Herbert R. Hill, "Lost
River Valley Meccas: West Baden and French Lick, A Classic Springs Rivalry,"
Outdoor Indiana 41 (Nov. 1976): 32; *Springs Valley Herald*, 19 Sept. 1957.

20. *The West Baden Journal*, 16 Dec. 1902.

21. Haupt, "History of the French Lick Springs Hotel," 101–2.

22. Ibid., 113–14; 1920 press release, 1920–28 File, TTP.

23. Haupt, "History of the French Lick Springs Hotel," 114–15.

24. Ibid., 115.

25. Ibid., 124–25; Eva Taggart Parsons, notes to author, 15 Oct. 1992.

26. Haupt, "History of the French Lick Springs Hotel," 149.

27. *Who's Who and What's What in Indiana Politics: This Book Is the Story
of Indiana Politics and Indiana Politicians* (Indianapolis: James E. Perry, 1944),
930; *Indiana Biography Series* (Indiana Division, Indiana State Library), 34:35;
C. Walter McCarty, ed., *Indiana Today* (New Orleans: The James O. Jones Co.,
1942), 138, 387. There is evidence that Thomas D. Taggart attended but did
not graduate from Howe Military School, Howe, Indiana. Jean Miller, development officer at Howe, to author, 25 Aug. 1993.

28. *Springs Valley Herald*, 19 Sept. 1957; West Baden ordinance, 1902, and
French Lick ordinances, 9 June 1902, French Lick Springs Hotel Company
File, TTP.

29. French Lick ordinance, 18 July 1905, ibid.

30. *Springs Valley Herald*, 14 Mar. 1929.

31. Commanding officer of U.S. Army General Hospital 35 (West
Baden) to Board of State Charities, 7 Apr. 1919, Commission on Public
Records, Indiana State Archives, Indiana State Library.

32. *Chicago Daily News,* 16 May 1903.

33. *French Lick Springs Hotel* (French Lick: French Lick Springs Hotel Co., 1915), 5; Auttie Shipman, interview by the author, 24 Aug. 1991.

34. *French Lick Springs Hotel,* 23–27.

35. Haupt, "History of the French Lick Springs Hotel," 126.

36. *To Help You Enjoy Your Stay: French Lick Springs Hotel* (French Lick: French Lick Springs Hotel, n.d.), 7, Indiana Clipping File, Indiana Division, Indiana State Library; *Indianapolis Times,* 31 Mar. 1957; *The Legend* (French Lick: French Lick Springs Resort, 1993).

37. "The French Lick Springs of Indiana," 30; *To Help You Enjoy Your Stay,* 8, 9, 11, 15; *French Lick Springs Hotel,* 33.

38. *Indianapolis News,* 19 May 1941.

39. "The French Lick Springs of Indiana," 32.

40. *Indianapolis Star,* 27 Sept. 1943.

41. *To Help You Enjoy Your Stay,* 9.

42. *French Lick Springs Hotel,* 5, 7–9; French Lick Scenic Railway brochure, Indiana Clipping File.

43. *Indianapolis News,* 24 Jan. 1903; Charles Edward "Ed" Ballard, Janet Kirk Johnson, and Anna Marie Borcia, *The Ballards in Indiana: A Story of Determination, Self-Education and Ultimate Success* ([Indianapolis]: C. E. Ballard-Literary Trust, 1984), 33. A copy of this book was given to the author by Wanda L. Willis.

44. Simons, "When Grandpa and Grandma Took the Waters"; Ballard, Johnson, and Borcia, *Ballards in Indiana,* 32.

45. Author's visit to French Lick, 26 Aug. 1992; "Welcome to French Lick and West Baden Springs," brochure (1989–90), Indiana Clipping File; *Springs Valley Herald,* 19 Sept. 1957.

46. *Indianapolis Star,* 8 Nov. 1936; "Welcome to French Lick and West Baden Springs"; Ballard, Johnson, and Borcia, *Ballards in Indiana,* 35–36.

47. Ballard, Johnson, and Borcia, *Ballards in Indiana,* 32.

48. Jim Ballard, interview by the author, 23 Aug. 1991.

49. "History of French Lick Springs," pamphlet, n.d., Indiana Health Resorts File, Indiana Clipping File.

50. *Chicago Tribune,* 14 Sept. 1905; *Indianapolis News,* 24 Jan. 1903.

51. Ballard, Johnson, and Borcia, *Ballards in Indiana,* 32.

52. *Indianapolis News,* 1 Mar. 1989.

53. *Indianapolis Times,* 29 July 1951.

54. *Anderson Herald-Bulletin,* 26 Jan. 1992.

55. Shipman interview.

56. Haupt, "History of the French Lick Springs Hotel," 78.

57. *To Help You Enjoy Your Stay,* 2–4; Haupt, "History of the French Lick Springs Hotel," 61.

58. Notes, Evelyn Chambers Denny Papers, Hyannis Port, Mass.

59. Simons,"When Grandpa and Grandma Took the Waters."

60. Trademark registration papers, 5 Oct. 1901, French Lick Springs Hotel Company File, TTP.

61. *French Lick Springs Hotel*, 15–23; Notes, Denny Papers.

62. *French Lick Springs Hotel*, no page number.

63. Haupt, "History of the French Lick Springs Hotel," 104–5, 116, 124, 128.

64. *Springs Valley Herald*, 19 Sept. 1957.

65. Address book listing Pluto water salesmen, TTP.

66. Simons, "When Grandpa and Grandma Took the Waters."

67. *Springs Valley Herald*, 19 Sept. 1957.

68. *Indianapolis Star*, 30 Aug. 1981.

69. Ibid., 12 June 1966.

70. Moster, "Whatever Happened to Pluto Water?," 8.

71. Haupt, "History of the French Lick Springs Hotel," 124; Minutes of Special Meeting of Board of Directors of the French Lick Springs Hotel Company, Dec. 1922, 1920–28 File, TTP; List of Stockholders of the French Lick Springs Hotel Company, 30 Nov. 1922, ibid.

Chapter 5

1. *Indianapolis Sentinel*, 5 June 1904.

2. Clifton J. Phillips, *Indiana in Transition: The Emergence of an Industrial Commonwealth, 1880–1920* (Indianapolis: Indiana Historical Bureau and Indiana Historical Society, 1968), 90.

3. *The American Monthly Review of Reviews* (June 1904): 653.

4. Mrs. Fremont Older, *William Randolph Hearst: American* (New York: D. Appleton-Century Co., 1936), 270; Oliver Carlson and Ernest Sutherland Bates, *Hearst: Lord of San Simeon* (New York: The Viking Press, 1936), 142–44.

5. *Boston Globe*, 11 July 1904.

6. Alton B. Parker to Wm. F. Sheehan, Alton B. Parker Papers, Library of Congress, Washington, D.C.

7. *The Campaign Text Book of the Democratic Party of the United States, 1904* (New York: Democratic National Committee, 1904), 53–61.

8. *New York Herald*, 11 July 1904.

9. James P. Hornaday, "Chairman Taggart and the Democratic Campaign," *The American Monthly Review of Reviews* (Sept. 1904): 292.

10. *New York Herald*, 11 July 1904.

11. Phillips, *Indiana in Transition*, 90–91.

12. *New York American,* 19 July 1904; *New York Daily Tribune,* 17 July 1904; *New York World,* 18 July 1904.

13. Grover Cleveland to Alton B. Parker, 14 July 1904, Parker Papers.

14. *New York Herald,* 18 July 1904.

15. *New York World,* 27 July 1904.

16. Ibid.

17. *New York Press,* 30 July 1904.

18. *Indianapolis News,* 3 Jan. 1905; *Louisville Courier-Journal,* 3 Aug. 1904; "Memories of the Campaign of 1904," Thomas Taggart Scrapbook, 1904, Indiana Historical Society Library, Indianapolis.

19. *New York Daily Tribune,* 4 Aug. 1904; J. Rogers Hollingsworth, *The Whirligig of Politics: The Democracy of Cleveland and Bryan* (Chicago: University of Chicago Press, 1963), 226.

20. *Harper's Weekly,* 24 Sept. 1904, p. 1457.

21. Hornaday, "Chairman Taggart and the Democratic Campaign," 290–92, 293.

22. Ibid., 292.

23. *Harper's Weekly,* 13 Aug. 1904, p. 1233.

24. Louis Ludlow, *From Cornfield to Press Gallery: Adventures and Reminiscences of a Veteran Washington Correspondent* (Washington, D.C.: W. F. Roberts Co., Inc., 1924), 143–44.

25. Address of acceptance, 10 Aug. 1904, Speeches 1904, Container 12, Parker Papers.

26. Letter to New York County Chairmen, 18 Aug. 1904, and W. S. Rodie to Alton B. Parker, 18 Aug. 1904, Correspondence State Committee, Container 11, ibid.

27. Hornaday, "Chairman Taggart and the Democratic Campaign," 293.

28. Biographical excerpts, Container 16, Parker Papers.

29. Hornaday, "Chairman Taggart and the Democratic Campaign," 289–90.

30. *New York World,* 14 July 1904.

31. Paolo E. Coletta, *William Jennings Bryan: Political Evangelist, 1860–1908,* 3 vols. (Lincoln: University of Nebraska Press, 1964), 1:349–50.

32. *New York Herald,* 18 Sept. 1904.

33. Parker speech, Speeches 1904, Container 12, Parker Papers.

34. Ibid.

35. Parker to W. S. Rodie, C. M. Preston, and Lawrence Van Etten, 18 Oct. 1904, Corrensponcence I–Z 1904, ibid.

36. Parker speech, Speeches 1904, ibid.

37. Ibid.

38. *Indianapolis Sentinel,* 13 May 1899.

39. *Harper's Weekly,* 24 Sept. 1904, p. 1456.

40. Elting E. Morison, ed., *The Letters of Theodore Roosevelt,* 8 vols. (Cambridge, Mass.: Harvard University Press, 1951), 4:963; William H. Harbaugh, "Election of 1904," in Arthur M. Schlesinger, Jr., ed., *History of American Presidential Elections, 1789–1968,* 9 vols. (New York: Chelsea House Publishers, 1985), 5:1988, 1992, 1993, 2046.

41. Morison, ed., *Letters of Theodore Roosevelt,* 4:1009.

42. *Indianapolis News,* 3 Jan. 1905.

43. *Harper's Weekly,* 5 Nov. 1904, p. 1684.

44. "To the Democracy of the Nation" statement, Speeches 1904, Container 12, Parker Papers.

45. *Indianapolis Star,* 27 Feb. 1966.

46. *Indianapolis News,* 19 Dec. 1904.

47. *Indianapolis Star,* 23 Apr. 1905.

Chapter 6

1. Evelyn Chambers Denny, notes to author, 28 Sept. 1992.

2. *Indianapolis News,* 27 Apr. 1910; *Indianapolis Star,* 27 Apr. 1910.

3. Dora Sinclair Loutrel, notes to author, Aug. 1992; William Richardson Sinclair obituary, *Indianapolis Star,* 23 Apr. 1965.

4. *Indianapolis Star,* 9 July 1914.

5. Louis Ludlow, *From Cornfield to Press Gallery: Adventures and Reminiscences of a Veteran Washington Correspondent* (Washington, D.C.: W. F. Roberts Co., Inc., 1924), 125–26.

6. *Indianapolis Star,* 1 June 1906.

7. Ibid., 11 June 1906.

8. *Indianapolis News,* 4 July 1906.

9. Ibid., 5 July 1906.

10. Ibid., 3 July 1906.

11. *Chicago Tribune,* 2 Aug. 1904; "Memories of the Campaign of 1904," Thomas Taggart Scrapbook, 1904, Indiana Historical Society Library, Indianapolis; *Indianapolis News,* 13, 16 July 1906.

12. *Indianapolis Star,* 18 July 1906.

13. *Indianapolis News,* 16 July 1906.

14. Clifton J. Phillips, *Indiana in Transition: The Emergence of an Industrial Commonwealth, 1880–1920* (Indianapolis: Indiana Historical Bureau and Indiana Historical Society, 1968), 97–98.

15. *Boston Herald,* 24 July 1927; *Indianapolis News,* 29, 30 Aug. 1906.

16. Phillips, *Indiana in Transition,* 101; *Indianapolis Star,* 27 Mar. 1908; *Fort Wayne Journal-Gazette,* 16 June 1913; Keith S. Montgomery, "Thomas R.

Marshall's Victory in the Election of 1908," *Indiana Magazine of History* 53 (June 1957): 150; H. S. K. Bartholomew, "Thomas R. Marshall," ibid. 37 (Mar. 1941): 39.

17. *Indianapolis Star,* 27 Mar. 1908.

18. Paolo E. Coletta, "Election of 1908," in Arthur M. Schlesinger, Jr., ed., *History of American Presidential Elections, 1789–1968,* 9 vols. (New York: Chelsea House Publishers, 1985), 5:2078.

19. John B. Stoll, *History of the Indiana Democracy, 1816–1916* (Indianapolis: Indiana Democratic Publishing Co., 1917), 1036.

20. *Indianapolis Star,* 15 June 1913.

21. Mrs. Fremont Older, *William Randolph Hearst: American* (New York: D. Appleton-Century Co., 1936), 320.

22. Ibid., 323.

23. Oliver Carlson and Ernest Sutherland Bates, *Hearst: Lord of San Simeon* (New York: The Viking Press, 1936), 159–61.

24. Phillips, *Indiana in Transition,* 105–6; Herbert R. Hill, "Lost River Valley Meccas: West Baden and French Lick, A Classic Springs Rivalry," *Outdoor Indiana* 61 (Nov. 1976): 35.

25. *Indianapolis Star,* 22, 23, 24 Jan. 1910.

26. Ibid., 15 June 1913; *Indianapolis News,* 26, 27, 28 Apr. 1910; Claude Bowers, *My Life: The Memoirs of Claude Bowers* (New York: Simon and Schuster, 1962), 63–64.

27. *Indianapolis News,* 28 Apr. 1910; *Indianapolis Star,* 15 June 1913. The suggestion that Taggart was a serious senatorial candidate in 1910 can also be found in Phillips, *Indiana in Transition,* 110 and David Sarasohn, *The Party of Reform: Democrats in the Progressive Era* (Jackson: University Press of Mississippi, 1989), 113–14.

28. *Fort Wayne Journal-Gazette,* 16 June 1913; Hill, "Lost River Valley Meccas," 36.

29. Jacob Piatt Dunn, *Greater Indianapolis: The History, the Industries, the Institutions, and the People of a City of Homes,* 2 vols. (Chicago: The Lewis Publishing Co., 1910), 2:1204.

30. E. A. Stoll, "'T. T.': An Appreciation," Miscellaneous Notes File, Thomas Taggart Papers, Indiana Division, Indiana State Library, Indianapolis (hereafter cited as TTP).

31. Phillips, *Indiana in Transition,* 113–14; *Washington Post,* 7 Mar. 1929; Rena Niles, "The Taggart Tradition Is to Start at the Bottom," newspaper clipping, TTP; Arthur S. Link, *The Higher Realism of Woodrow Wilson and Other Essays* (Nashville, Tenn.: Vanderbilt University Press, 1971), 236; Arthur S. Link, ed., *The Papers of Woodrow Wilson,* 69 vols. (Princeton, N.J.: Princeton University Press, 1966–94), 27:22 n. 2. This account includes John J. Fitzgerald with Taggart, Murphy, and Sullivan.

32. A. C. Sallee, "T. T.," unpublished manuscript, p. 174, Miscellaneous Notes File, TTP; Stoll, *History of the Indiana Democracy*, 1036. Not all sources credit Taggart with a critical role in Wilson's nomination. Russel Nye, for example, gives credit to William Jennings Bryan's opposition to Champ Clark. See Russel B. Nye, *Midwestern Progressive Politics: A Historical Study of Its Origins and Development, 1870–1950* (East Lansing: Michigan State College Press, 1951), 289.

33. W. G. McAdoo to Eva B. Taggart, 6 Apr. 1929, Dated-to-be-filed File, TTP.

34. *Indianapolis News*, 21 Jan. 1966; *Fort Wayne Journal-Gazette*, 16 June 1913; William F. McCombs, *Making Woodrow Wilson President* (New York: Fairview Publishing Co., 1921), 177; Stoll, *History of the Indiana Democracy*, 1037; Link, *Higher Realism of Woodrow Wilson and Other Essays*, 239–40; Sarasohn, *Party of Reform*, 141.

35. *Indianapolis Star*, 15 June 1913.

36. William O. Lynch, "Editor's Pages: Three Busy Years, 1911–1914," *Indiana Magazine of History* 34 (Sept. 1938): 360.

37. *Indianapolis News*, 13 July 1912.

38. *Indianapolis Star*, 9 July 1912.

39. Ibid., 13, 12, 10 July 1912.

40. Ibid., 10 July 1912.

41. Ibid., 29 Oct. 1912.

42. Joseph M. Dixon to Taggart, 16 Mar. 1914, 1874–1914 File, TTP; Will Irwin to Taggart, 3 June 1914, ibid.; Cornelius J. Sullivan to Taggart, 25 Aug. 1914, ibid.

43. Betty Blythe, undated newspaper article (ca. 1913), TTP.

44. *Indianapolis City Directory, 1913* (Indianapolis: R. L. Polk and Co., 1913).

45. *Indianapolis Times*, 20 June 1954; *House Beautiful* (June 1920): 510.

46. *Indianapolis Star*, 19 Apr. 1914.

47. Ibid., 30 Jan. 1914; *Indianapolis News*, 26 Jan. 1914.

48. *Miami Herald* (ca. 1925), TTP; Albert Nelson Marquis, ed., *Who's Who in America, 1914–15* (Chicago: A. N. Marquis and Co., 1914), 2297.

49. *Indianapolis News*, 19 Feb. 1915.

50. Ibid., 27 Feb. 1915.

51. "The Bribery Indictments in Indiana," *The Outlook* (7 July 1915): 537; newspaper article, scrapbook, State Press on Taggart and Bell Cases, June–Oct. 1915, p. 2, TTP.

52. *Minneapolis Journal*, 6 Mar. 1929; *Indianapolis Star*, 7 Mar. 1929.

53. *Indianapolis Star*, 20 Oct. 1915; *Indianapolis News*, 19 Oct. 1915. Taggart associate Walter D. Myers described Rucker many years later as "a man of rather strong partisan views." See Walter D. Myers interview by

Randall W. Jehs, 1970–71, Indiana Division, Indiana State Library, p. 48. Thomas Taggart had a personalized, bound copy of testimony and newspaper articles relating to the case of *State of Indiana v. Joseph E. Bell and Others.* The twelve jurors in the case included six Republicans, three Democrats, a Socialist, a Prohibitionist, and a Progressive. This bound copy was provided courtesy of Diana Chambers Leslie.

54. Taggart to Samuel M. Ralston, 21 Feb. 1914, Box 3, Ralston Correspondence, Jan.–Aug. 1914, 21–28 Feb. 1914, Samuel M. Ralston Papers, Lilly Library, Indiana University, Bloomington; Taggart to Ralston, 16 June 1913, Box 2, Ralston Correspondence, Dec. 1912–1913, 11–20 June 1913, ibid.; Taggart to Ralston, 19 May 1913, Box 2, Ralston Correspondence, Dec. 1912–1913, 16–31 May 1913, ibid.; Taggart to Ralston, 29 Apr. 1913, Box 2, Ralston Correspondence, Dec. 1912–1913, 20–30 Apr. 1913, ibid.; Taggart to Ralston, 24 Apr. 1913, Box 2, Ralston Correspondence, Dec. 1912–1913, 20–30 Apr. 1913, ibid.; Taggart to Ralston, 21 Mar. 1913, Box 2, Ralston Correspondence, Dec. 1912–1913, 21–31 Mar. 1913, ibid.

Chapter 7

1. Letitia Sinclair Mumford, notes to author, autumn 1992.
2. *Boston Globe* interview, Aug. 1923, 1924 Democratic National Convention File, Thomas Taggart Papers, Indiana Division, Indiana State Library, Indianapolis (hereafter cited as TTP); *New Bedford (Mass.) Standard,* 6 Mar. 1929; *Indianapolis Sun,* 23 Aug. 1899.
3. Paul Fairbanks Herrick and Larry G. Newman, *Old Hyannis Port, Massachusetts: An Anecdotal, Photographic Panorama* (New Bedford, Mass.: Reynolds-DeWalt, 1968), 17.
4. Ibid., 52–53.
5. Ibid., 38.
6. *Boston Globe* interview, Aug. 1923; Real estate deeds to Thomas Taggart from Emily E. Whelden (23 Sept. 1912), Martha Keough (10 Oct. 1912), and Wendell L. Hinckley (25 Oct. 1912), Barnstable County (Mass.) Registry of Deeds; Land Court title records dated 26 Oct. 1912 and 23 Apr. 1913, ibid.
7. *Boston Sunday Advertiser,* 10 Oct. 1920; *New York World,* 27 July 1924; Commitment sheets for 1914–17, Assessor's Office, Barnstable, Mass.; Letitia Sinclair Mumford and Dora Sinclair Loutrel, interview by the author, Aug. 1992; Letitia Sinclair Mumford, phone conversation with the author, Jan. 1994; Eva Taggart Parsons, notes to author, 10 Mar. 1994; Joseph E. Garland, *Eastern Point: A Nautical, Rustical, and Social Chronicle of Gloucester's Outer Shield and Inner Sanctum, 1606–1950* (Peterborough, N.H.: William L. Bauhan, Publisher, 1971), 341; Caroline Latham and Jeannie Sakol, *The*

Kennedy Encyclopedia: An A-to-Z Illustrated Guide to America's Royal Family (New York: NAL Books, 1989), 99.

8. Mrs. Fisk Landers, interview by the author, 5 Aug. 1992; Mumford and Loutrel interviews.

9. Mumford and Loutrel interviews.

10. Yacht guest book, TTP.

11. *Indianapolis News,* 20 Mar. 1916.

12. *Bluffton Evening Banner,* 21 Mar. 1916.

13. Taggart to Samuel M. Ralston, 20 Mar. 1916, Box 5, Ralston Correspondence, July 1915–20 Mar. 1916, 18–20 Mar. 1916, Samuel M. Ralston Papers, Lilly Library, Indiana University, Bloomington.

14. E. P. Honan to Ralston, 20 Mar. 1916, ibid.

15. *Indianapolis Times,* 21 Mar. 1916.

16. *Washington Democrat,* 22 Mar. 1916.

17. *Indianapolis News,* 20 Mar. 1916.

18. Ibid.

19. Press release by Associated Prohibition Press Bureau of the Prohibition National Committee, Mar. 1916, 1915–July 1916 File, TTP.

20. Oscar Reed McKay to Ralston, 20 Mar. 1916, Box 5, Ralston Correspondence, July 1915–20 Mar. 1916, 18–20 Mar. 1916, Ralston Papers.

21. "Senator Taggart, of Indiana," *The Outlook* (29 Mar. 1916): 724.

22. Taggart to Ralston, 29 Mar. 1916, Box 6, Ralston Correspondence, 21 Mar.–31 Aug. 1916, 26–31 Mar. 1916, Ralston Papers.

23. *Indianapolis Star,* 28 Mar. 1916.

24. A. C. Sallee to Taggart, 31 Mar. 1916, 1915–July 1916 File, TTP.

25. Lew M. O'Bannon, telegram to Ralston, 1 Apr. 1916, Box 6, Ralston Correspondence, 21 Mar.–31 Aug. 1916, 1–5 Apr. 1916, Ralston Papers.

26. *Indianapolis Times,* 1 Apr. 1916.

27. Bernard Korbly to Taggart, 5 Apr. 1916, 1915–July 1916 File, TTP.

28. Carl Painter, "The Progressive Party in Indiana," *Indiana Magazine of History* 16 (Sept. 1920): 270.

29. *Indianapolis Star,* 21 Oct. 1916.

30. Sallee telegram to Taggart, 5 May 1916, 1915–July 1916 File, TTP.

31. Taggart telegram to Sallee, 20 Apr. 1916, ibid.

32. Taggart telegram to Sallee, 20 May 1916, ibid.

33. Taggart to Sallee, undated, and Taggart telegram to Sallee, 10 July 1916, ibid.

34. Taggart to Sallee, 6 Aug. 1916, Aug.–Dec. 1916 File, ibid.

35. Korbly to Taggart, 25 July 1916, 1915–July 1916 File, ibid.

36. Lists of federal government employees from Indiana secured by Taggart; Korbly to Taggart, 29 May 1916, 1915–July 1916 File, TTP. These lists included Hoosier employees in the Government Printing Office, Department

of Agriculture, Civil Service Commission, Department of Labor, Post Office Department, Department of Justice, Department of State, U.S. Capitol, Interstate Commerce Commission, Navy Department, War Department, Commerce Department, and Department of the Treasury.

37. Sallee to Taggart, 4 Aug. 1916, Aug.–Dec. 1916 File, TTP.

38. John Barnett to Taggart, 23 Aug. 1916, ibid.; Homer L. Cook to Taggart, 14 Aug. 1916, ibid.; Taggart to Korbly, 13, 28 Aug. 1916, ibid.; Cedric C. Cummins, *Indiana Public Opinion and the World War, 1914–1917,* vol. 28 of *Indiana Historical Collections* (Indianapolis: Indiana Historical Bureau, 1945), 201 n.

39. Taggart to Korbly, 31 Aug. 1916, and Spaulding Grafton to J. C. Cantrill, 26 Aug. 1916, Aug.–Dec. 1916 File, TTP.

40. Korbly to Taggart, 30 Aug., 4 Sept. 1916, and Taggart to Korbly, 19 Aug. 1916, ibid.

41. Korbly to Taggart, 4 Sept. 1916, ibid.

42. Korbly telegram to Taggart, 6 Sept. 1916, and Taggart telegram to Korbly, 7 Sept. 1916, ibid.

43. Thomas Taggart's secretary to Korbly, 29 Aug. 1916, ibid.

44. 1920 campaign press release, 1920–28 File, and Taggart to Sallee, 7 May 1916, 1915–July 1916 File, ibid.

45. Newspaper clipping, 29 July 1916, ibid.

46. Taggart to Ralston, 7 Apr. 1916, Box 6, Ralston Correspondence, 21 Mar.–31 Aug. 1916, 6–10 Apr. 1916, Ralston Papers. The remaining six of the nine-member Committee on Forest Reservations and Protection of Game were Lee S. Overman (North Carolina), Robert F. Broussard (Louisiana), Harry Lane (Oregon), George P. McLean (Connecticut), John W. Weeks (Massachusetts), and Lawrence Y. Sherman (Illinois). Harold Zink, "Tom Taggart" (unpublished manuscript), 35, in possession of Diana Chambers Leslie; Richard A. Baker, historian of the United States Senate, to the author, 29 Nov. 1994.

47. Taggart's remarks to the Senate on the River and Harbor Appropriation Bill, 23 May 1916, Dated-to-be-filed File, TTP.

48. Taggart's remarks on the River and Harbor Appropriation Bill, 29 May 1916, TTP; White House invitation to the Taggarts from Mrs. Woodrow Wilson, Miscellaneous Notes File, ibid.

49. David M. Silver, ed., "Richard Lieber and Indiana's Forest Heritage," *Indiana Magazine of History* 67 (Mar. 1971): 49, 52.

50. Clifton J. Phillips, *Indiana in Transition: The Emergence of an Industrial Commonwealth, 1880–1920* (Indianapolis: Indiana Historical Bureau and Indiana Historical Society, 1968), 222.

51. Letters from men offering to serve in Taggart's regiment in the event of war with Mexico, 1915–July 1916 File, TTP; *Indianapolis Star,* 25 June 1916.

52. David Laurance Chambers to Taggart, 7 July 1916, 1915–July 1916 File, TTP.

53. Chambers to Taggart, 12 July 1916, ibid.

54. "Government Should Practice Same Kind of Economy That a Good Business Man Would Follow," *Speeches of Hon. Thomas Taggart of Indiana in the Senate of the United States* (Washington, D.C.: Government Printing Office, 1916), 12. This speech was delivered by Taggart on 12 Aug. 1916 and is quoted in Claude G. Bowers, "Why Thomas Taggart Should Be Returned to the United States Senate," pamphlet, Indiana State Library. Bowers was editor of the *Fort Wayne Journal-Gazette*.

55. *Washington Times,* 12 Aug. 1916, quoted in *Indianapolis Times,* 21 Oct. 1916.

56. *South Bend News-Times,* 16 Aug. 1916, quoted in ibid.

57. *Indianapolis News,* Aug. 1916, quoted in ibid.

58. *Washington Times,* 12 Aug. 1916, quoted in ibid; Taggart to Grace Julian Clarke, 21 Aug. 1916, 1916–1917 File, Grace Julian Clarke Papers, Indiana Division, Indiana State Library.

59. "Wealth Must Bear Its Just Proportion of the Burden of Taxation," *Speeches of Hon. Thomas Taggart of Indiana in the Senate of the United States,* 11–12. This speech was delivered by Taggart on 12 Aug. 1916. In a speech during the senatorial campaign in 1916, Taggart endorsed the income tax law. Speech provided courtesy of Diana Chambers Leslie.

60. Taggart to Korbly, 3 Sept. 1916, Aug.–Dec. 1916 File, TTP.

61. Byford E. Long to Paul Swartz, 6 Oct. 1916, ibid.

62. Sallee telegram to Taggart, 5 Sept. 1916, ibid.

63. Taggart to Willis Thompson, 4 Sept. 1916, ibid.

64. Newspaper clipping, n.d. (1916), TTP.

65. Louis Ludlow, *From Cornfield to Press Gallery: Adventures and Reminiscences of a Veteran Washington Correspondent* (Washington, D.C.: W. F. Roberts Co., Inc., 1924), 290–91.

66. *Indianapolis Star,* 28 Mar. 1916.

67. Ibid., 13 Oct. 1916; Suellen M. Hoy, "Governor Samuel M. Ralston and Indiana's Centennial Celebration," *Indiana Magazine of History* 71 (Sept. 1975): 260–61, 262–65. See also Harlow Lindley, ed., *The Indiana Centennial, 1916* (Indianapolis: Indiana Historical Commission, 1919), 300–10.

68. William Bauchop Wilson to Woodrow Wilson, 16 Oct. 1916, in Arthur S. Link, ed., *The Papers of Woodrow Wilson,* 69 vols. (Princeton, N.J.: Princeton University Press, 1966–94), 38:457; *Indianapolis Star,* 22 Oct. 1916; Cummins, *Indiana Public Opinion and the World War,* 221.

69. *Indianapolis News,* 10 Nov. 1916; *Year Book of the State of Indiana for the Year 1917* (Indianapolis: William B. Burford, 1918), 683.

70. Phillips, *Indiana in Transition,* 125; *Union Labor Bulletin,* 3 Nov. 1916, p. 1. For a discussion of Senator Kern's reelection campaign and the general election of 1916 in Indiana see George C. Roberts, "Woodrow Wilson, John W. Kern and the 1916 Indiana Election: Defeat of a Senate Majority Leader," *Presidential Studies Quarterly* 10 (1980).

71. Byford E. Long to Stanton T. Spencer, 18 Nov. 1916, Aug.–Dec. 1916 File, TTP.

72. *Indianapolis Star,* 30 Jan. 1917; *Battle Creek (Mich.) Enquirer News,* 7 Mar. 1929.

73. Taggart to Ralston, 29 Apr. 1917, Box 7, Ralston Correspondence, Sept. 1916–Oct. 1917, 11–30 Apr. 1917, Ralston Papers.

74. Phillips, *Indiana in Transition,* 597.

75. Taggart to Ralston, 11 Dec. 1917, Box 8, Ralston Correspondence, Nov. 1917–Mar. 1921, 11–20 Dec. 1917, Ralston Papers; Walter Greenough, *The War Purse of Indiana: The Five Liberty Loans and War Savings and Thrift Campaigns in Indiana during the World War,* vol. 8 of *Indiana Historical Collections* (Indianapolis: Indiana Historical Commission, 1922), 203 n.

76. Washington, D.C., newspaper clipping, n.d. (1917 or 1918), TTP.

77. Woodrow Wilson to Taggart, 27 Apr. 1918, Woodrow Wilson Papers, Manuscript Division, Library of Congress, Washington, D.C.

78. Taggart to Ralston, 22 Jan. 1919, Box 8, Ralston Correspondence, Nov. 1917–Mar. 1921, 16–31 Jan., Ralston Papers.

79. Frederick Van Nuys to Ralston, 2 Aug. 1919, and Taggart to Ralston, 2 Aug. 1919, Box 8, Ralston Correspondence, Nov. 1917–Mar. 1921, Aug. 1919, ibid.

80. Marriage certificate of Irene Taggart and William J. Young, Evelyn Chambers Denny Papers, Hyannis Port, Mass. The story goes that Mrs. Taggart, concerned that Irene was not married in her mid-thirties, set out to draw Dr. Young's attention to Irene. Mrs. Taggart loved chocolate candies and would often sit with family members on the balcony outside the Taggart penthouse apartment in the deluxe wing of the French Lick Springs Hotel. One day she and Irene were on the balcony and Dr. Young was walking below. Mrs. Taggart dropped candies in his direction so he would look up and notice Irene. The ploy worked. Irene later confided that her parents gave the Taggart daughters one million dollars each as wedding gifts. Author interview with Berta-Ann Barkhausen Steinkamp, 22 July 1996.

81. *Indianapolis News,* 2 Mar. 1920.

82. Ibid., 9, 10 Mar. 1920.

83. Ibid., 27 Mar. 1920.

84. Senate campaign advertisement, *Hammond Lake County Times,* 16 Apr. 1920; *Indianapolis News,* 3 May 1920.

85. *Indianapolis News,* 7 May 1920.

86. *Indianapolis Star,* 10 May 1920. Edmond H. Moore, manager of Ohio governor James M. Cox's presidential effort in 1920, met in May at French Lick with Taggart, Charles F. Murphy, and other urban leaders opposed to William Gibbs McAdoo. David Burner, *The Politics of Provincialism: The Democratic Party in Transition, 1918–1932* (New York: Alfred A. Knopf, 1968), 62–63.

87. *Indianapolis News,* ibid.

88. I*ndianapolis Times,* 13 May 1920.

89. Newspaper clippings, n.d. (May 1920), scrapbook (1920), TTP; Taggart's speech to the Democratic State Convention, 20 May 1920, Dated-to-be-filed File, TTP.

90. Newspaper clipping, n.d. (1920), scrapbook (1920), ibid.

91. *Greensburg News,* 19 June 1920.

92. *New York Evening Post,* 18 June 1920.

93. Ibid.

94. Newspaper clipping, n.d. (1920), TTP.

95. List of delegates and alternates to the national convention in 1920, 1920–28 File, and newspaper clipping, 19 May 1920, scrapbook (1920), ibid.

96. Newspaper clippings, n.d. (1920), scrapbook (1920), ibid.; *Indianapolis Star,* 6 July 1920. Taggart's comments and actions at the convention regarding McAdoo are at odds with reports that he was part of an anti-McAdoo alliance with Murphy, Brennan, and Ed Moore of Ohio. See Douglas B. Craig, *After Wilson: The Struggle for the Democratic Party, 1920–1934* (Chapel Hill: University of North Carolina Press, 1992), 17.

97. *New York Evening Sun,* 10 July 1920.

98. Walter D. Myers interview by Randall W. Jehs, 1970–71, Indiana Division, Indiana State Library, pp. 25–27; *Indianapolis News,* 7 July 1920.

99. Newspaper clipping, 24 July 1920, scrapbook (1920), TTP.

100. *Fort Wayne News and Sentinel,* 2 Aug. 1920.

101. *Indianapolis News,* 27 Aug. 1920. Nicholson's statement of support was also published in a campaign brochure titled "Indiana Campaign Song: 'Taggart, We Want a Man Like You' for Senator" (Indianapolis: Halcyon Pub. Co., Inc., 1920). A copy can be found in the Indiana State Library.

102. Indianapolis newspaper clipping, Sept. 1920, scrapbook (1920), TTP.

103. Wesley M. Bagby, *The Road to Normalcy: The Presidential Campaign and Election of 1920* (Baltimore: Johns Hopkins Press, 1962), 151; *Indianapolis News,* 23 Sept. 1920.

104. *Indianapolis News,* 14 Sept. 1920.

105. Newspaper clipping, n.d. (1920), scrapbook (1920), TTP. For Senator Watson's comments on Woodrow Wilson and the League of Nations see James E. Watson, *As I Knew Them: Memoirs of James E. Watson, Former United*

States Senator from Indiana (Indianapolis: The Bobbs-Merrill Co., 1936), 184–206.

106. Newspaper clippings, n.d. (1920), scrapbook (1920), TTP.

107. "Indiana Campaign Song."

108. *Indianapolis News,* 14 Sept. 1920; newspaper clipping, n.d. (1920), scrapbook (1920), TTP.

109. Taggart to Warren B. Allison, 11 Oct. 1920, 1920–28 File, TTP.

110. *Yearbook of the State of Indiana for the Year 1920* (Fort Wayne: Fort Wayne Printing Co., 1921), 61–66.

111. *Indianapolis Star* clippings, n.d., TTP.

Chapter 8

1. Florence Kling Harding to Thomas Taggart, 6 Apr. 1921, Dated-to-be-filed File, Thomas Taggart Papers, Indiana Division, Indiana State Library, Indianapolis (hereafter cited as TTP).

2. Warren G. Harding to Taggart, 1 Apr. 1922, 1920–28 File, ibid.

3. See Robert K. Murray, *The Harding Era: Warren G. Harding and His Administration* (Minneapolis: University of Minnesota Press, 1969); Receipt from the Harding Memorial Association, 14 Apr. 1924, 1920–28 File, TTP; Thank-you note from Mrs. Harding, Miscellaneous Notes File, ibid.

4. *Indianapolis Star,* 9 June 1922. The only eyewitness account of the Taggart-Pringle wedding is that of David Laurance Chambers, Jr., telephone conversation with the author, Nov. 1993.

5. Taggart to Samuel M. Ralston, 16 Sept. 1922, Box 9, Ralston Correspondence, Apr. 1921–Sept. 1922, 16–20 Sept. 1922, Ralston Papers, Lilly Library, Indiana University, Bloomington; Herbert R. Hill, "Lost River Valley Meccas: West Baden and French Lick, A Classic Springs Rivalry," *Outdoor Indiana* 61 (Nov. 1976): 36.

6. Certificate of appointment to the Lincoln Memorial Commission, 5 May 1923, 1920–28 File, TTP.

7. Taggart to Claude G. Bowers, 25 June 1923, Bowers Papers, Lilly Library.

8. Frank R. Kent, "The City Boss: How He Gets His Power and His Fortune," *World's Work* 47, no. 3 (Jan. 1924): 290; W. A. Swanberg, *Citizen Hearst: A Biography of William Randolph Hearst* (New York: Charles Scribner's Sons, 1961), 366.

9. *Indianapolis News,* 22 Sept. 1923.

10. Taggart to Ralston, 16 Jan. 1924, Box 10, Ralston Correspondence, Oct. 1922–10 Feb. 1924, 16–20 Jan. 1924, Ralston Papers; Taggart to Ralston,

2 Feb. 1924, Box 10, Ralston Correspondence, Oct. 1922–10 Feb. 1924, 1–5 Feb. 1924, ibid.; Taggart to Ralston, 13 Feb. 1924, Box 11, Ralston Correspondence, 11 Feb. 1924–31 July 1924, 11–13 Feb. 1924, ibid.; newspaper clipping, n.d., TTP.

11. Taggart letter to annual banquet of the IDEA, 1924, TTP.

12. Passenger list of R.M.S.P. *Orca*, 20 Feb. 1924, Dated-to-be-filed File, ibid.; *Indianapolis News*, 18 Feb. 1924; Taggart to Ralston, 6 Feb. 1924, Box 10, Ralston Correspondence, Oct. 1922–10 Feb. 1924, 6–10 Feb. 1924, Ralston Papers. The Taggarts visited Nassau, the Bahamas; Havana, Cuba; Kingston, Jamaica; Colon, Panama Canal; Cartagena, Colombia; Curacao; La Guayra, Venezuela; Trinidad; Barbados; Martinique; St. Thomas; San Juan, Puerto Rico; and Bermuda.

13. Taggart to Ralston, 25 Mar. 1924, Box 11, Ralston Correspondence, 11 Feb. 1924–31 July 1924, 23–25 Mar. 1924, Ralston Papers.

14. "Brethren of the Senate: Senator Ralston," *The Indiana Freemason* 48, no. 7 (Dec. 1970): 34; Robert Sobel and John W. Raimo, *Biographical Directory of the Governors of the United States, 1789–1978*, vol. 1, *Alabama–Indiana* (Westport, Conn.: Meckler Books, 1978), 414.

15. Taggart to Ralston, 30 Mar. 1924, Box 11, Ralston Correspondence, 11 Feb. 1924–31 July 1924, 29–31 Mar. 1924, Ralston Papers.

16. Taggart to Ralston, 7 Apr. 1924, Box 11, Ralston Correspondence, 11 Feb. 1924–31 July 1924, 6–8 Apr. 1924, ibid.

17. Taggart to Ralston, 21 Apr. 1924, Box 11, Ralston Correspondence, 11 Feb. 1924–31 July 1924, 21–25 Apr. 1924, ibid.

18. Taggart to Ralston, 23 May 1924, Box 11, Ralston Correspondence, 11 Feb. 1924–31 July 1924, 21–25 May 1924, ibid.

19. Ralston to Taggart, 19 June 1924, 1920–28 File, TTP.

20. Ralston telegram to Taggart, 20 June 1924, ibid.

21. Articles, scrapbook, Democratic National Convention 1924, ibid.; *Indianapolis Star*, 21 June 1924; William H. Harbaugh, *Lawyer's Lawyer: The Life of John W. Davis* (New York: Oxford University Press, 1973), 216; Claude Bowers, *My Life: The Memoirs of Claude Bowers* (New York: Simon and Schuster, 1962), 113.

22. *Indianapolis News*, 24 June 1924; *Indianapolis Star*, 29 June 1924.

23. Article, 25 June 1924, and Associated Press article, 25 June 1924, scrapbook, Democratic National Convention 1924, TTP; *Indianapolis Star*, 1 July 1924.

24. Article, scrapbook, Democratic National Convention 1924, TTP.

25. Article, 28 June 1924, ibid.; Robert K. Murray, *The 103rd Ballot: Democrats and the Disaster in Madison Square Garden* (New York: Harper and Row, Publishers, 1976), 73; Harold Feightner, interview by Thomas Krasean,

28 Feb. 1968, Indiana Division, Indiana State Library, pp. 29–30. Feightner, an Indianapolis newspaperman in New York City covering the convention, stated that Taggart asked Ralston to withdraw from the presidential nomination contest.

26. Articles, scrapbook, Democratic National Convention 1924, TTP.

27. Article, scrapbook, ibid.; Murray, *103rd Ballot*, 154.

28. Murray, *103rd Ballot*, 154.

29. Articles, scrapbook, Democratic National Convention 1924, TTP.

30. Article, 28 June 1924, scrapbook, ibid.

31. Sexson E. Humphreys, "The Nomination of the Democratic Candidate in 1924," *Indiana Magazine of History* 31 (Mar. 1935): 5–7.

32. Ralston telegrams to Taggart, 23, 24, 29 June, 1, 3, 4 July 1924, 1920–28 File, TTP.

33. *Boston Herald*, 24 July 1927.

34. *Indianapolis Star*, 15 May 1949.

35. Ralston to Maurice P. Murphy, 14 July 1924, Box 11, Ralston Correspondence, 11 Feb. 1924–31 July 1924, 11–15 July 1924, Ralston Papers.

36. Humphreys, "Nomination of the Democratic Candidate in 1924," 5–8; article, 9 July 1924, scrapbook, Democratic National Convention 1924, TTP.

37. *Indianapolis Star*, 10 July 1924; Murray, *103rd Ballot*, 211; Alfred E. Smith, *Up to Now: An Autobiography* (New York: The Viking Press, 1929), 290.

38. *Indianapolis News*, 24 June 1924.

39. Ralston to Taggart, 29 June 1924, 1920–28 File, TTP; David Burner, *The Politics of Provincialism: The Democratic Party in Transition, 1918–1932* (New York: Alfred A. Knopf, 1968), 123–24 n.

40. Ralston telegram to Taggart, 11 July 1924, Box 11, Ralston Correspondence, 11 Feb. 1924–31 July 1924, 11–15 July 1924, Ralston Papers.

41. Murray, *103rd Ballot*, 198; Burner, *Politics of Provincialism*, 123–24 n; A. C. Sallee to Thomas D. Taggart, 1 Nov. 1929, 1929–50 File, TTP.

42. Harbaugh, *Lawyer's Lawyer*, 206.

43. A. C. Sallee, "T. T.," unpublished manuscript, p. 187, Miscellaneous Notes File, TTP.

44. *Miami Herald*, 7 Mar. 1929.

45. *Miami Daily News*, 17 Feb. 1925. For a discussion of the Florida land boom and other development in that state in the early 1920s, see Frederick Lewis Allen, *Only Yesterday: An Informal History of the Nineteen-Twenties* (New York: Harper and Brothers, 1931).

46. *Miami Herald*, 12 Mar. 1925.

47. *Washington (Ind.) Herald,* 24 June 1924.

48. Taggart to Ralston, 24 May 1925, Box 12, Ralston Correspondence, Aug. 1924–May 1925, 21–25 May 1925, Ralston Papers.

49. *Shreveport (Louisiana) Times,* 7 Mar. 1929; Victor Wenzel to Taggart, 15 May 1926, 1920–28 File, TTP.

50. Taggart became chairman of the board of the Fletcher American National Bank on 19 May 1923, serving until his death in 1929. In 1921 Taggart was one of a group of businessmen personally selected by Stoughton A. Fletcher to assume his controlling interest in the bank when Fletcher encountered financial problems with his Midwest Engine Company, a manufacturer of marine turbine engines no longer needed by the government in the aftermath of World War I. This group of businessmen, along with other shareholders of the bank, subscribed to an additional one million dollars of bank stock authorized by the board in May 1923. For an account of the board meeting at which Taggart became chairman of the bank, one of Indiana's premier institutions, see the *Indianapolis News,* 19 May 1923, and the minutes of the meeting, Fletcher American National Bank Minute Book, provided courtesy of Tom Plimpton. Stoughton A. Fletcher, scion of one of Indianapolis's oldest and wealthiest families, lost his fortune amid financial and personal tragedy. For a brief account of his family see Kate Lenkowsky, *The Herman Kahn Center of the Hudson Institute* (Indianapolis: Hudson Institute, 1991), 5–11.

51. Ralston, Gates, Lairy, Van Nuys and Barnard law firm to Doubleday, Page and Company, 26 Aug. 1926, 1920–28 File, TTP; Greenbaum, Wolff and Ernst to Ralston, Gates, Lairy, Van Nuys and Barnard, 2 Sept. 1926, ibid.; Edna Ferber, *Show Boat* (New York: Grosset and Dunlap Publishers, 1926), 303; *New Bedford (Mass.) Mercury,* 3 Sept. 1926; *Indianapolis News,* 2 Sept. 1926.

52. *Boston Herald,* 24 July 1927.

53. *Indianapolis Star,* 7 Mar. 1929; Evans Woollen to Taggart, 29 June 1928, Dated-to-be-filed File, TTP.

54. J. Edward Krause to Sallee, 22 Sept. 1926, 1920–28 File, ibid.

55. Carleton B. McCulloch to Taggart, 16 Nov. 1926, ibid.

56. *Indianapolis News,* 18 June 1928; family photograph of the Taggarts' fiftieth wedding anniversary. Family members present for the golden anniversary celebration were Lucy Taggart; Mr. and Mrs. David Laurance Chambers and their three children, Evelyn Chambers, David L. Chambers, Jr., and Judy Chambers; Dr. and Mrs. William J. Young and their son, Thomas Taggart Young; Mr. and Mrs. Thomas D. Taggart and their daughter, Eva Taggart; Mr. and Mrs. William Richardson Sinclair and their three children, Dora Sinclair, Thomas Taggart Sinclair, and Letitia Sinclair.

57. Lisa Drake, "Mt. Airie, French Lick, Indiana" (paper, Melton Public Library, Mt. Airie-Taggart Mansion Clipping File, French Lick, circa 1986), 1–3, 6, 8; Eva Taggart Parsons, notes, 15 Oct. 1992. The transfer book in the Orange County auditor's office indicates that Tom and Eva Taggart transferred the 160 acres at Mt. Airie to the French Lick Springs Hotel Company on 21 Jan. 1926.

58. Eva Taggart Parsons, notes to author, 10 Mar. 1994; Joseph E. Garland, *Eastern Point: A Nautical, Rustical, and Social Chronicle of Gloucester's Outer Shield and Inner Sanctum, 1606–1950* (Peterborough, N.H.: William L. Bauhan, Publisher, 1971), 341; Barbara D. Tarr, site manager of "Beauport," to author, 1 Apr. 1996.

59. *Indianapolis News,* 20 Oct. 1928, 6 Mar. 1929; Smith, *Up to Now,* 403.

60. Letters to Taggart responding to his request for information on the 1928 election, 1920–28 File, TTP.

61. Sallee to Thomas D. Taggart, 30 Sept. 1929, 1929–50 File, ibid.

62. *Indianapolis Star,* 18 Nov. 1928.

63. *Springs Valley Herald,* 7 Mar. 1929; *Indianapolis Times,* 7 Mar. 1929; *Indianapolis Star,* 9 Mar. 1929.

64. Charles Roll, *Indiana: One Hundred and Fifty Years of American Development,* 5 vols. (Chicago and New York: The Lewis Publishing Co., 1931), 4:383–84.

65. For a survey of the literature on municipal government and politics, including machine bosses, see Jon C. Teaford, "Finis for Tweed and Steffens: Rewriting the History of Urban Rule," *Reviews in American History* 10 (Dec. 1982): 133–49. John M. Allswang, *Bosses, Machines, and Urban Voters: An American Symbiosis* (Port Washington, N.Y.: Kennikat Press, 1977), covers the career of Charles F. Murphy as boss of Tammany.

66. Senate campaign speech in 1916 provided courtesy of Diana Chambers Leslie.

67. Thomas R. Marshall, *Recollections of Thomas R. Marshall, Vice-President and Hoosier Philosopher: A Hoosier Salad* (Indianapolis: Bobbs-Merrill Co., 1925), 170–72. For a revisionist discussion of progressive ideology and practice see Samuel P. Hays, "The Politics of Reform in Municipal Government in the Progressive Era," *Pacific Northwest Quarterly* 55 (Oct. 1964): 157–69. For the role of individualism in the progressive movement see Richard Hofstadter, *The Age of Reform: From Bryan to F.D.R.* (New York: Alfred A. Knopf, 1955).

Epilogue

1. Last Will and Testament of Thomas Taggart, microfilm records, Marion County Probate Court; *Pittsburgh Press,* 14 Mar. 1929; *New York Times,* 7 Mar. 1929; *Detroit Free Press,* 14 Mar. 1929; *Springfield (Mass.) Republican,* 14 Mar. 1929; *Muncie Press,* 13 Mar. 1929; *Indianapolis Star,* 14 Mar. 1929.

2. Donation agreement, 31 Aug. 1929, 1929–50 File, Thomas Taggart Papers, Indiana Division, Indiana State Library, Indianapolis (hereafter cited as TTP).

3. *Springs Valley Herald,* 5 Dec. 1929.

4. Invitation to the dedication of the Thomas Taggart Memorial for Children in the Julius A. Hanson Unit of the Methodist Episcopal Hospital, 30 May 1930, Dated-to-be-filed File, TTP.

5. Caroline Latham and Jeannie Sakol, *The Kennedy Encyclopedia: An A-to-Z Illustrated Guide to America's Royal Family* (New York: NAL Books, 1989), 99.

6. Dora Sinclair Loutrel and Letitia Sinclair Mumford, interview by author, Aug. 1992. The Taggart-Kennedy dock case is not a published Massachusetts case according to the Barnstable County Superior Court library.

7. Evelyn Chambers Denny notes, 28 Oct. 1992.

8. *Indianapolis Star,* 11, 15 June 1931. An article in the *Indianapolis Star,* 14 June 1931, placed the cost of the Taggart memorial at nearly $50,000. An article in the 28 June 1987 *Indianapolis Star* listed the cost at $39,044 with the city contributing $25,000 and Thomas D. Taggart providing the balance.

9. Ibid., 25 Nov. 1931.

10. Ibid., 22 Jan. 1938

BIBLIOGRAPHY

GENERAL REFERENCES

Allen, Frederick Lewis. *Only Yesterday: An Informal History of the Nineteen-Twenties.* New York: Harper and Brothers, 1931.

Allswang, John M. *Bosses, Machines, and Urban Voters: An American Symbiosis.* Port Washington, New York: Kennikat Press, 1977.

Bagby, Wesley M. *The Road to Normalcy: The Presidential Campaign and Election of 1920.* Baltimore: Johns Hopkins Press, 1962.

Ballard, Charles Edward "Ed" with Janet Kirk Johnson and Anna Marie Borcia. *The Ballards in Indiana: A Story of Determination, Self-Education and Ultimate Success.* [Indianapolis]: C. E. Ballard-Literary Trust, 1984.

Biographical Directory of the United States Congress, 1774–1989. Washington, D.C.: Government Printing Office, 1989.

Book of Friendship. Privately printed by friends of Thomas Taggart, December 1927.

Bowers, Claude G. *Beveridge and the Progressive Era.* Cambridge, Massachusetts: Houghton Mifflin, 1932.

_____. *My Life: The Memoirs of Claude Bowers.* New York: Simon and Schuster, 1962.

Burner, David. *The Politics of Provincialism: The Democratic Party in Transition, 1918–1932.* New York: Alfred A. Knopf, 1968.

Calhoun, Charles W. *Gilded Age Cato: The Life of Walter Q. Gresham.* Lexington: University Press of Kentucky, 1988.

The Campaign Text Book of the Democratic Party of the United States, 1904. New York: Democratic National Committee, 1904.

Carlson, Oliver, and Ernest Sutherland Bates. *Hearst: Lord of San Simeon.* New York: The Viking Press, 1936.

Coletta, Paolo E. *William Jennings Bryan: Political Evangelist, 1860–1908.* 3 vols. Lincoln: University of Nebraska Press, 1964–1969.

Cottman, George S. *Centennial History and Handbook of Indiana.* Indianapolis: Max R. Hyman, Publishers, 1915.

Craig, Douglas B. *After Wilson: The Struggle for the Democratic Party, 1920–1934.* Chapel Hill: University of North Carolina Press, 1992.

Crunden, Robert M. *Ministers of Reform: The Progressives' Achievement in American Civilization, 1889–1920*. New York: Basic Books, 1982.

Cumback, Will, and J. B. Maynard, eds. *Men of Progress, Indiana*. Indianapolis: The Indianapolis Sentinel Company, 1899.

Cummins, Cedric C. *Indiana Public Opinion and the World War, 1914–1917*. *Indiana Historical Collections*, vol. 28. Indianapolis: Indiana Historical Bureau, 1945.

Dillard, Arthur L. *Orange County Heritage*. Paoli, Indiana: Stout's Print Shop, 1971.

Dunn, Jacob Piatt. *Greater Indianapolis: The History, the Industries, the Institutions, and the People of a City of Homes*. 2 vols. Chicago: The Lewis Publishing Company, 1910.

Foulke, William Dudley. *Lucius B. Swift: A Biography*. Indiana Historical Society *Publications*, vol. 9. Indianapolis: The Bobbs-Merrill Company, 1930.

Glad, Paul W. *McKinley, Bryan, and the People*. Philadelphia: Lippincott, 1964.

_____. *The Trumpet Soundeth: William Jennings Bryan and His Democracy, 1896–1912*. Lincoln: University of Nebraska Press, 1960.

Graham, Otis L., Jr. *The Great Campaigns: Reform and War in America, 1900–1928*. Englewood Cliffs, New Jersey: Prentice Hall, 1971.

Greenough, Walter. *The War Purse of Indiana: The Five Liberty Loans and War Savings and Thrift Campaigns in Indiana during the World War*. *Indiana Historical Collections*, vol. 8. Indianapolis: Indiana Historical Commission, 1922.

Gresham, Matilda. *Life of Walter Quintin Gresham, 1832–1895*. 2 vols. Chicago: Rand McNally and Company, 1919.

Harbaugh, William H. *Lawyer's Lawyer: The Life of John W. Davis*. New York: Oxford University Press, 1973.

_____. *Power and Responsibility: The Life and Times of Theodore Roosevelt*. New York: Farrar, Straus and Cudahy, 1961.

Herrick, Paul Fairbanks, and Larry G. Newman. *Old Hyannis Port, Massachusetts: An Anecdotal, Photographic Panorama*. New Bedford, Massachusetts: Reynolds-DeWalt, 1968.

Hicks, John D. *Republican Ascendancy, 1921–1933*. New York: Harper, 1960.

Hofstadter, Richard. *The Age of Reform: From Bryan to F.D.R.* New York: Alfred A. Knopf, 1955.

Hollingsworth, J. Rogers. *The Whirligig of Politics: The Democracy of Cleveland and Bryan*. Chicago: University of Chicago Press, 1963.

Hoogenboom, Ari. *Outlawing the Spoils: A History of the Civil Service Reform Movement, 1865–1883*. Urbana: University of Illinois Press, 1961.

Hubbard, Kin, ed. *A Book of Indiana.* The Indiana Biographical Association, 1929.

Indianapolis Men of Affairs, 1923. Indianapolis: American Biographical Society, 1923.

Jensen, Richard J. *The Winning of the Midwest: Social and Political Conflict, 1888–1896.* Chicago: University of Chicago Press, 1971.

Josephson, Matthew. *The Politicos, 1865–1896.* New York: Harcourt, Brace and Company, 1938.

_____. *The President Makers: The Culture of Politics and Leadership in an Age of Enlightenment, 1896–1919.* New York: Harcourt, Brace and Company, 1940.

Kalfus, Melvin. *Frederick Law Olmsted: The Passion of a Public Artist.* New York: New York University Press, 1990.

Kleppner, Paul. *The Cross of Culture: A Social Analysis of Midwestern Politics, 1850–1900.* 2d ed. New York: Free Press, 1970.

Latham, Caroline, and Jeannie Sakol. *The Kennedy Encyclopedia: An A-to-Z Illustrated Guide to America's Royal Family.* New York: NAL Books, 1989.

Lindley, Harlow, ed. *The Indiana Centennial, 1916.* Indianapolis: Indiana Historical Commission, 1919.

Link, Arthur S. *The Higher Realism of Woodrow Wilson and Other Essays.* Nashville: Vanderbilt University Press, 1971.

_____., ed. *The Papers of Woodrow Wilson.* 69 vols. Princeton, New Jersey: Princeton University Press, 1966–1994.

_____. *Wilson.* 5 vols. Princeton, New Jersey: Princeton University Press, 1947–.

Ludlow, Louis. *From Cornfield to Press Gallery: Adventures and Reminiscences of a Veteran Washington Correspondent.* Washington, D.C.: W. F. Roberts Company, 1924.

McCarty, C. Walter, ed. *Indiana Today.* New Orleans: The James O. Jones Company, 1942.

McCombs, William F. *Making Woodrow Wilson President.* New York: Fairview Publishing Company, 1921.

McCormick, Richard L. *The Party Period and Public Policy: American Politics from the Age of Jackson to the Progressive Era.* New York: Oxford University Press, 1986.

Madison, James H. *Indiana through Tradition and Change: A History of the Hoosier State and Its People, 1920–1945.* Indianapolis: Indiana Historical Society, 1982.

_____. *The Indiana Way: A State History.* Bloomington and Indianapolis: Indiana University Press and Indiana Historical Society, 1986.

Marshall, Thomas R. *Recollections of Thomas R. Marshall, Vice-President and Hoosier Philosopher: A Hoosier Salad.* Indianapolis: The Bobbs-Merrill Company, 1925.

Morison, Elting E., ed. *The Letters of Theodore Roosevelt*. Vol. 4. Cambridge, Massachusetts: Harvard University Press, 1951.

Mowry, George E. *The Era of Theodore Roosevelt, 1900–1912*. New York: Harper, 1958.

Murray, Robert K. *The Harding Era: Warren G. Harding and His Administration*. Minneapolis: University of Minnesota Press, 1969.

_____. *The 103rd Ballot: Democrats and the Disaster in Madison Square Garden*. New York: Harper and Row, Publishers, 1976.

_____. *The Politics of Normalcy: Governmental Theory and Practice in the Harding-Coolidge Era*. New York: W. W. Norton and Company, 1973.

Noble, Iris. *Frederick Law Olmsted: Park Designer*. New York: Julian Messner, 1974.

Nolan, Jeannette Covert. *Hoosier City: The Story of Indianapolis*. New York: Julian Messner, 1943.

Nye, Russel B. *Midwestern Progressive Politics: A Historical Study of Its Origins and Development, 1870–1950*. East Lansing: Michigan State College Press, 1951.

Older, Mrs. Fremont. *William Randolph Hearst: American*. New York: D. Appleton-Century Company, 1936.

Phillips, Clifton J. *Indiana in Transition: The Emergence of an Industrial Commonwealth, 1880–1920*. Indianapolis: Indiana Historical Bureau and Indiana Historical Society, 1968.

Pictorial and Biographical Memoirs of Indianapolis and Marion County, Indiana. Chicago: Goodspeed Brothers, 1893.

Rabb, Kate Milner, and William Herschell, eds. *An Account of Indianapolis and Marion County*. Dayton, Ohio: Dayton Historical Publishing Company, 1924.

Reed, George Irving, ed. *Encyclopedia of Biography of Indiana*. 2 vols. Chicago: Century Publishing and Engraving Company, 1899.

Roll, Charles. *Indiana: One Hundred and Fifty Years of American Development*. 5 vols. Chicago and New York: The Lewis Publishing Company, 1931.

Roper, Laura Wood. *FLO: A Biography of Frederick Law Olmsted*. Baltimore: The Johns Hopkins University Press, 1973.

Sarasohn, David. *The Party of Reform: Democrats in the Progressive Era*. Jackson: University Press of Mississippi, 1989.

Schlesinger, Arthur M., *The Crisis of the Old Order, 1919–1933*. Boston: Houghton Mifflin, 1956.

Schlesinger, Arthur M., Jr., ed. *History of American Presidential Elections, 1789–1968*. Vol. 5. New York: Chelsea House Publishers, 1985.

Smith, Alfred E. *Up to Now: An Autobiography*. New York: The Viking Press, 1929.

Sobel, Robert, and John W. Raimo. *Biographical Directory of the Governors of the United States, 1789–1978*. Vol. 1. *Alabama–Indiana*. Westport, Connecticut: Meckler Books, 1978.

Stevenson, Elizabeth. *Park Maker: A Life of Frederick Law Olmsted.* New York: Macmillan Publishing Company, 1977.

Stoll, John B. *History of the Indiana Democracy, 1816–1916.* Indianapolis: Indiana Democratic Publishing Company, 1917.

Swanberg, W. A. *Citizen Hearst: A Biography of William Randolph Hearst.* New York: Charles Scribner's Sons, 1961.

Thomas, Charles M. *Thomas Riley Marshall, Hoosier Statesman.* Oxford, Ohio: The Mississippi Valley Press, 1939.

Todd, John Emerson. *Frederick Law Olmsted.* Boston: Twayne Publishers, 1982.

Trissal, Francis M. *Public Men of Indiana: A Political History.* 2 vols. Hammond, Indiana: W. B. Conkey Company, 1923.

VanderMeer, Philip R. *The Hoosier Politician: Officeholding and Political Culture in Indiana, 1896–1920.* Urbana: University of Illinois Press, 1985.

Van Riper, Paul P. *History of the United States Civil Service.* Evanston, Illinois: Row, Peterson and Company, 1958.

Walsh, Justin E. ed. *A Biographical Directory of the Indiana General Assembly.* Vol. 2. Indianapolis: Indiana Historical Bureau, 1984.

Watson, James E. *As I Knew Them: Memoirs of James E. Watson, Former United States Senator from Indiana.* Indianapolis: The Bobbs-Merrill Company, 1936.

White, William Allen. *The Citizen's Business.* New York: Macmillan, 1924.

Who Was Who in America. Vol. 1. Chicago: The A. N. Marquis Company, 1943.

Who Was Who in America. Vol. 2. Chicago: The A. N. Marquis Company, 1950.

Who's Who and What's What in Indiana Politics: This Book Is the Story of Indiana Politics and Indiana Politicians. Indianapolis: James E. Perry, 1944.

Wiebe, Robert H. *The Search for Order, 1877–1920.* New York: Hill and Wang, 1967.

Year Book of the State of Indiana for the Year 1917. Indianapolis: Wm. B. Burford, 1918.

Yearbook of the State of Indiana for the Year 1920. Fort Wayne: Fort Wayne Printing Company, 1921.

ARTICLES

Bartholomew, H. S. K. "Thomas R. Marshall." *Indiana Magazine of History* 37 (March 1941).

Blackburn, Glen A. "Interurban Railroads of Indiana." *Indiana Magazine of History* 20 (September 1924).

"Brethren of the Senate: Senator Ralston." *The Indiana Freemason* 48, no. 7 (December 1970).

"Brethren of the Senate: Senator Taggart." *The Indiana Freemason* 48, no. 4 (September 1970).

"The Bribery Indictments in Indiana." *The Outlook* (7 July 1915).

Glossbrenner, Alfred M. "Tom Taggart Park." *The Shield* (January–February 1928).

Harper's Weekly. 13 August and 24 September 1904.

Hays, Samuel P. "The Politics of Reform in Municipal Government in the Progressive Era." *Pacific Northwest Quarterly* 55, no. 4 (October 1964).

Hill, Herbert R. "Lost River Valley Meccas: West Baden and French Lick, A Classic Springs Rivalry." *Outdoor Indiana* 61 (November 1976).

Hornaday, James P. "Chairman Taggart and the Democratic Campaign." *The American Monthly Review of Reviews* (September 1904).

Hoy, Suellen M. "Governor Samuel M. Ralston and Indiana's Centennial Celebration." *Indiana Magazine of History* 71 (September 1975).

Humphreys, Sexson E. "The Nomination of the Democratic Candidate in 1924." *Indiana Magazine of History* 31 (March 1935).

Kent, Frank R. "The City Boss: How He Gets His Power and His Fortune." *World's Work* (January 1924).

Lynch, William O. "Editor's Pages: Three Busy Years, 1911–1914." *Indiana Magazine of History* 34 (September 1938).

Montgomery, Keith S. "Thomas R. Marshall's Victory in the Election of 1908." *Indiana Magazine of History* 53 (June 1957).

Moster, Mary Beth. "Whatever Happened to Pluto Water?" *Indianapolis Star Magazine,* 27 July 1975.

Nicholson, Meredith. "T.T." *The Shield* (January–February 1928).

O'Malley, John W. "The Story of the West Baden Springs Hotel." *Indiana Magazine of History* 54 (December 1958).

Painter, Carl. "The Progressive Party in Indiana." *Indiana Magazine of History* 16 (September 1920).

"Politics and the Politicians." *The Illustrated Indiana Weekly* (9 September 1899).

Rodgers, Daniel J. "In Search of Progressivism." *Reviews in American History* 10 (December 1982).

"Senator Taggart, of Indiana." *The Outlook* (29 March 1916).

Silver, David M., ed. "Richard Lieber and Indiana's Forest Heritage." *Indiana Magazine of History* 67 (March 1971).

Simons, Richard S. "When Grandpa and Grandma Took the Waters." *Indianapolis Star Magazine,* 9 August 1959.

Teaford, Jon C. "Finis for Tweed and Steffens: Rewriting the History of Urban Rule." *Reviews in American History* 10 (December 1982).

Tyner, Martha Alice. "Walter Q. Gresham." *Indiana Magazine of History* 29 (December 1933).

PAMPHLETS, PAPERS, AND MISCELLANEOUS SOURCES

Birge, Jonathan L. "Past Imperfect." Paper read before the Indianapolis Literary Club on 3 December 1969.
Civil Service Chronicle.
Cottman, George S. Indiana Scrapbook Collection.
Dixie (19 May 1974).
Drake, Lisa. Paper on Mt. Airie, circa 1986, Melton Public Library, French Lick, Indiana.
French Lick Springs Hotel, published by the French Lick Springs Hotel Company, 1915.
Haupt, Richard Walter. "History of the French Lick Springs Hotel." Master's thesis, Indiana University, 1953.
The Hoosier Waltonian (fall 1977).
The Hotel Monthly.
Indiana Biography Series. Vols. 16, 34, 57, 59. Indiana Division, Indiana State Library.
"Indiana Campaign Song: 'Taggart, We Want a Man Like You' for Senator."
Indianapolis City Directory.
The Indianapolis Woman.
Sallee, A. C. "T. T." Unpublished manuscript.
Speeches of Hon. Thomas Taggart of Indiana in the Senate of the United States. Washington, D.C.: Government Printing Office, 1916.
To Help You Enjoy Your Stay: French Lick Springs Hotel. Published by the French Lick Springs Hotel, n.d.
Union Labor Bulletin (3 November 1916).
The West Baden Journal.
Zink, Harold. "Tom Taggart." Unpublished manuscript.

MANUSCRIPTS

Claude G. Bowers Papers. Lilly Library, Indiana University, Bloomington.
Evelyn Chambers Denny Papers. Hyannis Port, Massachusetts.
Grace Julian Clarke Papers. Indiana Division, Indiana State Library, Indianapolis.
Alton B. Parker Papers. Manuscript Division, Library of Congress, Washington, D.C.

Eva Taggart Parsons Papers. Indiana Historical Society Library, Indianapolis.
Samuel M. Ralston Papers. Lilly Library, Indiana University, Bloomington.
Thomas Taggart Papers. Indiana Division, Indiana State Library, Indianapolis.
Woodrow Wilson Papers. Microfilm, Indiana University Library, Bloomington.

INTERVIEWS

James Ballard
David Laurance Chambers, Jr.
Betty Cretors
Evelyn Chambers Denny
Harold Feightner
Claire Kearby
Mary Louise Landers
Dora Sinclair Loutrel

Elizabeth Mumford
Letitia Sinclair Mumford
Walter D. Myers
Eva Taggart Parsons
Auttie Shipman
Josephine M. Sinclair
Asa J. Smith
Berta-Ann Barkhausen Steinkamp

NEWSPAPERS

The Indianapolis newspapers were used extensively for this study of Taggart's life. The other newspapers listed below ran stories about Taggart, especially at the time of his death. Clippings from these newspapers can be found in the Thomas Taggart Scrapbook, Indiana Historical Society Library, Indianapolis.

Akron (Ohio) Beacon-Journal
Albany (N.Y.) Times-Union
Albion (Mich.) Evening Recorder
Albuquerque (N. Mex.) Journal
Altoona (Pa.) Mirror
Amsterdam (N.Y.) Recorder
Anderson Bulletin
Anniston (Ala.) Star
Ashland (Ky.) Independent
Atlanta (Ga.) Journal
Atlanta (Ga.) Constitution
Atlanta (Ga.) Georgian
Atlantic (N.J.) Press
Attica (Ind.) Tribune
Attleboro (Mass.) Sun
Auburn Star
Augusta (Ga.) Herald

Augusta (Maine) Journal
Baker (Ore.) Democrat
Baltimore Evening Sun
Baltimore Sun
Baltimore News
Bangor (Maine) Commercial
Batavia (N.Y.) News
Bath (Maine) Times
Battle Creek (Mich.) Enquirer News
Bayonne (N.J.) Evening News
Beardstown (Ill.) Star
Beaumont (Tex.) Enterprise
Beaver (Pa.) Daily Times
Beaver Dam (Wis.) Citizen
Beaver Falls (Pa.) News-Tribune
Bedford Times
Bend (Ore.) Bulletin

Binghamton (N.Y.) Press
Birmingham (Ala.) Post
Bismarck (N. Dak.) Tribune
Bloomington Evening World
Bluffton Banner
Bluffton News
Boise (Idaho) Capital-News
Boston Advertiser
Boston Christian Science Monitor
Boston Globe
Boston Herald
Boston News Bureau
Boston Post
Boston Transcript
Bowling Green (Ky.) Park City News
Bridgeport (Conn.) Times Star
Bristol (Va.-Tenn.) Herald Courier
Bronx (N.Y.) North Side News
Brooklyn (N.Y.) Citizen
Brooklyn (N.Y.) Eagle
Brooklyn (N.Y.) Standard Union
Brooklyn (N.Y.) Times
Brunswick (Ga.) News
Burlington (Vt.) Free Press
Burlington (Vt.) Press
Calexico (Calif.) Chronicle
Calgary (Alberta) Herald
Camden (N.J.) Courier
Canton (Ohio) Repository
Carbondale (Pa.) Leader
Charleston (Ill.) Courier
Charleston (S.C.) Post
Chattanooga (Tenn.) Times
Chester (Pa.) Times
Chicago American
Chicago Evening Post
Chicago Herald Examiner
Chicago Journal
Chicago Journal of Commerce
Chicago News
Chicago Tribune
Chillicothe (Ohio) Scioto Gazette

Cincinnati Commercial Tribune
Cincinnati Enquirer
Cincinnati Post
Cincinnati Press
Clarksburg (W. Va.) Telegram
Clearfield (Pa.) Progress
Cleveland (Ohio) News
Cleveland (Ohio) Plain Dealer
Cleveland (Ohio) Press
Clifton Forge (Va.) Review
Coatesville (Pa.) Record
Colorado Springs News
Columbia (Tenn.) Herald
Columbia City Commercial Mail
Columbus (Ga.) Inquirer-Sun
Columbus (Ind.)Daily Herald
Columbus (Ind.) Evening Republican
Columbus (Ohio) Citizen
Columbus (Ohio) Dispatch
Council Bluffs (Iowa) Nonpareil
Crawfordsville Journal
Cumberland (Md.) News
Cumberland (Md.) Times
Dallas (Tex.) News
Dayton (Ohio) Daily News
Dayton (Ohio) Journal
Dayton (Ohio) News
Decatur Daily Democrat
Denver (Colo.) Post
Denver (Colo.) Rocky Mountain News
Detroit Free Press
Detroit News
Dothan (Ala.) Eagle
Dover (N.H.) Democrat
Doylestown (Pa.) Intelligencer
Dubuque (Iowa) Herald
Easton (Pa.) Express
Edwardsburg (Mich.) Argus
Edwardsville (Ill.) Intelligencer
El Paso (Tex.) Post
Eldorado (Ill.) Journal
Elizabeth (N.J.) Journal

Elizabeth (N.J.) Times
Elkins (W. Va.) Inter-Mountain
Elmira (N.Y.) Advertiser
Elmira (N.Y.) Star
Enid (Okla.) Eagle
Evansville Journal
Fargo (N. Dak.) Forum
Findlay (Ohio) Courier
Fitchburg (Mass.) Sentinel
Fort Smith (Ark.) Record
Fort Wayne Journal-Gazette
Fort Worth (Tex.) Press
Fort Worth (Tex.) Star-Telegram
Frankfort Morning Times
Franklin City (Pa.) News
Galesburg (Ill.) Register Mail
Gardner (Mass.) News
Gastonia (N.C.) Gazette
Geneva (N.Y.) Times
Georgetown (Ky.) News
Glendale (Calif.) News
Gloversville (N.Y.) Leader-Republican
Goshen Democrat
Grand Rapids (Mich.) Herald
Greeley (Colo.) Tribune
Green Bay (Wis.) Press Gazette
Greencastle Banner
Greensboro (N.C.) News
Greensburg (Ind.) News
Greensburg (Pa.) Tribune
Hagerstown (Md.) Mail
Haleyville (Ala.) Advertiser
Hamilton (Ohio) Journal
Hamilton (Ohio) News
Hammond Lake County Times
Harrisburg (Ill.) Register
Hartford (Conn.) Times
Hazelton (Pa.) Standard-Sentinel
Hazleton (Pa.) Standard
Helena (Mont.) Independent
Herkimer (N.Y.) Telegram
Hoboken (N.J.) Observer

Hollywood (Calif.) Citizen
Hornell (N.Y.) Tribune-Times
Houston (Tex.) Post-Dispatch
Houston (Tex.) Press
Hudson (N.Y.) Register
Huntington Herald
Huntington Press
Indianapolis Journal
Indianapolis News
Indianapolis Sentinel
Indianapolis Star
Indianapolis Sun
Indianapolis Times
Iron Mountain (Mich.) News
Ironton (Ohio) News
Jackson Mississippian
Jacksonville (Fla.) Journal
Jeffersonville Evening News
Johnstown (Pa.) Democrat
Johnstown (Pa.) Tribune
Kansas City (Mo.) Journal
Kansas City (Mo.) Star
Kearney (Neb.) Hub
Kendallville News-Sun
Kenton (Ohio) Daily Democrat
Kewanee (Ill.) Star Courier
Key West (Fla.) Citizen
Kingston (N.Y.) Freeman
Knoxville (Tenn.) Journal
Knoxville (Tenn.) News-Sentinel
Lafayette Journal-Courier
Lake Charles (La.) Press
Lamar (Colo.) News
Lancaster (Pa.) New Era
Lansford (Pa.) Evening Record
Lansing (Mich.) Capital News
Lewiston (Maine) Sun
Lexington (Ky.) Herald
Lima (Ohio) News
Little Rock (Ark.) Democrat
Long Branch (N.J.) Record
Los Angeles Express

Los Angeles Herald
Los Angeles News
Los Angeles Times
Louisville Courier-Journal
Louisville Herald Post
Louisville Times
Lynbrook (N.Y.)/Nassau Daily Star
Lynchburg (Va.) News
Lynn (Mass.) Item
Macon (Ga.) News
Madison (Ind.) Courier
Madison (Wis.) State Journal
Manchester (N.H.) Union
Manning (Iowa) Monitor
Marion Leader-Tribune
Marlboro (Mass.) Enterprise
Marseilles (Ill.) Press
Mayfield (Ky.) Messenger
McAllen (Tex.) Daily Press
Medford (Ore.) Herald
Memphis (Tenn.) Press Scimitar
Meridian (Miss.) Star
Miami (Fla.) Herald
Miami (Fla.) News
Michigan City Dispatch
Michigan City News
Milwaukee Journal
Milwaukee Sentinel
Minneapolis Journal
Minneapolis Tribune
Mobile (Ala.) Item
Mobile (Ala.) Register
Moline (Ill.) Daily Dispatch
Monroe (Mich.) Evening News
Montgomery (Ala.) Advertiser
Monticello Democrat
Monticello Journal
Montreal (Quebec) Star
Mt. Clemens (Mich.) Leader
Mount Vernon (Ill.) Register-News
Mount Vernon (Ind.) Democrat
Muncie Press

Murphysboro (Ill.) Independent
Napa (Calif.) Register
Nashville (Tenn.) Banner
Nashville Tennessean
Naugatuck (Conn.) News
New Bedford (Mass.) Standard
New Castle Courier
New Haven (Conn.) Courier
New Haven (Conn.) Journal
New Haven (Conn.) Times Union
New Orleans Item
New Orleans States
New Orleans Times Picayune
New Orleans Tribune
New York American
New York Daily News
New York East Side Home News
New York Evening Post
New York Evening World
New York Graphic
New York Herald Tribune
New York National Hotel Review
New York Telegram
New York Times
New York World
Newark (N.J.) Evening News
Newark (N.J.) Ledger
Newark (N.J.) Star Eagle
Newport News (Va.) Press
Noblesville Daily Ledger
Nogales (Ariz.) Herald
Norfolk (Neb.) News
Norfolk Virginian Pilot
Oakland (Calif.) Tribune
Oklahoma City News
Oklahoma City Oklahoman
Olean (N.Y.) Herald
Omaha (Neb.) News-Bee
Oneonta (N.Y.) Star
Oroville (Calif.) Press
Oshkosh (Wis.) Northwestern
Para (Ill.) Paladium

South Bend News Times
South Manchester (Conn.) Herald
South Norwalk (Conn.) Evening Sentinel
Spokane Chronicle
Spokane Review
Springfield (Ill.) Register
Springfield (Ill.) State Journal
Springfield (Mass.) Republican
Springfield (Mass.) Union
Springs Valley Herald
Stamford (Conn.) Advocate
Staunton (Va.) Evening Leader
Stockton (Calif.) Independent
Stroudsburg (Pa.) Morning Press
Sturgis (Mich.) Daily Journal
Syracuse (N.Y.) Journal
Tacoma (Wash.) Ledger
Tampa (Fla.) Times
Tarrytown (N.Y.) News
Terre Haute Star
Texarkana (Tex.) Gazette
Tipton Tribune
Toledo (Ohio) Blade
Topeka (Kans.) Capital
Trenton (N.J.) Gazette
Trenton (N.J.) Times
Trenton (N.J.) Times Advertiser
Troy (Ala.) Messenger
Troy (N.Y.) Morning Record
Tulsa (Okla.) World
Uniontown (Pa.) Herald
Uniontown (Pa.) News Standard
Urbana (Ill.) Courier
Urbana (Ohio) Daily Citizen
Valdosta (Ga.) Times
Valparaiso Vidette Messenger
Vancouver (British Columbia) Daily Province
Ventura (Calif.) Press
Vincennes Commercial
Vincennes Sun
Waco (Tex.) News-Tribune

Waco (Tex.) Times
Walla Walla (Wash.) Bulletin
Warren (Pa.) Times
Washington (D.C.) Evening Star
Washington (D.C.) Herald
Washington (D.C.) Post
Washington (D.C.) News
Washington (D.C.) Star
Washington (D.C.) Times
Washington (Ind.) Herald
Washington (Pa.) Observer
Waterbury (Conn.) Republican
Waterford (Calif.) News
Waterloo (Iowa) Courier
Waterloo (Iowa) Tribune
Wayne (W. Va.) News
Westerly (R.I.) Sun
Weston (W. Va.) Independent
Wheeling (W. Va.) Intelligencer
Wheeling (W. Va.) News
Wheeling (W. Va.) Register
Wichita Falls (Tex.) Times
Wilkes-Barre (Pa.) News
Wilkes-Barre (Pa.) Record
Williamsport (Pa.) Sun
Willimantic (Conn.) Chronicle
Wilmington (Del.) Every Evening
Wilmington (Del.) Journal
Wilmington (Del.) News
Wilmington (Del.) News-Dispatch
Wilmington (N.C.) Star
Wilson (N.C.) Times
Worcester (Mass.) Gazette
Worcester (Mass.) Telegram
Yonkers (N.Y.) Statesmen
York (Pa.) Gazette Daily
Youngstown (Ohio) Telegram
Youngstown (Ohio) Vindicator
Ypsilanti (Mich.) Daily Press
Yuma (Ariz.) Sun
Zanesville (Ohio) Signal
Zanesville (Ohio) Times-Recorder

Index

Foley, Michael E., 206, 214
Ford, Henry, 185
Foster, Samuel M., Democratic senatorial candidate, 163
Foulke, William Dudley (Richmond, Ind.), 41
Fox, Charles, 160
Frances Shimer (school), 9
Francis, Right Rev. Joseph M., Episcopal bishop of Indianapolis, 106, 206, 214
Frazier, Edwin G., 8
French, Dr. R. C. (Natchez, Miss.), 119
French Lick: growth of town, 69–70, 112; Taggarts spend more time in, 180; and gambling, 198, 199; Taggart builds home for son, 202; and Taggart funeral, 208
French Lick and West Baden Railway, 69, 81–82
French Lick House, 61–62
French Lick Springs Casino, 109
French Lick Springs Company, 63, 72, 110
French Lick Springs Hotel Company, 63–64, 81, 118, 213; expansions, 65–69; noted for recreation, 72–74; gardens, 73; gambling, 74–78; and wedding of Tom and Adele Taggart, 180
Frenzel, John P., 47

Garfield Park (Indianapolis), 43
Garrett City Lodge Number 537, p. 26
Geiger, George W., 220 n. 15
German Democrats, defect to Republican party, 149
Gilman, Edward, 7
Gilman, Jeremiah, 7
Girls' Classical School, 25
Gloucester (Mass.), 140, 179, 202
Gompers, Samuel, 150
Goodrich, Gov. James P., 160, 162
The Gorge, supper club and casino outside French Lick, 74–75
Gorman, Sen. Arthur P. (Maryland), 89, 92
Graham, Sylvester, 80
Grand Hotel (Indianapolis), 22–23, 30, 33, 45, 101, 116, 130
Graves, John Temple, vice presidential nominee of Independence League, 118
Gray, Gov. Isaac P., 15, 19
Gray, Pierre, 47
Greenbaum, Wolff and Ernst, 198
Gresham, Walter Q., appointed Grover Cleveland's secretary of state, 21–22
Guffey, Col. James M. (Pennsylvania), Democratic national committeeman, 87, 91, 181, 182

Hagen, Paul, secretary of Home Brewing Company, 135
Hagen, Walter, 72
Hall, Alton Parker, 86
Hall, Bertha Parker, marriage, 86
Hall, Charles Mercer, 86, 88

Hall, Mary, 86
Hanly, Gov. J. Frank, 107, 111, 114, 118; raids casinos at French Lick and West Baden, 110; Prohibition presidential candidate in 1916, p. 114
Hanna, Mark, 137
Harding, Florence Kling, 179
Harding, Warren G., president, 169, 175, 177, 179, 185, 191, 194
Harding, William M., 43
Harold, Dr. I. S., 157
Harrison, Benjamin, president, 18, 19, 21, 30, 128; public school, 68, 105
Harrison, Sen. Byron Patton (Pat) (Mississippi), 193–94
Harrison, Louise, see Bryant, Louise Harrison
Harrity, William F., 19, 21
Haughville, Indianapolis suburb, 43
Haur, George, 74
Hawes, Dr. E. E., 182
Hawthorne, Charles, artist, 139
Haynes, Elwood, 34, 157
Hays, Will H., 160, 187, 188
Hearst, William Randolph, 84–85, 107, 111; seeks Democratic presidential nomination, 83, 84; reelected to Congress, 85; attacks gambling at French Lick, 108; forms third party, 118, 119; and Democratic party, 182
Hearst Clubs, 85
Hendricks-Gray Club, 26
Henry, F. A., 226 n. 16
Henry Drug Company (Louisville), 78
Herff, Jerome, 219 n. 15
Hickam, Willis, 219 n. 15
Hickman, Henry, secretary and treasurer of French Lick Springs Hotel Company, 64, 226 n. 16
Highland Square (Indianapolis), 37
Hinckley, Wendell (Hyannis Port), 138
Hisgen, Thomas L., presidential nominee of Independence League, 118
Hitchcock, Sen. Gilbert M. (Nebraska), 151
Hite, W. W., 226 n. 16
Hoffman House (New York), national Democratic headquarters, 89, 91, 93, 98
Holliday, John H., 157
Holt, Sterling R., 47
Home Brewing Company (Indianapolis), 135
Homestead Hotel (West Baden), 70, 75
Honan, E. P., 143
Hoover, Herbert, president, 203
Hoskins, James M., 219 n. 15
Hottle, M. B. (Salem, Ind.), 112
Hovey, Gov. Alvin P., 15
Howard, Dr. (Louisville), 78
Howard, John C., 226 n. 16
Howe Military School (Indiana), 68
Howland, Louis, 132, 133
Hughes, Charles Evans, 156, 158
Hunt, Union B., secretary of state, 64

4

Designer: Dean Johnson Design, Inc., Indianapolis, Indiana
Typeface: New Baskerville
Typographer: Shepard Poorman Communications Corporation, Indianapolis, Indiana
Paper: 60-pound Cougar Opaque Natural Smooth
Printer: Evangel Press, Nappanee, Indiana